Professional Text Production

Margaret Cashin

Consultant Editor Diana Jones

with Keyboarding

Kathleen Dulmage

PITMAN
PUBLISHING

PITMAN PUBLISHING
128 Long Acre, London WC2E 9AN

A Division of Longman Group UK Limited

© Longman Group UK Limited 1993

First published in Great Britain 1993

British Library Cataloguing in Publication Data
A catalogue record for this book is available from the British
Library

ISBN 0-273-03959-8

All rights reserved; no part of this publication may be reproduced,
stored in a retrieval system, or transmitted in any form or by any
means, electronic, mechanical, photocopying, recording, or
otherwise without either the prior written permission of the
Publishers or a licence permitting restricted copying in the United
Kingdom issued by the Copyright Licensing Agency Ltd, 90
Tottenham Court Road, London W1P 9HE. This book may not be
lent, resold, hired out or otherwise disposed of by way of trade
in any form of binding or cover other than that in which it is
published, without the prior consent of the Publishers.

Note: The material at the back of the book between pages 121
and 122 is copyright free and may be photocopied for use by the
student in carrying out exercises given in this book.

Typeset by 🅰 Tek-Art, Addiscombe, Croydon
Printed in Singapore

Contents

Introduction

Keyboarding

Look at the diagrams in Part 1 of this book and identify the parts of the machine or keyboard which you are using. Read the section on keyboarding skill – it is important that you learn how to position your body and hands correctly so that you will use the best method for fast, accurate and pain-free keyboard operation.

Then turn to Part 2 of this book, which contains the keyboarding section. It has been designed for mixed ability groups and so you should use as much of each page as necessary for you to master that key. Remember, though, that the quickest way to learn is through practice, by typing/keying in the whole page, with further practice gained by using the chaining in Part 3, the keyboard development section.

This is a quick and effective method of learning the keyboard, learning time being between 10–12 hours.

National Vocational Qualification Levels 1, 2 and 3

Parts 4, 5 and 6 of this book cover the theory and application related to NVQ Business Administration Levels 1, 2 and 3 typewriting and word processing competences. All sections are accompanied by achievement criteria applicable to NVQ training, as well as guidelines relevant to single subject preparation. Both typewriting and word processing references are made throughout and all units meet examination requirements. Each section stands alone, facilitating roll-on, roll-off training, and delivery allows for easy transition from Level 1 through to Level 3. On page vii is a table to help you plan your work.

As you progress, the work increases in complexity, requiring a good level of understanding of advanced applications. You are also deemed to have increased responsibility within the organisation. This is all part of NVQ strategy and active learning.

Although there are only certain units within NVQs specifically related to typewriting or word processing, the theory in this book will help in presenting material for *all* the NVQ units at Levels 1–3.

Organisation chart   On page *80* you will find an organisation chart which shows the structure of a fictitious company and how each sector relates to the others. You will need to refer to this chart as you work through the following sections of the book.

As you work through the next sections, you will find points of theory with the tasks to which they refer. You will need to read through all the theory points before you start a section and read through *all* instructions relating to a task before you begin. Although no time limit has been put on tasks while you are learning, you should always try to work as fast as you can, remembering that in the business world you will be expected to produce work within certain time limits and to mailable standard.

For each of the sections at Levels 1–3 you will be placed in a different sector of the organisation and given the name of the person you are working for. All the work you produce must be 'mailable', ie error-free, which means that you must proofread your work and correct errors before it is marked. You should always use a dictionary and check any spellings of which you are unsure.

At the end of every one of these sections you will find a checklist of the performance criteria you have achieved by successfully completing that section. If you type/key in the checklists, you can ask your tutor or supervisor to sign and date them and keep a copy in your record of achievement. All tasks within this book can be done on a manual, an electric or an electronic typewriter, a word processor, or a computer with word processing software. You will only be expected to use the facilities suggested if they are available on your system.

Acknowledgements

The authors would like to thank Valerie Brice, Pamela Gough, June Hubbard and Ann O'Hare at the Mid Kent College of Higher and Further Education, and Lee Cashin, for providing handwritten material for the assignments.

The authors and publishers are grateful to Hoverspeed Limited for permission to reproduce the two timetables in Task 1 of Element 5.2 in Part 6, and to the Royal Society of Arts Examinations Board, Pitman Examinations Institute and London Chamber of Commerce and Industry Examinations Board for permission to reproduce past examination papers at the end of this book.

Planning your way through Levels 1, 2 and 3

NVQ Business Administration

NVQ unit	Administration	Secretarial	Financial
Level 1			
1 Filing*	x	x	x
2 Communicating information	x	x	x
3 Data processing	x		x
4 Processing petty cash and invoices	x	x	
5 Stock handling	x	x	x
6 Mail handling	x	x	x
7 Reprographics	x	x	x
8 Liaising with callers and colleagues	x	x	x
9 Health and safety	x	x	x
Level 2			
10 Creating and maintaining business relationships	x	x	x
11 Providing information to customers/clients	x	x	x
12 Storing and supplying information	x	x	x
13 Information processing	x	x	x
14 Telecommunications and data transmission	x	x	
15 Reception	x	x	
16 Text processing		x	
17 Audio transcription		x	
or			
18 Shorthand transcription		x	
19 Arranging travel and meetings	x	x	
20 Processing payments	x		x
21 Processing documents relating to goods and services			x
22 Processing payroll			x
23 Maintaining financial records			x

* Unit 1 Filing is not a requirement for Level 2 but is covered in Unit 12.

NVQ Administration Level 3

After you have taken your route through Level 2, you can now work through the units in Level 3 (at Level 3 these are not separated into Administration, Secretarial and Financial).

NVQ unit

1 Communication systems

2 Researching and retrieving information

3 Reception

4 Arranging travel

5 Preparing and producing documents

6 Processing correspondence

7 Organising work schedules

8 Servicing meetings

9 Office resource administration

10 Health and safety at work

11 Shorthand transcription (optional)

Remember that you will need to produce *three* assignments at each level in order to achieve your elements of competence.

Index

Index   x

1 How to use this book

This part introduces you to the machine which you are going to use to gain your keyboard skills. Identify the parts on your typewriter or word processor/computer.

Then read the information on how to sit correctly at your keyboard, which is very important. To type/key in fast with the minimum of effort, you must be seated correctly at your machine and strike the keys in the correct way.

All the material has been thoroughly researched and applied in the classroom, and by following the instructions carefully you will learn to type in the safest, fastest and most efficient way.

Professional Text Production with Keyboarding
Assignments Pack

A portfolio facility with no additional workload for the teacher. This pack gives further assessment tasks and perfect examples together with forms and letterheads for use with Professional Text Production with Keyboarding. Written in conjunction with the main text, this copyright-free pack offers an excellent selection of practice assignments for use as homework or extra sessional tasks.

To order, simply photocopy the form below, or ask your local bookseller.

Order Form

☐ Please send me **sample pages** from the Assignment Pack (ISSN: 0994 001649)

☐ I wish to purchase the following:

Qty	ISBN	Title	Price
☐	0 273 03960 1	**Professional Text Production with Keyboarding** Assignments Pack	£9.99

NB Please add £2.35 to your order for postage & packing in the UK. Payment should be made in £ Sterling.

☐ I enclose a cheque (payable to **Pitman Publishing**) for £ _____

☐ Alternatively, please debit my credit card:

VISA ☐   Access ☐   AMERICAN EXPRESS ☐   DINERS CLUB ☐

Please supply cardholder's address below if paying by credit card.

Card No: ☐☐☐☐☐☐☐☐☐☐☐☐☐☐☐☐☐☐   Expiry Date: ☐☐☐☐☐

Signature _____

PLEASE USE CAPITALS
Mr/Mrs/Miss/Ms _____ Initials _____ Surname _____   My job title is: _____

Institute: _____

Address _____

Town _____   County _____   Postcode _____

Return this form with your remittance to
Customer Services Dept
Pitman Publishing
Southport Book Distributors
12-14 Slaidburn Crescent
Southport
PR9 9YF

OR Tel: 0704 26881   OR Fax: 0704 231970

Prices and availability are subject to change without notice.
Pitman Publishing, part of the Longman Group UK Limited. Registered office: 5 Bentinck Street, London W1M 5RN.

Manual typewriter

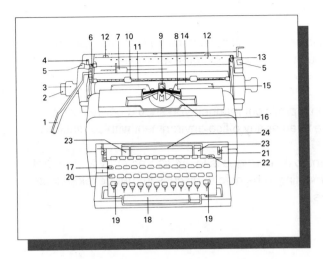

Parts of a manual typewriter

1 Carriage return lever	9 Card holder	17 Margin release key
2 Variable line spacer	10 Paper grips	18 Space bar
3 Cylinder knobs	11 Paper bail scale	19 Shift keys
4 Interliner	12 Margin stops	20 Shift lock
5 Carriage release levers	13 Paper release lever	21 Ribbon colour adjuster
6 Line space selector	14 Platen	22 Backspace key
7 Paper guide	15 Paper holders	23 Tabulator set and clear keys
8 Alignment scale	16 Typing point indicator	24 Tabulator bar/key

1 **The carriage return lever** takes you to the start of the next line.
2 **The variable line spacer** knob (which you either pull out or push in, depending on your machine) enables you to alter your typing line so you can type above or below it.
3 **The cylinder knob** allows you to move the paper up or down.
4 **The interliner** is a small lever which can be pulled forward to free the platen without losing the original typing line.
5 **The carriage release levers** release the paper and allow you to take it out of the machine.
6 **The line space selector** allows you to change from single to one-and-a-half or double line spacing.
7 You should insert paper with the left side against the **paper guide**. This will ensure that all your work starts at the same position when using the same margins.
8 **The alignment scale** helps in lining up your displayed work.
9 **The card holder** is a metal section above the centre of the typing line, used with the paper holders (**15**) to secure cards or thick envelopes.
10 **The paper grips** will hold the paper against the platen for you.
11 **The paper bail** scale allows you to see your typing point and helps you to plan your work.
12 **Margin stops** will set your left and right margins wherever you position them.

13 **The paper release lever**, when pulled forward, releases the paper and allows you to straighten it in the machine.
14 **The platen** (or cylinder) is the roller around which the paper is held – it can be replaced when worn.
15 **The transparent paper holders**: (a) indicate the bottom of the typing line on the alignment scale; (b) hold postcards and envelopes in position to make them easier to type; and (c) help you to rule in a straight line by inserting a fine black ballpoint pen into the two holes in the plastic, and moving the carriage along so a line is drawn.
17 **The margin release key** allows you to type into the margins if you want to extend your typing line.
18, **19**, and **20** will be explained in the keyboarding section.
21 **Colour change adjuster** – changes the colour of a dual-colour ribbon; set this on white to type stencils for duplication.
22 **Backspace key** moves the printing point one space back – its position on different makes of the keyboard varies.
23 **The tabulator set and clear keys** are used for marking and deleting the positions for indenting text (usually 5 spaces) from the left margin, or for column work.
24 **The tabulator key** or bar moves the carriage quickly across the page to the positions where tabulator stops (tabs) have been set.

Personal Assistant

Two years have elapsed. Susan Sharpe has left the Company, and you have been promoted to the position of PA to John Briggs.

Because of the very senior nature of the work involved, you will need to make sure that you carry out every Task to the very best of your ability, and much more of the material will require you to use your own initiative.

If you can work through this remaining material in a proficient manner, you should be well equipped to achieve NVQ Level 3 Administration and be able to enter any office environment with confidence.

One of your responsibilities as Personal Assistant to John Briggs is to act as Secretary for the Broker Group Meetings. Tasks 1-5 deal with a special meeting to be held to discuss further developments within the Group. Use plain paper for these tasks.

■ Task 1

Prepare the following Notice of Meeting and despatch it to those entitled to attend.

The Broker Group ← (CAPS & BOLD)

Notice is hereby given that a Meeting will take place on 16 Feb 19 _ _ at the Med Hotel, Fakenham, Norfolk at 1400 hrs to discuss proposed new devs within the Group

Vicky Wright
Secretary

20 Jan 19 _ _

Electric typewriter

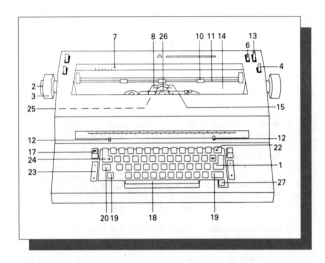

Parts of an electric typewriter

1 Carriage return key
2 Variable line spacer
3 Cylinder knobs
4 Interliner
6 Line space selector
7 Paper guide
8 Alignment scale
10 Paper grips

11 Paper bail scale
12 Margin stops
13 Paper release lever
14 Platen (cylinder)
15 Transparent paper holders
17 Margin release key
18 Space bar
19 Shift keys

20 Shift lock
22 Backspace key
23 Tabulator set and clear keys
24 Tabulator key
25 Carrier
26 Printing element (behind
   this is printing point indicator)
27 Half-space correction key

Explanations are the same as those for the manual typewriter.

Section 1, Task 1

N O T I C E

Would all guests please observe the following points:

<u>Keys</u>

No keys should be removed from the Hotel premises. Please hand in your key to Reception when going out and collect it on your return.

<u>Noise</u>

Would all guests please ensure that, when leaving or entering rooms after 2200 hrs, respect is shown for fellow guests who may be sleeping.

<u>Night Porter</u>

The Hotel operates a 24-hour service and when Reception is closed a Night Porter is always available to deal with any problems. He will either be in the Night Porter's Office on the Ground Floor or he can be contacted on Extension 11.

<u>Departure Time</u>

All rooms should be vacated by 1200 hrs, unless special arrangements have been made.

<u>Settlement of Accounts</u>

Accounts will be ready for collection at any time after 0900 hrs on the day of departure. Payments should be made <u>before</u> 1100 hrs. Charge cards, cheques or cash are acceptable.

Task 2

<u>SECURITY</u>

<u>Visitors Book</u>   All guests <u>must</u> sign the Visitors Book on arrival, stating their name, address, and date and time of arrival. When checking out of the Hotel, the date and time of departure should be inserted.

<u>Valuables</u>   The Hotel accepts no responsibility for valuables left in rooms. A safe is available for guests' use and no charge is made for this service. Please ask at Reception for details.

<u>Theft</u>   In the unlikely event that a guest notices any item missing from his or her room, this should be reported immediately, either to Reception or to the Hotel Manager.

<u>Main Entrance Closure</u>   The Hotel's Main Entrance and Reception will be closed from midnight to 0700 hrs each night for reasons of security. Guests requiring access during these times should ring the bell at the Main Entrance and inform the Night Porter of their name and room number. As long as he is satisfied, access will be granted.

<u>General Awareness</u>   Guests should at all times look after their property and not leave bags and cases lying around in Reception or corridors. They should also immediately report any suspicious packages they see to Reception or a member of staff. Any person suspected of theft will be questioned by the Manager and, if necessary, referred to the Police.

Task 3

RULES FOR RECEPTIONISTS

1   As a Receptionist you create the first impression of the Hotel for guests as they arrive. Make sure you are always perfectly groomed and that you greet the guests with a friendly, welcoming smile.

2   All guests should be treated with a courteous manner.

3   If you are ever frightened or unsure about a visitor to the Reception Desk, dial the emergency number immediately, or press the buzzer and another member of staff will come to your assistance. <u>Never</u> take chances.

4   Always make sure that any reservations taken either at the Desk or on the telephone, are immediately entered on the Reservations Chart, otherwise double booking will occur.

5   When answering the telephone, give the name of the Hotel, say "Good morning", "Good afternoon" or "Good evening", followed by "How may we help you?". Try to deal with the telephone call efficiently. If it is for a reservation, you can deal with it yourself. Otherwise connect the caller to the appropriate member of staff.

6   <u>Never</u> leave the Reception Desk unattended.

Task 4

<u>PERSONAL QUALITIES OF A SUCCESSFUL RECEPTIONIST</u>

a   Good typing knowledge

b   Experience on a word processor

c   A polite and courteous manner

d   Smart clothes and well-groomed appearance

e   Ability to cope in a crisis

f   Adaptable attitude to workload

g   Willingness to cover for colleagues' absences

h   Must be prepared to work shifts, plus weekends and Bank Holidays

Professional Text Production with Keyboarding   Assignments Pack   Ann Dobson   Pitman Publishing
© Longman Group UK Limited 1993

Electronic typewriter

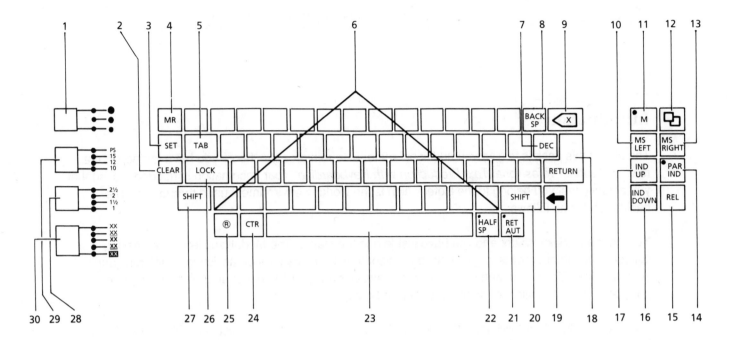

Parts of an electronic typewriter keyboard

1 Impression – the darkness of the type
  (up = heavy; centre = medium; low = light)
2 Tab clear
3 Tab set
4 Margin release
5 Tab key – moves carrier to tab stops
6 Alphanumeric keyboard
  (position of special characters, eg fractions, varies)
7 Decimal tab key
  (automatically aligns decimal point at tab stop)
8 Backspace key
9 Error correction key
10 Margin set key for left margin
11 Memory key – to store/recall text from phrase memory
12 Mode key – several functions
  (eg acts as a second shift key for certain symbols)
13 Margin set key for right margin
14 Paragraph indent key
15 Relocate key – several functions
  (eg to start memory printing; to return to original
  printing point after making a correction)
16 Index down – moves paper down half a line space (has
  repeat function)
17 Index up – moves paper up half a line space (has
  repeat function)

18 Carrier return (to start of next line)
19 Express backspace – fast return along same line
20 Shift key for upper case characters
21 Automatic return – automatically returns the carrier at
  the right margin to start a new line
22 Half-space key – moves the carrier half a space to the
  left for insertion of extra character
23 Space bar – moves the carrier one space to the right
24 Centre – centres automatically between margins;
  centres between tab stops when pressed after tab key;
  centres around any point where pressed on page
25 Repeat key – repeats character(s) just typed
26 Shift lock – use when typing several characters in
  upper case
27 Shift key (see 20)
28 Line space selector (set usually at 1 = single line
  spacing)
29 Pitch – to change type size (PS = proportional spacing;
  15 = 15 characters to the inch; 12 = 12 characters to
  the inch; 10 = 10 characters to the inch)
30 Print type – press this key to change the type to
  underlined, bold (double-typed), bold underlined or
  reversed out (white characters on black surround).
  Some electronic typewriters have a more simple or a
  more sophisticated keyboard than that given above.

Professional Text Production With Keyboarding
Assignments Pack - Sample pages

Introduction

The aim of this pack is to give you additional material to reinforce the theory you have learned in the main textbook, *Professional Text Production with Keyboarding*. Your imagination is needed too, so that you actually feel you belong to the Hotel which is the working environment used throughout. The background is as follows:

Your name is Vicky Wright and you have just joined the staff of The Medallion Hotel after leaving college. The Hotel policy is to give newcomers some experience through assisting in different junior secretarial positions, and then if you progress satisfactorily, you can either apply for a permanent position at The Medallion, or at one of the other hotels in the Group.

The Organisation Chart will show that you work first as a Junior Receptionist under the supervision of Ms Rose Prior and Mrs Pauline Sale, the Head Receptionists. There are, as you will see, two other Receptionists, and you will be expected to work with either Jayne Smith or Mandy Parker, carrying out various tasks as requested.

The Medallion Hotel has 100 bedrooms and is managed by Mr John Briggs. It is a busy hotel, set in pleasant East Anglian countryside, catering for both business people and holidaymakers.

As you proceed through the Sections, you will see that your position on the Organisation Chart changes. The Sections follow the general order of the theory covered in the main textbook. At the end of Section 4 you will have the opportunity to apply for your first permanent position.

Suggested answers are provided in the Worked examples of Tasks and Assignments at the end of this pack, but it should be stressed that these answers are only suggestions. Your interpretation of a particular task may be different and your tutor/supervisor will guide you on whether or not your answer is acceptable.

At the end of Sections 2, 5 and 6 are specimen assignments for NVQ Levels 1, 2 and 3. These, together with the assignments in the main textbook, provide the necessary material for accreditation at each level. In addition, the entire pack provides ample practice for all Stage 1 and 2 single subject examinations.

Finally, enjoy being Vicky Wright. Use your imagination to picture the Hotel and your part in it.

Note: Please refer to the main textbook, *Professional Text Production with Keyboarding*, if you are not sure how to produce a particular task.

Word processor/computer

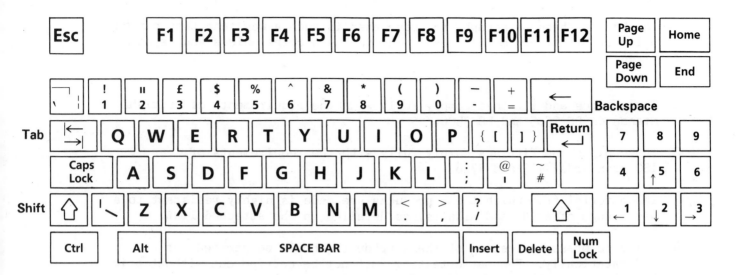

These are the basic keys generally found on word processor keyboards. There may be some differences on your particular keyboard. You may, for example, have a computer with a word processing software package on it rather than a dedicated word processor. You may have a 'mouse' to point with and click on the functions which you require, rather than use the **F** function keys on the word processor keyboard.

PRINTERS

There are 2 main types of printer:

1 Impact printers, such as the dot matrix or daisywheel – pressure is applied by a print head through a ribbon and an imprint is transferred to the paper.

2 Non-impact printers, such as the ink jet or laser printer – ink is placed on the paper without any direct contact being made between the print head and the paper (no ribbon is used).

Dot matrix printers   The image is formed by a series of dots made on the paper. Printing is very rapid. They are in widespread use for draft quality printout because of their speed and the use of cheaper continuous stationery. On most printers, quality can be improved by using the NLQ (near letter quality) function, when the printer goes over each character twice to improve the density. They can print graphics.

Daisywheel printers   The daisywheel is a small wheel, shaped rather like a daisy, with plastic typeheads at the end of flexible arms, known as petals. The wheel rotates to bring the required character to top centre, when a hammer hits it to leave an imprint through a ribbon on to the paper. Daisywheels can be changed to give different type styles and special characters, particularly useful for foreign language work. Quality of printing is good and printing can be very fast if the printer is bi-directional – goes in one direction across the page and then back again.

Ink jet printers   These spray tiny droplets of ink on to the paper to make the characters in dot form. The quality of the work is excellent for both graphics and text and they are fast and quiet.

Laser printers   Laser beams are used to transfer the original image on to a drum, which then transfers it to the paper. A variety of typestyles (fonts) is available in different sizes and styles of lettering. The quality is excellent for graphics and text, and they are used for desktop publishing.

ASSIGNMENT 4 - Candidate's Copy (Part 1)

Please key in these paragraphs and save them in such a way that they can be used later for boilerplating. Don't key in the numbers unless your system requires them.

1 These pipes and fittings comply fully with the requirements of British Standards BS 3505 and BS 3506.

2 These pipes and fittings comply fully with the requirements of ISO standards 4723 and 4726.

3 The material from which these products are made is highly resistant to a wide range of acids and alkalis, as detailed in the attached list.

4 All site pressure testing of these products should be carried out hydrostatically. Pneumatic testing must not be carried out without prior consultation with our Technical Services Department.

5 Solvent welded pipelines should not be pressure tested until at least 24 hours after the last solvent welded joint has been made.

6 Heat-welded pipelines may be pressure tested within 1 hour of the last weld being completed.

7 This product complies with the requirements of the Inner London Drainage Bye-Laws, specifically Bye-Law 3: subsoil drains.

8 This product complies with the requirements of the Inner London Drainage Bye-Laws, specifically Bye-Law 4: storm and emergency drains.

Keyboarding skill

In operating any keyboard, skill is based on technique. Before you produce any documents, therefore, you must learn and master proper technique.

Ignore errors for the time being. Technique is a process and accuracy is the product. Accuracy will result from proper technique.

A skill, by definition, is learned and improves with practice. In learning any skill, extra practice is most effective if it is done in short, frequent sessions. Two practices daily, say 15-20 minutes each, in addition to class time, will produce better results than 2 hours on the same afternoon every week.

TECHNIQUE

Technique is built upon 3 components – posture, stroking and chaining – and all the drills in this book will be geared towards mastery of these. To achieve your maximum potential, concentrate on mastering each of these components.

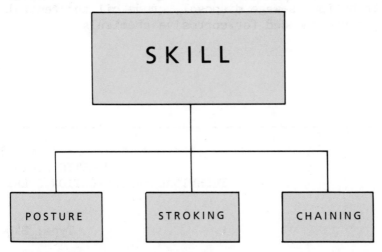

COMPONENT 1 – POSTURE

The first component is posture. Proper body positioning will help you to type without pain and fatigue. Frequent rests and moving around will prevent cramping of muscles.

The diagrams below show correct posture, so adjust your furniture accordingly.

Manual   Electric/   Computer
                electronic

The diagrams show the same person properly seated, on the same non-adjustable chair.

ASSIGNMENT 4 - Candidate's Copy (Part 2)

The skeletons of 2 documents are given below. Please key in this text on 2 separate pages. The headings must be flush to the right margin, and the first paragraph must be laid out as indicated.

To each page, add the standard paragraphs listed, in the order presented.

PLASTIC PIPING
TECHNICAL SPECIFICATION SHEET

Type: B52

Uses: Suitable for water distribution, sewage disposal, crude oil and general industrial purposes. Not recommended for corrosive chemicals.

(add paragraphs 1, 4, and 7)

_____

PLASTIC PIPING
TECHNICAL SPECIFICATION SHEET

Type: B40

Uses: Suitable for high-temperature fluids, including low-pressure gases. Recommended for hostile environments, including extremes of temperature.

(add paragraphs 2, 3, 5, and 8)

If you have an adjustable chair, adjust it to fit you. Otherwise, study the diagrams and make the necessary adjustments so that your posture will be correct.

Use a cushion, a footrest and, if necessary, a bike bag filled with soft cloths or a small padded bag at your back to create a proper working position.

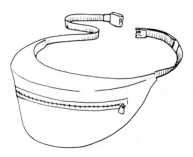

Use a bike bag positioned at the small of the back to provide support.

Sit like this

head – erect: tilting your head forward puts a strain on your neck, resulting in headaches; watching your hands increases this strain

shoulders – relaxed

elbows – close to your body

forearms – parallel to the keyboard slope

wrists – flat: keep your wrists in neutral position (a straight line from the knuckles of the middle fingers to the elbows)

fingers – curved: because a manual typewriter has a steeper slope, you must curve your fingers more tightly than for an electric, electronic or computer keyboard

back – straight

thighs – parallel to the floor

feet – flat on the floor

Sit back in the chair and lean slightly forward from the hips but do not slouch.

Well-designed furniture can reduce strain a great deal but it must be adjusted to fit you. Do not ever adjust your body to fit the furniture.

ASSIGNMENT 1

Type a copy of the following publicity sheet. Type each of the numbered items on a new line and display the task attractively.

NEW PREMISES - NEW SERVICES - NEW IMAGES

Our company has moved into larger premises on the Westward Business Site and can extend its services to businesses *and to the general public*.

NP COLOUR COPYING SERVICES [The following services are available on our laser copier:
1 Image distortion *to allow greater flexibility*. 2 Reduction *of* copy by 50%.
4 Combination of 2 originals into *one* copy in the position and size selected. 5 Change of colours of the original to give the copy a *special* effect. 6 Addition *of* colour to black and white originals or vice

NP versa. [Charges for these services are given below.

SERVICE	FIRST COPY		EXTRA COPIES each	
	A4 £	A3 £	A4 £	A3 £
Image Distortion	3.00	3.50	0.50	0.80
Reduction	5.30	7.80	1.00	1.20
Enlargement	5.30	7.80	1.00	1.20
Colour changes	6.90	7.20	1.30	1.50

We also offer a binding service for documents containing no more than 500 pages. 2 If you wish to have a document bound please telephone for an appointment when the binding can be done *and collect next day* immediately, or leave the document with us. Cost for this service depends upon the type of cover chosen and the thickness of the document.

NP [If you would like to view our facilities, meet our staff *and* discuss your requirements, telephone Gill Evans on 0403 192775 to arrange an appointment.

3 Enlargement of copy by 400%.

COPYING   BINDING   COLOURING

The steep slope on a manual typewriter requires a tight curve to the fingers.

The flatter keyboard on an electric/ electronic typewriter or a computer requires less curve to the fingers.

Do not crowd the machine. Sit far enough back so that your elbows will be slightly in front of your ribs. The average alphanumeric keyboard is about 12 inches wide and your hands come close together as you are typing. This forces your wrists to bend sideways, compressing the nerves.

Do not let the heel of your hand rest on the frame of the machine.

Sitting too close also forces your elbows out from your body, putting a strain on the muscles in your upper arms to hold that position.

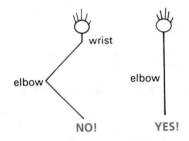

Don't let your elbows stick out.

Your wrists must never drop or angle to either side.

Some tables adjust but most do not; you may have to raise or lower the keyboard so your forearms are parallel to it.

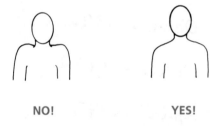

Relax your shoulders.

If your table is too high you will hunch your shoulders. If it is too low, you will bend your wrists.

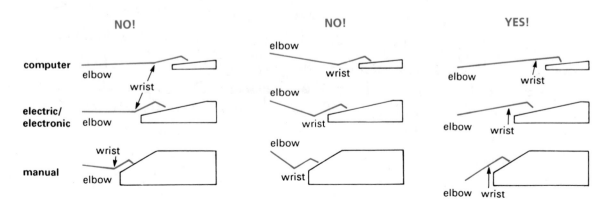

ASSIGNMENT 3

Type the following memorandum. Leave a clear line-space between the items in the table. Use the reference PM/2/92/3.

MEMORANDUM

To   Steven Jenkins   Ref
       Laboratory

From   Peter Morgan   Date
       General Manager

<u>Perfume Development</u>

I have had a preliminary discussion with Tom Evans of [uc] marketing following the decision by the Development Committee to proceed with marketing the new perfumes which your [NP] laboratory has produced. The following should be an effective plan.

Product

<u>Perfume</u>	<u>Replacing</u>	<u>Launch Date</u>
A	Domino	October 1992
B	Caress	October 1992
C	–	Spring 1993
D	–	Spring 1993

I enclose a copy of a memo in which Tom outlines a marketing strategy which I believe would be *most* effective. [stet] I think we should discuss the ~~probabilities~~ possibilities in detail before the next Product ~~Development~~ Development Committee meeting. If you are free for lunch on [uc] friday I will ask Tom and Alan Nichols of Production to join us. Please telephone me.

Enc

Copy holder

If you are using a typewriter, alternate your copy from left to right so you are not holding your neck in the same strained position all the time.

A computer screen can be raised to allow space for the copy holder between it and the keyboard. That eliminates any twisting of the neck.

Always use a document holder. If your copy is lying flat on the desk, you must stretch, twist or bend your neck to read it, and any of these actions is a strain. Furthermore, glossy copy can reflect light, causing a glare that is tiring to the eyes. If you do not have a copy holder, you can make one – for example, from a metal clothes hanger.

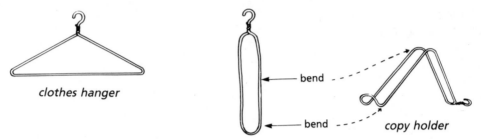

clothes hanger   *bend*   *bend*   *copy holder*

REPETITIVE STRAIN INJURY

A typist may suffer from more than one kind of repetitive strain injury. The only known cure is rest and the condition will recur if the same task is performed in the same way.

By learning and maintaining proper techniques, described in this book, pain from RSI can be prevented.

COMPONENT 2 – STROKING

The second component of typing skill is **ballistic stroking**. This is a special kind of stroking that uses strong, fast muscles on the inside of the forearm (flexors) instead of the slower ones on the outside (extensors).

Notice that your finger travels only a short distance, then relaxes. That gives your muscles the necessary rest time to recover from fatigue so your hands and arms will never get sore.

A ballistic stroke is always fast and very brief. It is the same on any keyboard, except that on a typewriter your fingers have a tighter curve than on a computer. It has been described in many ways – a kitten running across a carpet, fingers climbing a ladder, scratching, pulling gold dust from the keys into the palm. However you understand it best, the essence is that it is a pulling motion, inward toward the palm.

Ballistic stroking is the fastest, easiest, safest way to type. Practice it and master it.

COMPONENT 3 – CHAINING

This will be explained in the following pages of Part 2 as you learn to touch type.

Typewriting* First Level (April 1992) (*now Keyboarding)

ASSIGNMENT 1

Type the following letter. Use the reference PM/2/92/1 and address the letter to

Miss M J Hawke
O'Neill Advertising Agency Ltd
O'Neill House
Water Road
Nottingham
NG3 3SL

Dear Margaret

We have decided to discontinue production of the perfumes Caress
and Domino from /the end of July this year. Stocks should last at least
until December so we shall continue with a reduced advertising
NP programme until the end of November. [We are replacing these
perfumes with 2 others not yet named; these are aimed at the
same /market price range. The launch will be through magazine and other
stet uc advt advertisements and trade press announcements. Both these
perfumes are light based fragrances. Please phone me/soon to discuss
possible names for the perfumes, and a theme for the advertisements.

NP [We have also decided to add 2 new perfumes to our luxury range
and to launch these in September. Great emphasis is to be placed
upon
at a special presentation.

2) the use of natural products in production
3) environmentally friendly packaging
1) the quality of the perfumes

These themes are to be emphasised throughout the initial campaign.
NP [Please telephone Tom Evans, our Marketing Manager, for more details.
and let us have your suggestions for this campaign.

Yours sincerely

in due course

Peter Morgan
General Manager

2 Keyboarding

When you have completed this section, you should have the knowledge and skills to touch type and to operate a keyboard effectively – whether you are using a manual, electric or electronic typewriter or a computer.

This keyboarding section has been designed for mixed ability groups – use as much of the practice material as you find necessary. If you feel ready to move on to the next page, do so.

How to use this section

1 You will progress best if you read the drills aloud as you do them. This will help you to chain effectively. In a classroom, out of consideration for others, whisper or speak softly. Soon you will be able to read silently without spelling out words.

2 Ignore errors. They will go away as your skill grows.

3 Repeat any words that feel awkward to type or where you are aware of having made an error, but do not stop to make corrections. Continuity is important in developing fluency and ease in keyboard operation.

4 Watch your copy. If you forget the position of a letter, glance at the chart, but do not get into the habit of watching your hands.

5 Remember that typing skill is built on 3 factors – body positioning, ballistic stroking and chaining. Keep these factors in mind as you practise.

6 Check your posture before you begin.

7 Type at an easy pace. Do not try to rush. Let your fingers learn and then trust them to do what you have taught them.

8 Do not be discouraged if your speed does not seem to increase or you seem to be making no progress. Learning is still going on at a different level as new material is absorbed and the result will suddenly become apparent.

9 Work at your own pace. When you feel confident with a new letter, move on to the next page, even though you may not have completed the full page of drills. You will get plenty of further practice on the pages that follow.

Display the following

The Finance Bureau — SP CAPS

Correspondence Courses — CAPS & U/S

Below are details of Correspondence Courses which are now available from our offices.

uc Special introductory packs are obtainable (price £1·75 each incl post & packing) & these give basic information on the course content.

To obtain one (or more) of these packs, complete the attached slip & return it, together with your remittance, to: The Finance Bureau, Bankfield House, High St, MANCHESTER. (Please allow 28 days for delivery)

- -

Please send Introductory Pack(s) on the following Course(s) :- (Indicate number of packs required)

Financial Management ...
Book-keeping for the Small Business ...
Sales Analysis ...
Preliminary Budgeting ...
Investment matters ...
Statutory Statements ...
   TOTAL NO OF PACKS ...

I enclose Cheque/Postal Order* (payable to "The Finance Bureau") to the value of £ - - - -

NAME: - - - - - - - - -

ADDRESS: - - - - - - - - -
- - - - - - - - -

TEL NO: - - - - - - - - - -

* Delete as applicable

Home row

BEGINNING TO TYPE

If you are using a word processor, make sure the cursor is at the top left of your blank new document screen.

If you are using a typewriter, it is important that the paper be inserted so that you begin typing at the top of the page. Make a habit of the following procedure.

1 Set the paper guide at 0.

2 Pull the paper bail away from the roller (platen).

3 With the paper on your right, place your right hand, palm down, at the bottom of the sheet with your thumb holding the paper from the back, and pick the paper up.

4 Drop the paper behind the roller and against the paper guide. Then twirl the left cylinder knob with your left hand. Replace the paper bail to hold the page in place.

5 To remove the paper from the machine, pull the paper bail away from the roller, open the paper release and lift out the paper. This is a *silent* operation. Yanking the paper out can strip the gears in the roller. Furthermore, you can very easily tear the paper, and your work will have to be retyped.

HOME ROW

Place your fingers on the middle row of alphabet keys with your index fingers on **F** and **J**, and the other fingers on **D**, **S** and **A** with your left hand and **K**, **L** and **;** with your right hand.

This is the home row and we use it for guidance, as a landmark, a starting place. Your hands should hover close to the keys or barely touch them, but avoid resting on them. Resting on the keys of a computer can give you unwanted letters.

Using a ballistic stroke, look at your hands and type `fjfjfjfj`

Now, look at your script (the paper in your typewriter or the monitor screen of your computer) and type again `fjfjfjfj`, so you will see that you are typing what you think you are typing.

Type `dkdkdkdk` looking first at your hands, then at your script.
Type `slslslsl` in the same way, then `a;a;a;a;`

RETURN

Manual typewriter   When you reach the end of the line, use the return lever with your left hand, catching the lever between the 1st and 2nd knuckles of your index finger. Keep your palm down. Do not push or hold the lever; strike it smartly and drop your hand immediately to the home row.

Electrics, electronics and computers   These use a return key, on the right side of the keyboard. Keep your **J** finger close to home and stretch your hand to tap the return with your little finger. Do not lift your right hand from the keyboard to press return. Do not hold the return key down.

Please display the following Notice to its best advantage.

GRIEVANCE PROCEDURES

Stage 1   Any grievance you may have must always be raised first of all with your immediate supervisor.

Stage 2   Only if yr supervisor can not solve the matter should you approach yr Departmental Manager.

Stage 3   If the grievance is still unresolved ~~you must~~ approach the Personnel Manager within <u>one</u> week. This approach must be made in writing. A copy of your letter should ∧ be handed to yr Dept Mgr.

fig

∧ also/

Stage 4   If agreement still cannot be found the matter must then be brought to the attention of the Company Personnel Director at Head Office.

Stage 5   Failure to resolve the matter at stage 4 may result in the ~~situation~~ matter being referred to the Advisory Conciliation and Arbitration Service (ACAS) for their independent advice which shall be binding on both parties.

stet

SPACE BAR

Your thumb controls the long bar across the bottom of the keyboard. It is the space bar and the space is automatically attached to the end of a word as part of the word. Do not pause between the word and the space. Choose whichever thumb is easier for you and stick with it. Strike the space bar with a ballistic motion, which, on the thumb, is sideways, going toward the palm.

■ EXERCISE

Type the following lines twice each.
First, look at your hands – then look at your script.
Use a ballistic stroke.

```
fj fj fj fj fj fj fj
dk dk dk dk dk dk dk
sl sl sl sl sl sl sl
a; a; a; a; a; a; a;
```

You may find that your fingers and hands are moving a great deal as you type. This excessive motion is common in the early stages of any skill and will soon disappear.

As you type, do not worry about mistakes and don't correct them. If you are aware that you have made an error, type the word correctly and continue without stopping.

Watch your copy as you type. Looking at your hands puts your neck into an angle of at least 60 degrees and is a great strain. Glance at the keyboard chart if you forget where a letter is; there is a chart on every exercise page so there is no need to look at your hands except to locate the new key and confirm your ballistic stroke.

Check your posture and type the drill below. Be sure your wrists are flat and that the heel of your hand never rests on the frame.

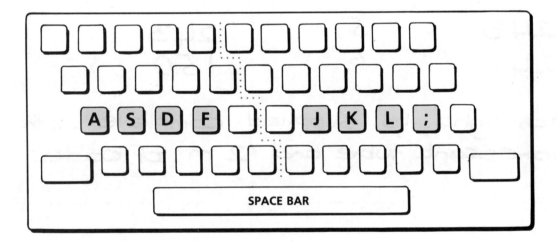

```
fj dk sl a; ;a ls kd jf as ask all adds
ad fall dad lad sass lass sad fads alas

all ads; dads ask a lad; sad lads fall;
sad falls; ask dad; sad salad; add all;

flasks fall; add ads; all lads; as dad;
all dads; a sad lad; ask lads; sad dad;
```

Display the following information. Your work should be centred horizontally.

BUDGET LINK-LIGHT SYSTEM

Code No	Watt	Length (mm)
0930	30	930
0625	18	625
0243	15	243
0241	6	150

Each light is supplied complete with fluorescent tube and 2 m of cable

CHAINING

The third component in building typing skill is chaining.

Your fingers will not move any faster than they are moving now. Trying to move them faster will result in tension through the arms up to the shoulder.

Fast typists type often, they do not move their fingers faster. They have shorter pauses between the strokes.

The only way to type faster is to shorten the pauses between strokes.

Shorten the pauses by typing a pair of letters as a single response. These pairs of letters are called chains and the more chains you use, the faster you will type.

Type `la` not `l a`.

Type this drill and read each chain aloud quietly as you type it. By reading the drills aloud you cannot spell because you can only say one thing at a time. Spelling (typing letter by letter) holds you to a slow rate.

```
sa sa ld ld af af al al as as alas alas
lf lf ad ad sk sk fa fa ll ll fall fall
ff ff da da lf lf la la ss ss lass lass
```

Some words are composed of several chains, others will combine chains and single letters and your fingers will choose the easiest combinations.

Inward motions are easier than outward, ie AF is easier than FA. Fingers farther apart strike letters more easily than those adjacent, ie FA is easier than SA.

Type `flask` several times and experiment with different possibilities – `fl as k` and `f la sk` and `fl a sk`.

Concentrate on chaining as you type this drill. Read aloud.

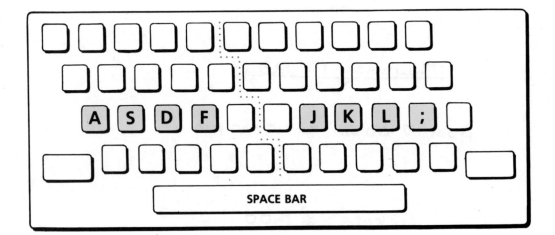

```
af ad al sl la lk ak ld da sa fa as ask
ss dd ll ff kk ja fl ls ds ks fs ad add

as ask ad alas lad dad sad fad lass all
add fall flask ads sass add flask salad

a lass falls; add all ads; alas a fall;
add a dad; sad fads; alas a lass falls;
```

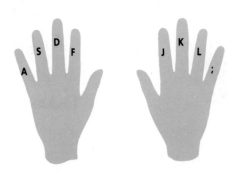

Display the following Notice as attractively as possible using any acceptable style.

RIVERGLEN COMMUNITY SCHOOL

UPPER SCHOOL DISCO

will be held

in the

MAIN HALL

on

Thursday 19 May

from 7.00pm to 10.00pm

Tickets: £1.00

Refreshments Available

Talent Spotting Competition

RELATED KNOWLEDGE

Punctuation

This becomes part of the word it follows; do not hesitate before typing a full stop. Space after punctuation, not before.

Margins

These are easy to set on the typewriter; consult the instruction manual if you need to do so. Computer programs and word processors have default (preset) settings that you can adjust as needed.

Print size

On manual and electric typewriters, print size is described as pica (10 characters to the inch) or elite (12 characters to the inch). Some electric typewriters also have proportional spacing (each character takes up a different amount of space).

Electronics and computers call print size 10 and 12 pitch; some also have 15 pitch. The print size cannot be changed on a manual typewriter, but the element on an electric can be 10 pica or 12 elite, and the daisywheel on an electronic typewriter or word processor/computer's daisywheel printer can be changed to give different typefaces and sizes.

```
This is 10 pitch (pica).
This is 12 pitch (elite).
```

Line spacing

This is set on manuals and electrics with a lever, usually on the top of the frame. Electronics have a fraction key or a sliding scale indicator. Word processors have a default (preset) setting but allow for choice.

There are 6 lines to the vertical inch, although word processors can be modified.

Line 1	This	This	This	This
Line 2	is			
Line 3	single	is	is	
Line 4	spacing	1 1/2		is
Line 5			double	
Line 6		spacing		
Line 7			spacing	triple
Line 8				
Line 9				
Line 10				spacing

PRACTICE

Short, frequent practices are most effective in building your skill so practice as often as you can.

When you do not have a keyboard to practise on, you can use a table top. You will notice the improvement in your chaining and ballistic stroking the next time you practise at a keyboard.

You can also practise very effectively in your mind. Imagine that you are typing the last line of each drill. There will be a minute muscular response, below your recognition level but there nonetheless, and the improvement will surprise you. After you have learned all the keys you can still use this practice technique.

> Put all the items in the Order code section into numerical order, under each heading, eg <u>Cushions</u>
>
> CS30 . . . .
> CS32 . . . .

PRAXI GARDEN FURNITURE — ACCESSORIES

Accessories are available in thoughtfully chosen floral and plain fabrics, in a variety of colours.

> Rule as shown

Order code	Description of items	Fabric information	
		Price code*	Fabrics available
<u>Cushions</u>			
CS32	Bench 72" x 18"	B	Plain
CS36	Lounger chair	C	Floral
CS30	Bench 48" x 18"	B	Plain
CS35	Highback chair	B	Floral
<u>Parasols</u>**			
PS49	Tasselled edge 90"	D	Plain
PS47	Fringed edge 72"	C	Floral
PS46	Scalloped edge 67"	C	Floral
PS48	Pleated edge 84"	D	Plain
<u>Tableware</u>	(Machine washable items)	A sample service of all fabric designs is available on request, free of charge.	
Tablecloths, placemats and napkins:	All tableware is edged with contrast cord piping for a top quality finish.		
TW54	Circular tablecloth 54"	B	Floral
TW53	Circular tablecloth 35"	B	Floral
TW55	Oval tablecloth 68" x 88"	C	Plain
TW60	Oval quilted placemat	A	Plain
TW61	Square napkin	A	Plain

*   See our separate list of price codes.

**   Supplied with easy tilt action and adjustable height.

Letter E

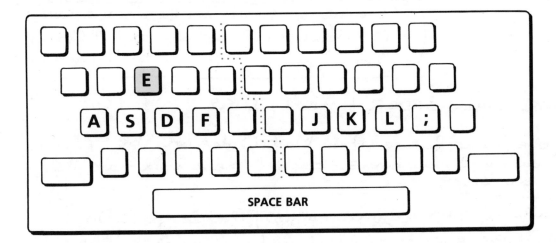

Locate **E–D** finger, upper row

Look at your hands – say and type de de de de
Look at the script – say and type de de de de
Watch the copy – say and type the drill below

Remember – flat wrists and a ballistic stroke

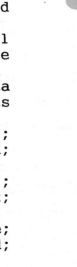

```
el ek ed es se ea le de fe ef ke je eel
elf elk el else sled fled led less lead

dell deal dead deaf desks fed safe fell
feed deed seed seek eke lake fake flake

sea seal sell self ease easel lease lea
fade ades ales dales sales sakes slakes

a jaded flea; flakes fell; a dead leaf;
sell eels; see a lake; deaf seals fled;

lead ladles; leased desks; seal a deal;
a fake elf; seek sleds; feed sleek elk;

sell easels; see a keel; a deeded lake;
added sales; kale seeds; as seals fled;

see a sleek flea flee; false lease fee;
feed a faded elf; sell sad lads a sled;

a lad sasses a dad; as sleek as a seal;
sad fleas fled; feed seals a dead leaf;

sell eels; see a lake; sell dad a flea;
a jelled leaf salad; see a safe saddle;
```

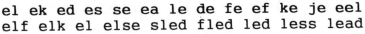

Speed in typing is calculated in words per minute; a word is calculated as 5 characters/
spaces. Across the bottom of each of the following pages there is a word count.

TASK 3

Please key in the details below and save under: NEWLINES. Print one copy. Choose either ragged or justified right margin

PRAXI MAIL ORDER - NEW LINES

In the/very near future Praxi Mail Order wl. be introducing 3 new lines. Each of these will have its own banner.

Details of them are given below. The Compact Disc Club is going to be run on similar lines to other mail order cos. offering this item but w. special features. ~~Its will appear in more than~~ ~~membership must last 18 mths.~~ Members will be asked to buy only 2 discs in their first year as members. They will be asked to remain members for 18 months. They can purchase ~~a specially priced extra disc with~~ one disc at bonus price for each disc they order at the normal club charge of £12.99 each.

Inset 15 spaces from left margin

Paperback Plus ~~gives~~ offers members the opp. to purchase ✓ newly published books with somewhat more sturdy covers at no extra cost. The only extra exp. will be postage + packing wh. will work out at approx. £1.50 per book.

Garden Direct shd. offer avid gardeners the chance to rec. advice at low cost. They can purchase seeds and bulbs at discount prices. Some shrubs and plants will also be offered. These are likely to be the more unusual species. at any time of yr.

Please ensure that all members of our other mail order clubs are ~~worked~~ ~~In receipt of full details of all these~~ ~~3 new clubs~~ placed on the mailing list for these new ones.

Details of ~~the new clubs will be released~~ these new ventures will be given to the press very shortly. Adverts. in the major journals will follow after that.

Double line spacing for this paragraph

Letter H

Locate **H**–**J** finger, adjacent

Look at your hands – say and type jh jh jh jh
Look at the script – say and type jh jh jh jh
Watch the copy – say and type the drill below

Remember – flat wrists and a ballistic stroke

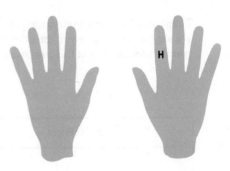

```
he ha ah sh she sheds shell shelf sheaf
he heed heel heal head held ah lah shah

haha has had hale half hall shall shale
ash dash hash flash slash sashes lashes

he has; she shall; he had; he has held;
she dashed; he shall see; she has half;

she has a shell; he has all; she heeds;
a hall shelf; shaded sheds; dead ashes;

she has half a desk; she has had fleas;
he has had a hall shelf; she has a dad;

he held a sash; shake fleas; he healed;
she flashes lashes; he shall see a she;

she dashes; he sees a flash; he shakes;
she has shed a sash; he has shed fleas;

she shakes shells; he has held a shelf;
a seal has shed a flea; she has a shad;

he shakes a leaf; a fake elk has fleas;
she held a dead hake; she seeks shades;
```

PLEASE ENTER YOUR NAME AND CENTRE NUMBER AND INSERT THE FORM INTO YOUR ANSWER BOOK AT THE END OF THE EXAMINATION. IF BOTH SIDES OF THE FORM ARE USED ONE ATTEMPT MUST BE CANCELLED. **YOU MAY TYPE ALL ENTRIES IN CAPITALS IF YOU WISH.**

NAME: _____ CENTRE NUMBER: _____

To	Date

Thank you for your enquiry received _____
We are pleased to give you the information required. Prices and delivery periods are valid for at least one month from the date of this quotation.

Goods/Services	Price	Delivery period

VAT is/is not* included in the prices quoted.

* Delete as appropriate

Photocopy this form for use with the task on page 226.

Letter O

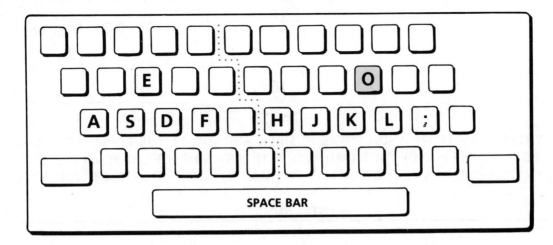

Locate **O-L** finger, upper row

Look at your hands — say and type `lo lo lo lo`
Look at the script — say and type `lo lo lo lo`
Watch the copy — say and type the drill below

Remember — flat wrists and a ballistic stroke

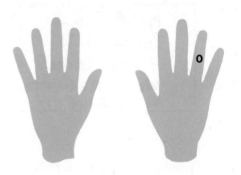

```
of oo so lo jo ho fo oa oe os od ok oho
ko do does doll dole ode shod shoe joke

shoo floods oodles aloof foe folk folds
hod hold hole hose lo lose losses lodes

kohl kodak koala so sole sold solo sofa
old oleo oak oaf oases oh aloha off odd

odd shoes; he sold a loaf; lose a doll;
desk of old oak; hold food; fool foals;

she shook a soda; shoe a hoof; he does;
do a solo; she loses shoes; old koalas;

she sold floss; she does sad old jokes;
a soaked oaf; flooded oases; load hods;

a loose sod; hold off; a load of sofas;
loaded lodes; a folded oak leaf; so so;

oodles of old shoe soles; a loose hose;
a fool shook a loofah; he loses a shoe;

oh oh she sloshed a soda; he looks old;
a doe flees a koala; so does a sad elk;
```

`. . . . 1 . . . . 2 . . . . 3 . . . . 4 . . . . 5 . . . . 6 . . . . 7 . . . . 8`

Please type these details on the attached blank form

PLEASE ENTER YOUR NAME AND CENTRE NUMBER AND INSERT THE FORM INTO YOUR ANSWER BOOK AT THE END OF THE EXAMINATION. IF BOTH SIDES OF THE FORM ARE USED ONE ATTEMPT MUST BE CANCELLED. **YOU MAY TYPE ALL ENTRIES IN CAPITALS IF YOU WISH.**

NAME: _____   CENTRE NUMBER: _____

To **Mr R Black**
Running Wild
7 High Street
WOLVERHAMPTON
WV2 5TN

Date

Thank you for your enquiry received   *last week*
We are pleased to give you the information required. Prices and delivery periods are valid for at least one month from the date of this quotation.

Goods/Services	Price	Delivery period
Pentagon trainers	£35	1 week
Cheetah racers	£50	2 weeks
Classic spikes	£60	2 weeks

VAT is/~~is not~~* included in the prices quoted.

* Delete as appropriate

Building good work habits

As in all skills, keyboarding habits are quick to form and slow to break, so it is important that you build good working practices. Bad habits interfere with your skill. If you find any developing, make a concentrated effort to break them.

Do not
  – watch your hands – keep your eyes on the copy
  – lean your hands on the frame of your machine
  – 'spell' as you type
  – slump in your chair
  – sit rigidly
  – cross your knees
  – lift your hand to press return
  – neglect to use your copy holder
  – stop to make corrections in this section
  – neglect to adjust your workstation
  – panic

Do
  – rest
  – move

Watching your hands
This habit has several bad effects. First of all, you cut your speed in half because you are reading half the time and typing the other half.

Then, each time you look away from the copy you have to find your place again and more time is lost. It is very easy to go back to the wrong place.

There is enormous strain upon your neck. The weight of your head (about 8 pounds) shifts from the skeletal system to the muscles as you bend your head forward and the further it is bent, the greater the strain.

Put your fingers on the back of your neck. Hold your head erect and notice that the muscles are relaxed. Now, bend your head forward and feel the muscles tighten more and more as your chin gets closer to your chest. Your neck will tolerate no more than 20 degrees of tilt before strain begins. See how far it bends forward when you watch your hands.

Watch the copy from which you are typing; do not watch your hands.

60° slope

Leaning your hands on the frame
This habit forces you to use a fixed muscle motion instead of a ballistic stroke. It also places and keeps your wrists in a strained, awkward position that will compress the nerves and blood vessels in the carpel tunnel. Keep your hands and wrists in the positions shown on page 8.

PRAXI SPORTS CLOTHING SPONSORED EVENTS

Once again we are sponsoring a series of events around the country. Our goods, including commemorative tee shirts, will be on sale at each venue.

Name of Event	Venue	Month
Cannock Chase half marathon	Cannock	June
Daventry 10k dash	Daventry	June
Round the Wrekin run	Telford	June
Ilkley Moor cross country	Ilkley Moor	July
Men of Kent marathon	Canterbury	August
Tamar Valley half marathon	Plymouth	July
Bristol ladies' fun run	Bristol	August
Wyre Forest jog	Bewdley	September
Yorkshire lasses' fun run	Leeds	September
Kings Lynn turkey trot	Kings Lynn	December

Spelling   You can only say one thing at a time and if you are spelling out words in your head as you type them, you cannot be chaining. Spelling keeps your speed to the rate you can spell; you can never type any faster than you can spell.

Slumping   Relaxing and slumping are not the same thing. You should relax your muscles, but slumping is allowing the lumbar curve in the spine to change from its natural inward curve to a outward one that squeezes the discs on the inside and forces them to push against the ligament on the outside.

Stand up, put your hands on your back at your waist and feel the lumbar curve, the inward curve of your spine. Now sit, maintaining that curve. To do so, you must sit up.

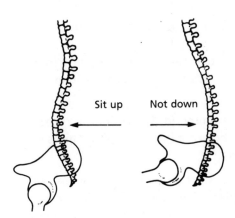

Sit up   Not down

Sitting rigidly   To keep your shoulder and back muscles relaxed, lean forward slightly from the hip, so gravity will keep you balanced instead of having to tense your back muscles.

Crossing your knees   Your body is thrown off balance when you take your weight off one or both of your feet. Then energy is needed to keep your body stable on the chair.

Lifting your hand to return   It is slow to lift your hand or use any other finger than the little one if you are pressing the return key. Stretch your hand but do not lift it. When you move it away from the home keys, it's easy to get lost.

Neglecting to use your copy holder   Using your copy holder keeps your head erect and allows for minimum twisting of your neck. Laying your copy flat on the desk forces a forward bend and often a twisted and rigid position to your neck.

Not resting   You must take regular breaks to relax your muscles. Lean back in your chair, stretch your legs out straight, let your arms hang loose.

Not moving   Walk around at intervals to allow the muscles to dispel the toxins that have accumulated and cause fatigue. This is particularly important if using a computer/word processor.

Stopping to make corrections   In building skill, technique is the first priority. If you stop to make corrections, you are putting emphasis on the product instead of concentrating on the process. When you stop, you interfere with your continuity, the fluency that makes you a skilled operator. When you are aware of having made an error, type the word again correctly, but do not stop.

Neglecting to adjust your workstation   Adjust your workstation before you begin and later on in the day, especially if someone else may have been using it. It must fit you.

Panicking   We learn best in a relaxed but alert state of mind. Allowing an emotional state to take over makes you react instead of acting in a positive way. Don't dawdle but do let your fingers do what you have taught them to do. Trust them and trust yourself.

Organise and arrange the copying, collating and binding of documents

In order to achieve this competence you are required to:

1 Copy, collate and bind all the tasks that you produced for Element 5.1.

2 Enlarge the graph you produced for Element 5.2 to twice its original size so that it can be displayed on a flip board for a presentation which Mr Dubuc is giving.

3 Reduce the graph to half its size so that Mr Dubuc can have it for easy reference on his journey.

4 a Place both Task 1 and Task 2 of Element 5.2 together on the photocopier and reproduce them on a sheet of A3. Take 3 copies.

  b Take a photocopy of Task 3 on page 209. Cut out the table. Take a photocopy of Task 2 on page 222. Now paste the 2 tables on to a single sheet of paper. Take 3 copies of this.

On the top of each of these 3 copies put the names of J Hammond, P Farrah and J Cozna. Then indicate which copy is to go to each, either with a tick or a highlight pen. This is so that they can have a copy when they visit their customers.

5 Ask a fellow student to play the part of a new member of staff at your company, and show them how to enlarge and reduce on the photocopier. Give them 3 tasks. You can choose these from Element 5.1 (page 205). Instruct them to enlarge one document, reduce one in size, and photocopy one the same size. Monitor their progress.

6 Keep records of your work.

You can now present this as evidence.

Letter R

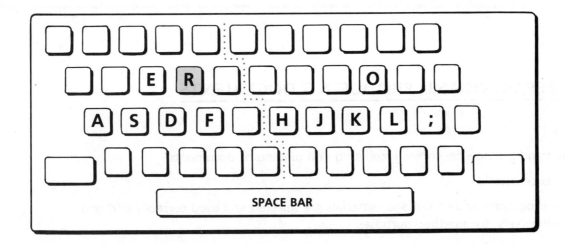

Locate **R–F** finger, upper row

Look at your hands – say and type `fr fr fr fr`
Look at the script – say and type `fr fr fr fr`
Watch the copy – say and type the drill below

Remember – flat wrists and a ballistic stroke

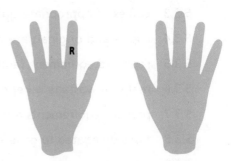

```
fr rf rk rl ar ra dr rd ro or rr er red
real rear read fore fare dare hare here

erred errors horror sorrel jarred arras
area ark ajar share freed fresher freak

fork hark lark dark jerk era eral erase
drear dread dress droll drake jeer deer

or ore oral floral ordered adore shores
rah rare rash radar raked raffle herald

ford lord lard harder herd horde afford
rod rodeo roe rose role rolls hero aero

he heard her jeers; a rare horror reel;
share red folders; free offers for her;

errors are erased; her hero adores her;
she fears lasers; a droll role for her;

her red roses are real; fares are dear;
her dad hoarded jars; a darker dresser;

here are orders for jars of kale salad;
he offered fresh fodder for her horses;
```

Administration

Level 3

UNIT 5   PREPARING AND PRODUCING DOCUMENTS

Element 5.3

Organise and arrange the copying, collating and binding of documents

Performance criteria

5.3.1   reprographic equipment and materials are selected and used correctly and cost effectively, for specified purposes

5.3.2   documents for reproduction are prepared correctly

5.3.3   copies of appropriate quality are produced from original documents

5.3.4   copies and originals are collated, fastened and distributed correctly

5.3.5   reported equipment faults are dealt with promptly

5.3.6   material wastage is kept to a minimum

5.3.7   precise requirements are conveyed to colleagues and confirmed where appropriate

5.3.8   tasks delegated to others are accurately defined and progress monitored

5.3.9   work progress is planned and monitored to meet all deadlines

5.3.10 records are kept up to date, legible and accurate

5.3.11 safe working practices are always followed and implemented

5.3.12 security and confidentiality procedures are always followed and implemented

Letter U

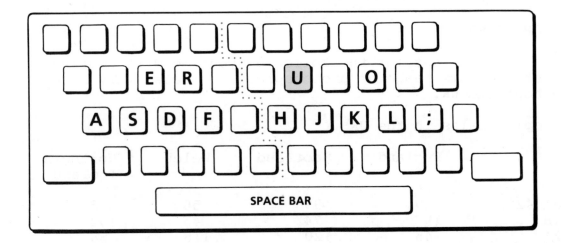

Locate **U–J** finger, upper row
Look at your hands – say and type ju ju ju ju
Look at the script – say and type ju ju ju ju
Watch the copy – say and type the drill below

Remember – flat wrists and a ballistic stroke

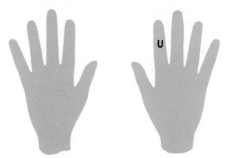

```
lu su hu ju ru ku fu au ou ur ul us use
ue ud ua du duel dues duo dull dud duke

us uses usual aura frau fraud laud haul
sure surf suds sulk flue hue sued suede

hull hulk husk hush rush ruse rude rule
fur furl fuel fuse fuss full fluff huff

our four sour dour hour flour shoulders
lulu lull lurk lured lush slush slurred

sure of full kudos for us; house fuses;
use our sour flour; a dull duo of duds;

a frau has furs; all four of our rules;
rush for hours; ruses eluded all of us;

a rude slur; for four hours; our house;
sure of our usual allure; full of suds;

a doused louse; assure us of a shuffle;
full of fuss; hurrah for us; loud surf;

a house full of rules; she should hula;
a duke has sued a dude for foul frauds;
```

■ TASK 2

The following information should be produced and sent with the memo to John Stephenson.
Display the figures in an appropriate graph form.

PHOTOCOPIER SALES

We have decided that for the following year we will continue
to offer the same range of photocopiers, as sales vary so much
throughout the UK.

Photocopier sales in the UK

	England	Scotland	Wales	Northern Ireland
Chanex 420	89	99	56	38
Rex 18	197	74	45	102
Rex 24	45	120	118	58
Rex 26	136	69	74	45

Shift keys

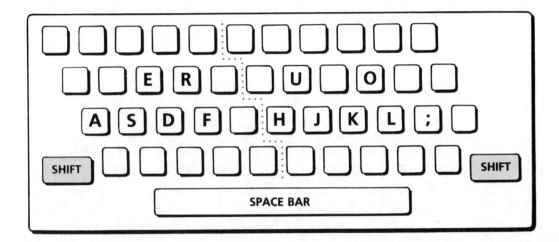

Every key will produce 2 characters, upper and lower case. Small letters are called lower case and capital letters are called upper case.

To type an upper case character, press the **SHIFT** key with the little finger of one hand and, while it is fully depressed, strike the letter key, using the fingers of the other hand.

There are 2 shift keys, one at each lower corner of the keyboard. It is important that you press shift with one hand and strike the letter key with the other, rather than trying to shift and strike with the same hand, a slow and very awkward motion.

The shift keys are controlled with the little fingers.

Stretch your hand and keep your index fingers close to their home keys.

Use a count of 3 – shift, strike, release.

Try **A** Shift with your right little finger and hold the key down
      Strike **A**
      Release the shift key

Type A A A D D D E E E F F F R R R S S S

Try **J** Shift with your left little finger and hold the key down
      Strike **J**
      Release the shift key

Type J J J K K K L L L H H H O O O U U U

Chain capitals by shifting and striking simultaneously if you can; that will use a count of 2.

Shift lock/caps lock

Use the **SHIFT LOCK** key on a typewriter or the **CAPS LOCK** key on a computer to type a word or more all in capitals.

Type this drill.

```
Ella Leo Fred Karl Sarah Joe Deke Lara
Ross Ursula Ada Hedda SAL OSLO AL LULU
```

. . . . 1 . . . . 2 . . . . 3 . . . . 4 . . . . 5 . . . . 6 . . . . 7 8

SeaCat timetable

DOVER TO CALAIS

APRIL

Service	Dep.	W	T	F	S	S	M	T	W	T	F	S	S	M	T	W	T	F	S	S	M	T	W	T	F	S	S	M	T	W	T
No.	Time	1	2	3	4	5	6	7	8	9	10	11	12	13	14	15	16	17	18	19	20	21	22	23	24	25	26	27	28	29	30
332	08.00	D	D	D	D	D	D	D	D	D	D	D	D	D	D	D	D	C	D	D	D	D	D	D	D	D	D	D	D	D	D
345	11.15	C		C	C		C	C	C		C	C	C	C	C	C	C	C	C	C	C	C	C	C	C	C	C	C	C	C	C
358	14.30	C		C	C		C	C	C		C	C	C	C	C	C	C	C	C	C	C	C	C	C	C	C	C	C	C	C	C
363	15.45		C			C				C																					
372	18.00	C		C	C		C	C	C		C																				
373	18.15											C	C	C	C	C	C	C	C	C	C	C	C	C	C	C	C	C	C	C	C
375	18.45		C			C				C																					
382	20.30	D	D	D	D	D	D	D	D	D	D	D	D	D	D	D	D	D	D	D	D	D	D	D	D	D	D	D	D	D	D

MAY

Service	Dep.	F	S	S	M	T	W	T	F	S	S	M	T	W	T	F	S	S	M	T	W	T	F	S	S	M	T	W	T	F	S	S
No.	Time	1	2	3	4	5	6	7	8	9	10	11	12	13	14	15	16	17	18	19	20	21	22	23	24	25	26	27	28	29	30	31
324	06.00																															D
332	08.00	D	D	D	D	D	D	D	D	D	D	D	D	D	D	D	D	D	D	D	D	D	B	B	D	D	D	D	D	D	D	
336	09.00																															C
345	11.15	C	C	C	C	C	C	C	C	C	C	C	C	C	C	C	C	C	C	C	C	C	B	B	C	C	C	C	C	C	C	
348	12.00																															C
358	14.30	C	C	C	C	C	C	C	C	C	C	C	C	C	C	C	C	C	C	C	C	C	B	B	C	C	C	C	C	C	C	
360	15.00																															C
372	18.00																															C
373	18.15	C	C	C	C	C	C	C	C	C	C	C	C	C	C	C	C	C	C	C	C	C	C	C	C	C	C	C	C	C	C	
382	20.30	D	D	D	D	D	D	D	D	D	D	D	D	D	D	D	D	D	D	D	D	D	D	D	D	D	D	D	D	D	D	
384	21.00																															D
392	23.00																															E

JUNE

Service	Dep.	M	T	W	T	F	S	S	M	T	W	T	F	S	S	M	T	W	T	F	S	S	M	T	W	T	F	S	S	M	T
No.	Time	1	2	3	4	5	6	7	8	9	10	11	12	13	14	15	16	17	18	19	20	21	22	23	24	25	26	27	28	29	30
324	06.00	D	D	D	D	D	D	D	D	D	D	D	D	D	D	D	D	D	D	D	D	D	D	D	D	D	D	D	D	D	D
336	09.00	C	C	C	C	C	C	C	C	C	C	C	C	C	C	C	C	C	C	C	C	C	C	C	C	C	C	C	C	C	C
348	12.00	C	C	C	C	C	C	C	C	C	C	C	C	C	C	C	C	C	C	C	C	C	C	C	C	C	C	C	C	C	C
360	15.00	C	C	C	C	C	C	C	C	C	C	C	C	C	C	C	C	C	C	C	C	C	C	C	C	C	C	C	C	C	C
372	18.00	C	C	C	C	C	C	C	C	C	C	C	C	C	C	C	C	C	C	C	C	C	C	C	C	C	C	C	C	C	C
384	21.00	D	D	D	D	D	D	D	D	D	D	D	D	D	D	D	D	D	D	D	D	D	D	D	D	D	D	D	D	D	D
392	23.00	E	E	E	E	E	E	E	E	E	E	E	E	E	E	E	E	E	E	E	E	E	E	E	E	E	E	E	E	E	E

JULY

Service	Dep.	W	T	F	S	S	M	T	W	T	F	S	S	M	T	W	T	F	S	S	M	T	W	T	F	S	S	M	T	W	T	F
No.	Time	1	2	3	4	5	6	7	8	9	10	11	12	13	14	15	16	17	18	19	20	21	22	23	24	25	26	27	28	29	30	31
306	01.30										E	E	E					E	E	E					E	E	E					E
324	06.00	D	D	D	D	D	D	D	D	D	C	C	C	C	C	C	C	C	C	C	C	C	C	C	C	C	C	C	C	C	C	C
336	09.00	C	C	C	C	C	C	C	C	C	B	B	C	C	C	C	C	B	B	C	C	C	C	B	B	B	C	C	C	C	C	B
348	12.00	C	C	C	C	C	C	C	C	C	B	B	C	C	C	C	C	B	B	C	C	C	C	B	B	B	C	C	C	C	C	B
360	15.00	C	C	C	C	C	C	C	C	C	B	B	C	C	C	C	C	B	B	C	C	C	C	B	B	B	C	C	C	C	C	B
372	18.00	C	C	C	C	C	C	C	C	C	B	C	C	C	C	C	C	B	C	C	C	C	C	B	C	C	C	C	C	C	C	B
384	21.00	D	D	D	D	D	D	D	D	D	D	D	D	D	D	D	D	D	D	D	D	D	D	D	D	D	D	D	D	D	D	D
392	23.00	E	D	D	D	E	E	E	E	D	D	D	E	E	E	E	D	D	D	E	E	E	E	D	D	D	E	E	E	E	D	D

AUGUST

Service	Dep.	S	S	M	T	W	T	F	S	S	M	T	W	T	F	S	S	M	T	W	T	F	S	S	M	T	W	T	F	S	S	M
No.	Time	1	2	3	4	5	6	7	8	9	10	11	12	13	14	15	16	17	18	19	20	21	22	23	24	25	26	27	28	29	30	31
306	01.30	E	E					E	E	E					E	E	E					E	E	E					E	E	E	
324	06.00	D	D	D	D	D	D	D	D	D	D	D	D	D	D	D	D	D	D	D	D	D	D	D	D	D	D	D	D	D	D	D
336	09.00	B	C	C	C	C	C	B	B	C	C	C	C	C	B	B	C	C	C	C	C	B	B	C	C	C	C	C	B	B	C	C
348	12.00	B	C	C	C	C	C	B	B	C	C	C	C	C	B	B	C	C	C	C	C	B	B	C	C	C	C	C	B	B	C	C
360	15.00	B	C	C	C	C	C	B	B	C	C	C	C	C	B	B	C	C	C	C	C	B	B	C	C	C	C	C	B	B	C	C
372	18.00	B	C	C	C	C	C	B	C	C	C	C	C	C	B	C	C	C	C	C	C	B	C	C	C	C	C	C	B	C	C	C
384	21.00	C	D	D	D	D	C	C	C	D	D	D	D	C	C	C	D	D	D	D	C	C	C	D	D	D	D	C	C	C	D	D
392	23.00	D	E	E	E	E	D	D	D	E	E	E	E	D	D	D	E	E	E	E	D	D	D	E	E	E	E	D	D	D	E	E

SEPTEMBER

Service	Dep.	T	W	T	F	S	S	M	T	W	T	F	S	S	M	T	W	T	F	S	S	M	T	W	T	F	S	S	M	T	W
No.	Time	1	2	3	4	5	6	7	8	9	10	11	12	13	14	15	16	17	18	19	20	21	22	23	24	25	26	27	28	29	30
306	01.30				E	E	E																								
324	06.00	D	D	D	D	D	D	D	D	D	D	D	D	D	D	D	D	D	D	D	D	D	D	D	D	D	D				
330	07.30																											D	D	D	D
334	08.30																											D	D	D	D
336	09.00	C	C	C	C	C	C	C	C	C	C	C	C	C	C	C	C	C	C	C	C	C	C	C	C	C	C				
346	11.30																											C	C	C	C
348	12.00	C	C	C	C	C	C	C	C	C	C	C	C	C	C	C	C	C	C	C	C	C	C	C	C	C	C				
358	14.30																											C	C	C	C
360	15.00	C	C	C	C	C	C	C	C	C	C	C	C	C	C	C	C	C	C	C	C	C	C	C	C	C	C				
370	17.30																											C	C	C	C
372	18.00	C	C	C	C	C	C	C	C	C	C	C	C	C	C	C	C	C	C	C	C	C	C	C	C	C	C				
382	20.30																											D	D	D	D
384	21.00	D	D	D	D	D	D	D	D	D	D	D	D	D	D	D	D	D	D	D	D	D	D	D	D	D	D				
392	23.00	E	E	D	D	D	E	E	E	E	D	D	D	E	E	E	E	D	D	D	E	E	E	E	D	D	D				

CALAIS TO DOVER

APRIL

Service	Dep.	W	T	F	S	S	M	T	W	T	F	S	S	M	T	W	T	F	S	S	M	T	W	T	F	S	S	M	T	W	T
No.	Time	1	2	3	4	5	6	7	8	9	10	11	12	13	14	15	16	17	18	19	20	21	22	23	24	25	26	27	28	29	30
442	10.30	D	D	D	D	D	D	D	D	D	D	D	D	D	D	D	D	D	D	D	D	D	D	D	D	D	D	D	D	D	D
455	13.45	C		C	C		C	C	C		C	C	C	C	C	C	C	C	C	C	C	C	C	C	C	C	C	C	C	C	C
468	17.00											C	C	C	C	C	C	C	C	C	C	C	C	C	C	C	C	C	C	C	C
469	17.15	C		C	C		C	C	C		C																				
473	18.15		C			C				C																					
482	20.30											D	D	D	D	D	D	D	D	D	D	D	D	D	D	D	D	D	D	D	D
483	20.45	D		D	D		D	D	D		D																				
485	21.15		D			D				D																					
492	23.00	E	E	E	E	E	E	E	E	E	E	E	E	E	E	E	E	E	E	E	E	E	E	E	E	E	E	E	E	E	E

MAY

Service	Dep.	F	S	S	M	T	W	T	F	S	S	M	T	W	T	F	S	S	M	T	W	T	F	S	S	M	T	W	T	F	S	S
No.	Time	1	2	3	4	5	6	7	8	9	10	11	12	13	14	15	16	17	18	19	20	21	22	23	24	25	26	27	28	29	30	31
434	08.30																															D
442	10.30	D	D	D	D	D	D	D	D	D	D	D	D	D	D	D	D	D	D	D	D	D	D	D	D	D	D	D	D	D	D	
446	11.30																															C
455	13.45	C	C	C	C	C	C	C	C	C	C	C	C	C	C	C	C	C	C	C	C	C	C	C	C	C	C	C	C	C	C	
458	14.30																															C
468	17.00	C	C	C	C	C	C	C	C	C	C	C	C	C	C	C	C	C	C	C	C	C	C	C	C	C	C	C	C	C	C	
470	17.30																															C
482	20.30	D	D	D	D	D	D	D	D	D	D	D	D	D	D	D	D	D	D	D	D	D	D	D	D	D	D	D	D	D	D	D
492	23.00	E	E	E	E	E	E	E	E	E	E	E	E	E	E	E	E	E	E	E	E	E	E	E	E	E	E	E	E	E	E	
494	23.30																															E

JUNE

Service	Dep.	M	T	W	T	F	S	S	M	T	W	T	F	S	S	M	T	W	T	F	S	S	M	T	W	T	F	S	S	M	T
No.	Time	1	2	3	4	5	6	7	8	9	10	11	12	13	14	15	16	17	18	19	20	21	22	23	24	25	26	27	28	29	30
416	04.00	E	E	E	E	E	E	E	E	E	E	E	E	E	E	E	E	E	E	E	E	E	E	E	E	E	E	E	E	E	E
434	08.30	D	D	D	D	D	D	D	D	D	D	D	D	D	D	D	D	D	D	D	D	D	D	D	D	D	D	D	D	D	D
446	11.30	C	C	C	C	C	C	C	C	C	C	C	C	C	C	C	C	C	C	C	C	C	C	C	C	C	C	C	C	C	C
458	14.30	C	C	C	C	C	C	C	C	C	C	C	C	C	C	C	C	C	C	C	C	C	C	C	C	C	C	C	C	C	C
470	17.30	C	C	C	C	C	C	C	C	C	C	C	C	C	C	C	C	C	C	C	C	C	C	C	C	C	C	C	C	C	C
482	20.30	D	D	D	D	D	D	D	D	D	D	D	D	D	D	D	D	D	D	D	D	D	D	D	D	D	D	D	D	D	D
494	23.30	E	E	E	E	E	E	E	E	E	E	E	E	E	E	E	E	E	E	E	E	E	E	E	E	E	E	E	E	E	E

JULY

Service	Dep.	W	T	F	S	S	M	T	W	T	F	S	S	M	T	W	T	F	S	S	M	T	W	T	F	S	S	M	T	W	T	F
No.	Time	1	2	3	4	5	6	7	8	9	10	11	12	13	14	15	16	17	18	19	20	21	22	23	24	25	26	27	28	29	30	31
408	02.00										E	E	E					E	E	E					E	E	E					E
416	04.00	E	E	E	E	E	E	E	E	E	E	E	E	E	E	E	E	E	E	E	E	E	E	E	E	E	E	E	E	E	E	E
434	08.30	D	D	D	D	D	D	D	D	D	C	C	C	C	C	C	C	C	C	C	C	C	C	C	C	C	C	C	C	C	C	C
446	11.30	C	C	C	C	C	C	C	C	C	C	B	B	C	C	C	C	C	B	B	C	C	C	C	C	B	B	C	C	C	C	C
458	14.30	C	C	C	C	C	C	C	C	C	C	B	B	C	C	C	C	C	B	B	C	C	C	C	C	B	B	C	C	C	C	C
470	17.30	C	C	C	C	C	C	C	C	C	C	B	B	C	C	C	C	C	B	B	C	C	C	C	C	B	B	C	C	C	C	C
482	20.30	D	D	D	D	D	D	D	D	D	C	C	C	C	C	C	C	C	C	C	C	C	C	C	C	C	C	C	C	C	C	C
494	23.30	E	E	E	E	E	E	E	E	E	E	D	D	D	D	D	D	D	D	D	D	D	D	D	D	D	D	D	D	D	D	D

AUGUST

Service	Dep.	S	S	M	T	W	T	F	S	S	M	T	W	T	F	S	S	M	T	W	T	F	S	S	M	T	W	T	F	S	S	M
No.	Time	1	2	3	4	5	6	7	8	9	10	11	12	13	14	15	16	17	18	19	20	21	22	23	24	25	26	27	28	29	30	31
408	02.00	E	E					E	E	E					E	E	E					E	E	E					E	E	E	
416	04.00	E	E	E	E	E	E	E	E	E	E	E	E	E	E	E	E	E	E	E	E	E	E	E	E	E	E	E	E	E	E	E
434	08.30	C	C	C	C	C	C	C	C	C	C	C	C	C	C	C	C	C	C	C	C	C	C	C	C	C	C	C	C	C	C	C
446	11.30	B	B	C	C	C	C	C	B	B	C	C	C	C	C	B	B	C	C	C	C	C	B	B	C	C	C	C	C	B	B	C
458	14.30	B	B	C	C	C	C	C	B	B	C	C	C	C	C	B	B	C	C	C	C	C	B	B	C	C	C	C	C	B	B	C
470	17.30	B	B	C	C	C	C	C	B	B	C	C	C	C	C	B	B	C	C	C	C	C	B	B	C	C	C	C	C	B	B	C
482	20.30	C	C	C	C	C	C	C	C	C	C	C	C	C	C	C	C	C	C	C	C	C	C	C	C	C	C	C	C	C	C	C
494	23.30	D	D	D	D	D	D	D	D	D	D	D	D	D	D	D	D	D	D	D	D	D	D	D	D	D	D	D	D	D	D	D

SEPTEMBER

Service	Dep.	T	W	T	F	S	S	M	T	W	T	F	S	S	M	T	W	T	F	S	S	M	T	W	T	F	S	S	M	T	W
No.	Time	1	2	3	4	5	6	7	8	9	10	11	12	13	14	15	16	17	18	19	20	21	22	23	24	25	26	27	28	29	30
408	02.00				E	E	E																								
416	04.00	E	E	E	E	E	C	E	E	E	E	E	E	E	E	E	E	E	E	E	E	E	E	E	E	E	E	E			
434	08.30	C	C	C	C	C	C	D	D	D	D	D	D	D	D	D	D	D	D	D	D	D	D	D	D	D	D				
436	09.00																											D	D	D	D
440	10.00																											D	D	D	D
446	11.30	C	C	C	C	C	B	C	C	C	C	C	C	C	C	C	C	C	C	C	C	C	C	C	C	C	C				
452	13.00																											C	C	C	C
458	14.30	C	C	C	C	B	B	C	C	C	C	C	C	C	C	C	C	C	C	C	C	C	C	C	C	C	C				
464	16.00																											C	C	C	C
470	17.30	C	C	C	C	B	B	C	C	C	C	C	C	C	C	C	C	C	C	C	C	C	C	C	C	C	C				
476	19.00																											C	C	C	C
482	20.30	C	C	C	C	B	B	D	D	D	D	D	D	D	D	D	D	D	D	D	D	D	D	D	D	D	D				
488	22.00																											D	E	E	E
494	23.30	D	D	D	D	C	C	D	D	D	D	D	D	D	D	D	D	D	D	D	D	D	D	D	D	D	D				

All SeaCat services from Dover depart from the Eastern Docks.

All SeaCat services from Calais depart from the Calais hoverport.

Minimum check-in time is 30 minutes before departure for motorists, and 45 minutes before departure for foot passengers.

All times are local. The time in France is one hour ahead of that in the UK except between 27th September and 24th October inclusive when times are the same.

All services subject to confirmation.

The company reserves the right to alter schedules without prior notice.

Full stop/period

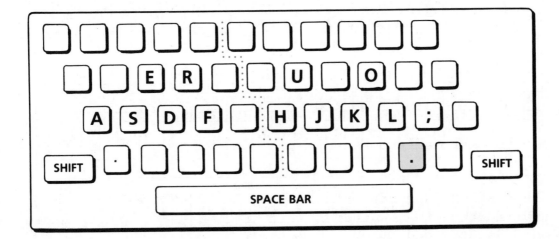

Locate .–**L** finger, lower row

Look at your hands – say and type 1. 1. 1. 1.
Look at the script – say and type 1. 1. 1. 1.
Watch the copy – say and type the drill below

Remember, when you reach to the lower row with one finger, the other fingers will rise a little.

A full stop, or period, at the end of a sentence is followed by 2 spaces. There is only one space following the full stop after an abbreviation.

Punctuation is part of the word it follows, so do not hesitate before typing a punctuation mark.

```
Here.  See.  Look.  Do.  Lead her here.
Lulu has a red dress.  Derek sees Jake.

Four of us are here.  Karl fled Alaska.
Joe heard Adelle.  She reads her rules.

He rushed here.  Ask us.  See her desk.
Sell our house.  Hal asked her.  Shush.

Ed looked for Sarah.  He has her shoes.
Jo hears Darla or Flora.  Harold reads.

Jeff looks sad.  He fell for Dee Drake.
Lola Lee asked Lou Dare for her orders.

Rose feared fleas.  Laurel has a horse.
Ella sold all her shares.  Al has ours.

Ask Dora for food.  Her folks are here.
She shared her oak desk.  Use our sofa.

Look for our house.  Our doors are oak.
Four of us are here for her old horses.
```

. . . . 1 . . . 2 . . . 3 . . . 4 . . . 5 . . . 6 . . . 7 . . . 8

Hovercraft timetable

DOVER TO CALAIS

MAY

Service	Dep.	F	S	S	M	T	W	T	F	S	S	M	T	W	T	F	S	S	M	T	W	T	F	S	S	M	T	W	T	F	S	S
No.	Time	1	2	3	4	5	6	7	8	9	10	11	12	13	14	15	16	17	18	19	20	21	22	23	24	25	26	27	28	29	30	31
524	06.05	D	D	D				D	D	D	D				D	D	D	D				D	C	C	D				D	D	D	
528	07.05	D	D	D	D	D	D	D	D	D	D	D	D	D	D	D	D	D	D	D	D	D	C	C	D	D	D	D	D	D	D	D
532	08.05	D	D	D				D	D	D	D				D	D	D	D				D	C	C	D				D	D	D	D
536	09.05	C	C	C	C	C	C	C	C	C	C	C	C	C	C	C	C	C	C	C	C	C	C	C	C	C	C	C	C	C	C	C
540	10.05	C	C	C				C	C	C	C				C	C	C	C				C	B	B	C				C	C	C	C
544	11.05																															C
546	11.35	C	C	C	C	C	C	C	C	C	C	C	C	C	C	C	C	C	C	C	C	C	B	B	C	C	C	C	C	C	C	
548	12.05																															C
552	13.05	C	C	C	C	C	C	C	C	C	C	C	C	C	C	C	C	C	C	C	C	C	B	B	C	C	C	C	C	C	C	C
556	14.05																															C
560	15.05	C	C	C	C	C	C	C	C	C	C	C	C	C	C	C	C	C	C	C	C	C	B	B	C	C	C	C	C	C	C	C
564	16.05																															C
568	17.05																															C
572	18.05	C	C	C	C	C	C	C	C	C	C	C	C	C	C	C	C	C	C	C	C	C	B	B	C	C	C	C	C	C	C	
576	19.05																															C

JUNE

Service	Dep.	M	T	W	T	F	S	S	M	T	W	T	F	S	S	M	T	W	T	F	S	S	M	T	W	T	F	S	S	M	T
No.	Time	1	2	3	4	5	6	7	8	9	10	11	12	13	14	15	16	17	18	19	20	21	22	23	24	25	26	27	28	29	30
528	07.05	D	D	D	D	D	D	D	D	D	D	D	D	D	D	D	D	D	D	D	D	D	D	D	D	D	D	D	D	D	D
532	08.05	D	D	D	D	D	D	D	D	D	D	D	D	D	D	D	D	D	D	D	D	D	D	D	D	D	D	D	D	D	D
536	09.05					C	C	C					C	C	C					C	C	C					C	C	C		
540	10.05	C	C	C	C	C	C	C	C	C	C	C	C	C	C	C	C	C	C	C	C	C	C	C	C	C	C	C	C	C	C
544	11.05	C	C	C	C	C	C	C	C	C	C	C	C	C	C	C	C	C	C	C	C	C	C	C	C	C	C	C	C	C	C
548	12.05					C	C	C					C	C	C					C	C	C					C	C	C		
552	13.05	C	C	C	C	C	C	C	C	C	C	C	C	C	C	C	C	C	C	C	C	C	C	C	C	C	C	C	C	C	C
556	14.05	C	C	C	C	C	C	C	C	C	C	C	C	C	C	C	C	C	C	C	C	C	C	C	C	C	C	C	C	C	C
560	15.05	C	C	C	C	C	C	C	C	C	C	C	C	C	C	C	C	C	C	C	C	C	C	C	C	C	C	C	C	C	C
564	16.05					C	C	C					C	C	C					C	C	C					C	C	C		
568	17.05	C	C	C	C	C	C	C	C	C	C	C	C	C	C	C	C	C	C	C	C	C	C	C	C	C	C	C	C	C	C
576	19.05	D	D	D	D	D	D	D	D	D	D	D	D	D	D	D	D	D	D	D	D	D	D	D	D	D	D	D	D	D	D

JULY

Service	Dep.	W	T	F	S	S	M	T	W	T	F	S	S	M	T	W	T	F	S	S	M	T	W	T	F	S	S	M	T	W	T	F
No.	Time	1	2	3	4	5	6	7	8	9	10	11	12	13	14	15	16	17	18	19	20	21	22	23	24	25	26	27	28	29	30	31
528	07.05	C	C	C	C	C	C	C	C	C	C	C	C	C	C	C	C	C	C	C	C	C	C	C	B	B	C	C	C	C	C	B
532	08.05	C	C	C	C	C	C	C	C	C	C	C	C	C	C	C	C	C	C	C	C	C	C	C	B	B	C	C	C	C	C	B
536	09.05	C	C	C	C	C	C	C	C	C	B	B	C	C	C	C	C	B	B	C	C	C	C	B	A	A	C	C	C	C	C	A
540	10.05	C	C	C	C	C	C	C	C	C	B	B	C	C	C	C	C	B	B	C	C	C	C	B	A	A	C	C	C	C	C	A
544	11.05	C	C	C	C	C	C	C	C	C	B	B	C	C	C	C	C	B	B	C	C	C	C	B	A	A	C	C	C	C	C	A
548	12.05	C	C	C	C	C	C	C	C	C	B	B	C	C	C	C	C	B	B	C	C	C	C	B	A	A	C	C	C	C	C	A
552	13.05	C	C	C	C	C	C	C	C	C	B	B	C	C	C	C	C	B	B	C	C	C	C	B	A	A	C	C	C	C	C	A
556	14.05	C	C	C	C	C	C	C	C	C	B	B	C	C	C	C	C	B	B	C	C	C	C	B	A	A	C	C	C	C	C	A
560	15.05	C	C	C	C	C	C	C	C	C	B	B	C	C	C	C	C	B	B	C	C	C	C	B	A	A	C	C	C	C	C	A
564	16.05	C	C	C	C	C	C	C	C	C	C	C	C	C	C	C	C	C	C	C	C	C	C	C	B	B	C	C	C	C	C	B
568	17.05	C	C	C	C	C	C	C	C	C	C	C	C	C	C	C	C	C	C	C	C	C	C	C	B	B	C	C	C	C	C	B
576	19.05	C	C	C	C	C	C	C	C	C	C	C	C	C	C	C	C	C	C	C	C	C	C	C	B	B	C	C	C	C	C	B

AUGUST

Service	Dep.	S	S	M	T	W	T	F	S	S	M	T	W	T	F	S	S	M	T	W	T	F	S	S	M	T	W	T	F	S	S	M
No.	Time	1	2	3	4	5	6	7	8	9	10	11	12	13	14	15	16	17	18	19	20	21	22	23	24	25	26	27	28	29	30	31
528	07.05	B	C	C	C	C	C	B	B	C	C	C	C	C	B	B	C	C	C	C	C	B	B	C	C	C	C	C	B	B	C	C
532	08.05	B	C	C	C	C	C	B	B	C	C	C	C	C	B	B	C	C	C	C	C	B	B	C	C	C	C	C	B	B	C	C
536	09.05	A	C	C	C	C	C	A	A	C	C	C	C	C	A	A	C	C	C	C	C	A	A	C	C	C	C	C	A	A	C	C
540	10.05	A	C	C	C	C	C	A	A	C	C	C	C	C	A	A	C	C	C	C	C	A	A	C	C	C	C	C	A	A	C	C
544	11.05	A	C	C	C	C	C	A	A	C	C	C	C	C	A	A	C	C	C	C	C	A	A	C	C	C	C	C	A	A	C	C
548	12.05	A	C	C	C	C	C	A	A	C	C	C	C	C	A	A	C	C	C	C	C	A	A	C	C	C	C	C	A	A	C	C
552	13.05	A	C	C	C	C	C	A	A	C	C	C	C	C	A	A	C	C	C	C	C	A	A	C	C	C	C	C	A	A	C	C
556	14.05	A	C	C	C	C	C	A	A	C	C	C	C	C	A	A	C	C	C	C	C	A	A	C	C	C	C	C	A	A	C	C
560	15.05	A	C	C	C	C	C	A	A	C	C	C	C	C	A	A	C	C	C	C	C	A	A	C	C	C	C	C	A	A	C	C
564	16.05	B	C	C	C	C	C	B	B	C	C	C	C	C	B	B	C	C	C	C	C	B	B	C	C	C	C	C	B	B	C	C
568	17.05	C	C	C	C	C	C	C	C	C	C	C	C	C	C	C	C	C	C	C	C	C	C	C	C	C	C	C	C	C	C	C
576	19.05	C	C	C	C	C	C	C	C	C	C	C	C	C	C	C	C	C	C	C	C	C	C	C	C	C	C	C	C	C	C	C

SEPTEMBER

Service	Dep.	T	W	T	F	S	S	M	T	W	T	F	S	S	M	T	W	T	F	S	S	M	T	W	T	F	S	S	M	T	W
No.	Time	1	2	3	4	5	6	7	8	9	10	11	12	13	14	15	16	17	18	19	20	21	22	23	24	25	26	27	28	29	30
528	07.05	D	D	D	D	D	D	D	D	D	D	D	D	D	D	D	D	D	D	D	D	D	D	D	D	D	D				
532	08.05	D	D	D	D	D	D	D	D	D	D	D	D	D	D	D	D	D	D	D	D	D	D	D	D	D	D				
536	09.05				C	C	C					C	C	C					C	C	C					C	C				
540	10.05	C	C	C	C	C	C	C	C	C	C	C	C	C	C	C	C	C	C	C	C	C	C	C	C	C	C				
544	11.05	C	C	C	C	C	C	C	C	C	C	C	C	C	C	C	C	C	C	C	C	C	C	C	C	C	C				
548	12.05				C	C	C					C	C	C					C	C	C					C	C				
552	13.05	C	C	C	C	C	C	C	C	C	C	C	C	C	C	C	C	C	C	C	C	C	C	C	C	C	C				
556	14.05	C	C	C	C	C	C	C	C	C	C	C	C	C	C	C	C	C	C	C	C	C	C	C	C	C	C				
560	15.05	C	C	C	C	C	C	C	C	C	C	C	C	C	C	C	C	C	C	C	C	C	C	C	C	C	C				
564	16.05				C	C	C					C	C	C					C	C	C					C	C				
568	17.05	C	C	C	C	C	C	C	C	C	C	C	C	C	C	C	C	C	C	C	C	C	C	C	C	C	C				
576	19.05	D	D	D	D	D	D	D	D	D	D	D	D	D	D	D	D	D	D	D	D	D	D	D	D	D	D				

CALAIS TO DOVER

MAY

Service	Dep.	F	S	S	M	T	W	T	F	S	S	M	T	W	T	F	S	S	M	T	W	T	F	S	S	M	T	W	T	F	S	S
No.	Time	1	2	3	4	5	6	7	8	9	10	11	12	13	14	15	16	17	18	19	20	21	22	23	24	25	26	27	28	29	30	31
632	08.05	D	D	D				D	D	D	D				D	D	D	D				D	D	D	D				D	D	D	
636	09.05	D	D	D	D	D	D	D	D	D	D	D	D	D	D	D	D	D	D	D	D	D	D	D	D	D	D	D	D	D	D	D
640	10.05	D	D	D				D	D	D	D				D	D	D	D				D	D	D	D				D	D	D	D
644	11.05	C	C	C	C	C	C	C	C	C	C	C	C	C	C	C	C	C	C	C	C	C	C	C	C	C	C	C	C	C	C	C
648	12.05	C	C	C				C	C	C	C				C	C	C	C				C	C	C	C				C	C	C	C
652	13.05																															C
654	13.35	C	C	C	C	C	C	C	C	C	C	C	C	C	C	C	C	C	C	C	C	C	C	C	C	C	C	C	C	C	C	
656	14.05																															C
660	15.05	C	C	C	C	C	C	C	C	C	C	C	C	C	C	C	C	C	C	C	C	C	C	C	C	C	C	C	C	C	C	C
664	16.05																															C
668	17.05	C	C	C	C	C	C	C	C	C	C	C	C	C	C	C	C	C	C	C	C	C	C	C	C	C	C	C	C	C	C	C
672	18.05																															C
676	19.05																															D
680	20.05	D	D	D	D	D	D	D	D	D	D	D	D	D	D	D	D	D	D	D	D	D	D	D	D	D	D	D	D	D	D	
684	21.05																															D

JUNE

Service	Dep.	M	T	W	T	F	S	S	M	T	W	T	F	S	S	M	T	W	T	F	S	S	M	T	W	T	F	S	S	M	T
No.	Time	1	2	3	4	5	6	7	8	9	10	11	12	13	14	15	16	17	18	19	20	21	22	23	24	25	26	27	28	29	30
636	09.05	D	D	D	D	D	D	D	D	D	D	D	D	D	D	D	D	D	D	D	D	D	D	D	D	D	D	D	D	D	D
640	10.05	D	D	D	D	D	D	D	D	D	D	D	D	D	D	D	D	D	D	D	D	D	D	D	D	D	D	D	D	D	D
644	11.05					C	C	C					C	C	C					C	C	C					C	C	C		
648	12.05	C	C	C	C	C	C	C	C	C	C	C	C	C	C	C	C	C	C	C	C	C	C	C	C	C	C	C	C	C	C
652	13.05	C	C	C	C	C	C	C	C	C	C	C	C	C	C	C	C	C	C	C	C	C	C	C	C	C	C	C	C	C	C
656	14.05					C	C	C					C	C	C					C	C	C					C	C	C		
660	15.05	C	C	C	C	C	C	C	C	C	C	C	C	C	C	C	C	C	C	C	C	C	C	C	C	C	C	C	C	C	C
664	16.05	C	C	C	C	C	C	C	C	C	C	C	C	C	C	C	C	C	C	C	C	C	C	C	C	C	C	C	C	C	C
668	17.05	C	C	C	C	C	C	C	C	C	C	C	C	C	C	C	C	C	C	C	C	C	C	C	C	C	C	C	C	C	C
672	18.05					C	C	C					C	C	C					C	C	C					C	C	C		
676	19.05	D	D	D	D	D	D	D	D	D	D	D	D	D	D	D	D	D	D	D	D	D	D	D	D	D	D	D	D	D	D
684	21.05	D	D	D	D	D	D	D	D	D	D	D	D	D	D	D	D	D	D	D	D	D	D	D	D	D	D	D	D	D	D

JULY

Service	Dep.	W	T	F	S	S	M	T	W	T	F	S	S	M	T	W	T	F	S	S	M	T	W	T	F	S	S	M	T	W	T	F
No.	Time	1	2	3	4	5	6	7	8	9	10	11	12	13	14	15	16	17	18	19	20	21	22	23	24	25	26	27	28	29	30	31
636	09.05	D	D	D	D	D	D	D	D	D	D	C	C	C	C	C	C	C	C	C	C	C	C	C	C	C	C	C	C	C	C	C
640	10.05	D	D	D	D	D	D	D	D	D	D	C	C	C	C	C	C	C	C	C	C	C	C	C	C	C	C	C	C	C	C	C
644	11.05	C	C	C	C	C	C	C	C	C	C	C	C	C	C	C	C	C	C	C	C	C	C	C	C	C	C	C	C	C	C	C
648	12.05	C	C	C	C	C	C	C	C	C	C	B	B	C	C	C	C	C	B	B	C	C	C	C	C	B	B	C	C	C	C	C
652	13.05	C	C	C	C	C	C	C	C	C	C	B	B	C	C	C	C	C	B	B	C	C	C	C	C	B	B	C	C	C	C	C
656	14.05	C	C	C	C	C	C	C	C	C	C	B	B	C	C	C	C	C	B	B	C	C	C	C	C	B	B	C	C	C	C	C
660	15.05	C	C	C	C	C	C	C	C	C	C	B	B	C	C	C	C	C	B	B	C	C	C	C	C	B	B	C	C	C	C	C
664	16.05	C	C	C	C	C	C	C	C	C	C	B	B	C	C	C	C	C	B	B	C	C	C	C	C	B	B	C	C	C	C	C
668	17.05	C	C	C	C	C	C	C	C	C	C	B	B	C	C	C	C	C	B	B	C	C	C	C	C	B	B	C	C	C	C	C
672	18.05	C	C	C	C	C	C	C	C	C	C	B	B	C	C	C	C	C	B	B	C	C	C	C	C	B	B	C	C	C	C	C
676	19.05	D	D	D	D	D	D	D	D	D	D	C	C	C	C	C	C	C	C	C	C	C	C	C	C	C	C	C	C	C	C	C
684	21.05	D	D	D	D	D	D	D	D	D	D	C	C	C	C	C	C	C	C	C	C	C	C	C	C	C	C	C	C	C	C	C

AUGUST

Service	Dep.	S	S	M	T	W	T	F	S	S	M	T	W	T	F	S	S	M	T	W	T	F	S	S	M	T	W	T	F	S	S	M
No.	Time	1	2	3	4	5	6	7	8	9	10	11	12	13	14	15	16	17	18	19	20	21	22	23	24	25	26	27	28	29	30	31
636	09.05	C	C	C	C	C	C	C	C	C	C	C	C	C	C	C	C	C	C	C	C	C	C	C	C	C	C	C	C	C	C	C
640	10.05	C	C	C	C	C	C	C	C	C	C	C	C	C	C	C	C	C	C	C	C	C	C	C	C	C	C	C	C	C	C	C
644	11.05	C	C	C	C	C	C	C	C	C	C	C	C	C	C	C	C	C	C	C	C	C	C	C	C	C	C	C	C	C	C	C
648	12.05	A	A	C	C	C	C	C	A	A	C	C	C	C	C	A	A	C	C	C	C	C	A	A	C	C	C	C	C	A	A	C
652	13.05	A	A	C	C	C	C	C	A	A	C	C	C	C	C	A	A	C	C	C	C	C	A	A	C	C	C	C	C	A	A	C
656	14.05	A	A	C	C	C	C	C	A	A	C	C	C	C	C	A	A	C	C	C	C	C	A	A	C	C	C	C	C	A	A	C
660	15.05	A	A	C	C	C	C	C	A	A	C	C	C	C	C	A	A	C	C	C	C	C	A	A	C	C	C	C	C	A	A	C
664	16.05	A	A	C	C	C	C	C	A	A	C	C	C	C	C	A	A	C	C	C	C	C	A	A	C	C	C	C	C	A	A	C
668	17.05	A	A	C	C	C	C	C	A	A	C	C	C	C	C	A	A	C	C	C	C	C	A	A	C	C	C	C	C	A	A	C
672	18.05	A	A	C	C	C	C	C	A	A	C	C	C	C	C	A	A	C	C	C	C	C	A	A	C	C	C	C	C	A	A	C
676	19.05	B	B	C	C	C	C	C	B	B	C	C	C	C	C	B	B	C	C	C	C	C	B	B	C	C	C	C	C	B	B	C
684	21.05	C	C	C	C	C	C	C	C	C	C	C	C	C	C	C	C	C	C	C	C	C	C	C	C	C	C	C	C	C	C	C

SEPTEMBER

Service	Dep.	T	W	T	F	S	S	M	T	W	T	F	S	S	M	T	W	T	F	S	S	M	T	W	T	F	S	S	M	T	W
No.	Time	1	2	3	4	5	6	7	8	9	10	11	12	13	14	15	16	17	18	19	20	21	22	23	24	25	26	27	28	29	30
636	09.05	C	C	C	C	B	A	D	D	D	D	D	D	D	D	D	D	D	D	D	D	D	D	D	D	D	D				
640	10.05	C	C	C	C	B	A	D	D	D	D	D	D	D	D	D	D	D	D	D	D	D	D	D	D	D	D				
644	11.05				C	A	A					C	C	C					C	C	C					C	C				
648	12.05	C	C	C	C	A	A	C	C	C	C	C	C	C	C	C	C	C	C	C	C	C	C	C	C	C	C				
652	13.05	C	C	C	C	A	A	C	C	C	C	C	C	C	C	C	C	C	C	C	C	C	C	C	C	C	C				
656	14.05				C	A	A					C	C	C					C	C	C					C	C				
660	15.05	C	C	C	C	A	A	C	C	C	C	C	C	C	C	C	C	C	C	C	C	C	C	C	C	C	C				
664	16.05	C	C	C	C	A	A	C	C	C	C	C	C	C	C	C	C	C	C	C	C	C	C	C	C	C	C				
668	17.05	C	C	C	C	A	A	D	D	D	D	D	D	D	D	D	D	D	D	D	D	D	D	D	D	D	D				
672	18.05				C	A	A					D	D	D					D	D	D					D	D				
676	19.05	C	C	C	C	A	A	D	D	D	D	D	D	D	D	D	D	D	D	D	D	D	D	D	D	D	D				
684	21.05	C	C	C	C	A	A	D	D	D	D	D	D	D	D	D	D	D	D	D	D	D	D	D	D	D	D				

All hovercraft flights from Dover depart from the hoverport in the Western Docks.

All hovercraft services from Calais depart from the Calais hoverport.

Minimum check-in time is 30 minutes before departure.

All times are local. The time in France is one hour ahead of that in the UK except between 27th September and 24th October inclusive when times are the same.

All services subject to confirmation.

The company reserves the right to alter schedules without prior notice.

Judging your progress

There are 3 ways to assess your progress in typing.

1 SPEED

Typing speed is measured in words per minute, 5 characters or spaces equalling 1 typing word. To find your rate, divide the number of words you typed by the number of minutes:

- If you type 100 words in 5 minutes, your rate is 100 divided by 5, which equals 20 words per minute.
- If you type for 1 minute, your score is the total words typed:
  30 seconds timing = No of words multiplied by 2 (1/2 minute)
  20 seconds timing = No of words multiplied by 3 (1/3 minute)
  15 seconds timing = No of words multiplied by 4 (1/4 minute)

2 CONTROL

Your control of the keyboard will show in your accuracy – the number of errors you make. Your accuracy depends on the speed you are typing, not on what you are typing, and is an indication of your control. Typing accidents, like car accidents, are caused by moving at a faster rate than you can control, so when accuracy is required, slow down to a more controlled rate. You will be surprised how little you have to slow down to be accurate.

In the early stages of learning to type, you may be discouraged at the number of errors you make. At this stage, they are not important. They will go away. Special drills later on will help you to attack any persistent errors but, for now, simply notice how they are decreasing on their own. When they begin to fall away, they will do so quickly. Right now, technique is far more important.

3 FLUENCY

As you become more fluent, typing becomes easier; you are more efficient. After each practice, ask yourself these questions:
1 Did I type faster?
2 Did I have better control?
3 Did I type with more ease and fluency?
Answering 'yes' to any of these shows progress.

SKILL DEVELOPMENT

Proper technique gives you a solid base for your skill and it is important that you practise technique as your first priority. Speed and accuracy will follow but they do not grow together. If you seem to be stuck on a speed or accuracy plateau, just concentrate on technique. Learning is taking place on another level and you will find sudden jumps in speed and sudden drops in errors.

15-SECOND TIMING

Being timed will help you to judge your day-to-day improvement in speed.

Start to type at a comfortable speed and let your rate build up. If you panic or freeze when you are told to start, count yourself in. When you hear 'Go', say to yourself '3, 2, 1' and start.

Use each line below for a 15-second timing. Multiply the total words typed by 4 to get your rate.

```
Fred asked her for a share of her shelf.
Ella has a use for our four house rules.
He heard fares are four dollars or less.
```

```
. . . . 1 . . . . 2 . . . . 3 . . . 4 . . . . 5 . . . 6 . . . . 7 . . . . 8
```

■ **TASK 1**

For this task you are working for Patrick Dubuc. Type/key in the following memo to John Stephenson, using today's date and ref PD/Eur/(your initials).

I have now contacted our representative in Paris and he will be happy to meet you at Gare du Nord station and take you to your hotel. You will need to catch the

(insert the time of the crossing. You will have to look up the hovercraft and SeaCat times from Dover – given at the end of the task – and work out which one will get him to Boulogne in time to catch the 1430 train to Paris. Remember that there is a one-hour time difference.)

Hovercraft/SeaCat crossing from Dover. Your tickets will be sent to you shortly.

RAIL SCHEDULE

Date	Departure Days	Service No	Depart Boulogne	Arrive Paris
01.3.9- to 01.6.9- and	Daily	789	1430	1700
01.9.9- to 01.3.9-	Daily	780	1630	1900
01.6.9- to 01.9.9-	Daily	789	1430	1700
	Daily	780	1630	1900
	Daily	790	1830	2100
	Daily	799	2030	2300

A graph of figures for UK photocopier sales is enclosed.

Letter I

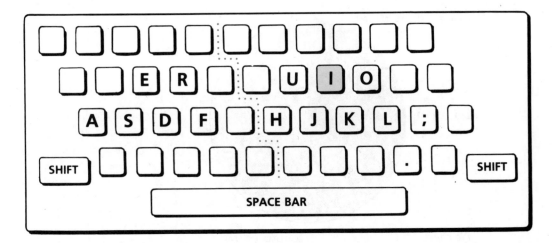

Locate **I–K** finger, upper row
Look at your hands – say and type `ki ki ki ki`
Look at the script – say and type `ki ki ki ki`
Watch the copy – say and type the drill below

Remember – flat wrists and a ballistic stroke

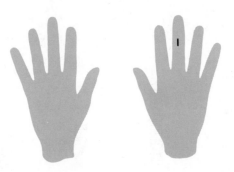

```
is si ai ia id di if fi ji ki ik il I I
li ei ie hi ir ri ui iu io oi Ida Idaho

isle arise frisk kids kissed kills kirk
iris irk ire afire shire oils foil soil

sill silk silo sir sire desired residue
did dial dill dish disk dirk dire diode

slide slid skid id idle ideal ides idol
air ail aid aide aisle alias friar liar

odious usurious orioles serious furious
rid ride rife rise risk rill riled sari

fill file fire fir fish fiddlers filial
life lids liar likes lie lied lieu lira

his hiss hill hid hide hifi hired hiked
rallied skier afield dried shield adieu

He likes his old skis.  Lil hired Lila.
I like Jill.  File his deed.  He flies.

She liked his ideas for a radio series.
Lisa said she should ask if he is here.
```

Examples

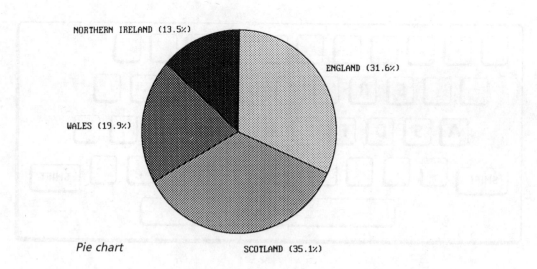

Pie chart

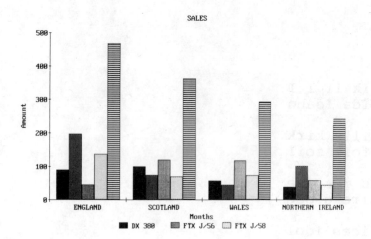

Bar graph

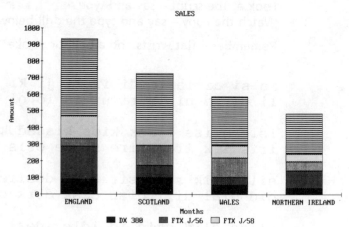

Stacked bar graph

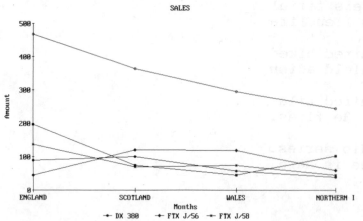

Hi-lo graph

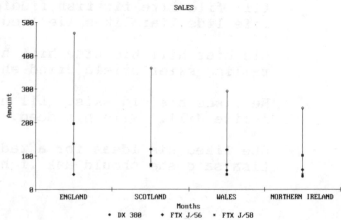

Line graph

Letter N

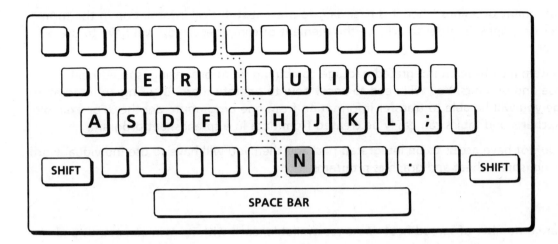

Locate **N–J** finger, lower row

Look at your hands – say and type jn jn jn jn
Look at the script – say and type jn jn jn jn
Watch the copy – say and type the drill below

Remember – flat wrists and a ballistic stroke

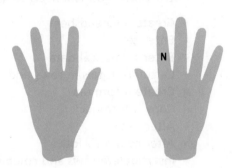

```
an na nd nk ne en un nu rn kn ni in N N
nn sn on no nor nod non none nose donor

an and flan elan anon knife kneel knell
on one shone onus lion iron ikon onions

inner dinner fennel funnel fanned annul
in ink shin shine inane infer skin akin

land sand rand hand hind find fund fend
lank sank dank rank rink sink sunk junk

sane lane line lone done dune dine fine
nine finish junior denied denial senile

nasal nadir ulna naked nuns null nurses
sneer sniff snuffle snake snare snooker

under unfair unusual unkind union shuns
fern horn shorn furnish darn kern learn

ended endure endorsed enrol ensue arena
Ned Nell Nola Noah Nora Norris Nan Nash

Donna needs fine noodles in her dinner.
Ken found a use for all his odd dishes.
```

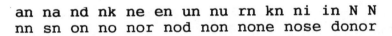

ELEMENT 5.2

Present narrative, graphic and tabular information using an alphanumeric keyboard

There are many occasions when it is necessary to present statistical information in the form of tables or graphs. In order to achieve this element of competence you will have to use a computer.

Your system may have an integrated package combining word processing, spreadsheet, database and graphics. You will need to know how to operate these. By using an integrated package you will be able to transfer information from one program to another. For example, graphs, charts and tables can easily be created from data in a spreadsheet program.

If you do not have access to an integrated package then you will have to use individual word processing, spreadsheet and graphics programs.

Spreadsheets

There are a number of spreadsheet packages available, each with its own commands and instructions. You will need to know how to:

- Create a spreadsheet
- Enter text
- Enter numerical data
- Calculate totals in rows and columns
- Create a formula
- Copy a formula
- Alter data
- Alter column widths
- Insert/delete rows and columns
- Save and print a spreadsheet

Graphics

You can transfer information from the database to the spreadsheet, or use information already on the spreadsheet, to form a graph.

Several different types of graph can be produced. Examples of a variety of graphs that have been produced from a spreadsheet are shown on page 218.

Letter T

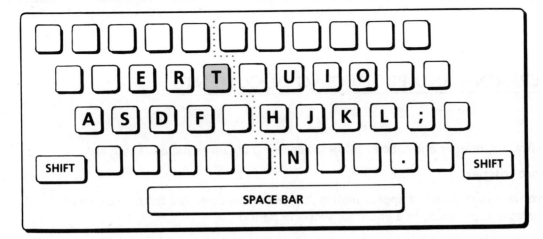

Locate **T–F** finger, upper row

Look at your hands – say and type `ft ft ft ft`

Look at the script – say and type `ft ft ft ft`

Watch the copy – say and type the drill below

Remember – flat wrists and a ballistic stroke

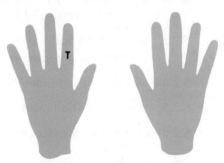

```
it ti at ta te et rt tr ut tu ot to T T
th nt lt st tt ft left lift rift rafter

tide tire tike tile tilt tint tiff anti
rent sent lent lint flat slat fiat that

unit flit skit edit shut utensils flute
tan tank task talk tall tale take taste

ten tell test tense rate late fate date
jet diet duet suet tattoo letter little

hurt hart dirt dart tart tort fort sort
trek true trio trod trial trust trailer

that than then thin this thus the there
turn tun tuna tundra tutu tutor tuition

halt hilt jilt silt salt shot slot knot
to toss toll toddle ton torn tore torte

stet stun star last dust fast just east
Turk Tudor Taurus Tess Toronto Tina Tod

Ted Tate tried not to retire till then.
Their files are here for use as needed.
```

National Vocational Qualification
Administration

Level 3

UNIT 5 PREPARING AND PRODUCING DOCUMENTS

Element 5.2

Present narrative, graphic and tabular information using an alphanumeric keyboard

Performance criteria

5.2.1 *error-free* documents of approximately 300 words are compiled from a variety of sources and produced in a one-hour working period

5.2.2 any uncertainty in the source material is identified and remedied so that the intended meaning is conveyed

5.2.3 narrative, graphic and tabular styles and formats conform to organisational house style and/or accepted presentation conventions

5.2.4 all deadlines are met or delays reported and accepted

5.2.5 the information produced correctly reflects the source material

5.2.6 safe working practices are always followed and implemented

5.2.7 security and confidentiality procedures are always followed and implemented

Competence must be demonstrated on a minimum of 3 separate occasions within a 2.5 hour working period.

A different set of materials must be produced on each occasion.

When completing the following tasks, if you do not have access to an integrated package, you may therefore not be able to combine the graph with the text. If so, produce the text on one sheet of paper, leaving sufficient space for the graph to be pasted on later. This can then be photocopied and pasted in.

Letter G

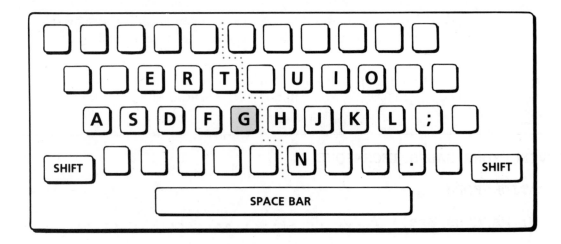

Locate **G–F** finger, adjacent

Look at your hands – say and type fg fg fg fg
Look at the script – say and type fg fg fg fg
Watch the copy – say and type the drill below

Remember – flat wrists and a ballistic stroke

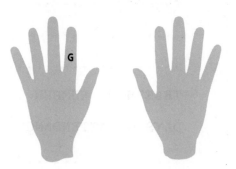

```
ag ge eg og go gg ng gl gr gi ig gn G G
gh gu ug ga gas gal gale gaff saga toga

flag drag shag slag snag stag aged agog
get gent gene urge edge sage rage tiger

go gone gosh gore goggle ergo logo sago
rigged ragged jagged jogged jugged eggs

ogre ogle frog grog sign gnat signature
king ring rang rung sung sang sing song

glue glad glee glen glut glide glistens
grin grog gross grass grill green gruel

sigh nigh high ought right night lights
gull gush gust gulf gun gut rogue fugue

slug drug snug thug igloo ignore origin
gift gird girl gill digit rigid legions

Greta Gordon Gloria Gertie Gail Gunther
Go and get Glenn to sing a hiking song.

Georgina is going golfing then jogging.
All of us are glad he got here at last.
```

```
. . . . 1 . . . . 2 . . . . 3 . . . . 4 . . . . 5 . . . . 6 . . . . 7 . . . . 8
```

■ **TASK 9**

I have received an application from Ms Margaret Marshall, 64 Pennington Road, Catford, LONDON, SE6 9YT, to attend the Staff Conference Week. You can contact her on extension 2229. Will you let her know that the form has not yet been printed but that we will fill in her details when it is ready. She can only attend on Tuesday, Wednesday and Thursday am and will be taking her own car. Please note also that she is a vegetarian and is allergic to eggs.

Please prepare a copy of the following application form for places on the Staff Conference Week to be held at The Viking, 85 Albany Road, BRIGHTON, BN6 9GR. Fill in Ms Marshall's details.

```
IMPROVING YOUR SALES TECHNIQUE

APPLICATION FORM

NAME (Mr/Ms/Miss/Mrs)* ..............................

ADDRESS   ...........................................

..................................................

..................................................

TELEPHONE NUMBER ....................................

DAYS OF ATTENDANCE ..................................

..................................................

..................................................

SPECIAL DIETARY REQUIREMENTS ........................

..................................................

..................................................

TRANSPORT NEEDED YES/NO*

DATE .................... SIGNED ....................


* Delete as applicable
```

Letter Y

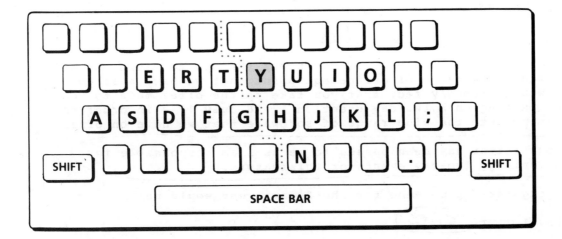

Locate **Y–J** finger, upper row

Look at your hands – say and type `jy jy jy jy`
Look at the script – say and type `jy jy jy jy`
Watch the copy – say and type the drill below

Remember – flat wrists and a ballistic stroke

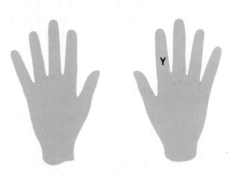

```
ey oy ya yo ye ly ry ty ny gy sy dy Y Y
ay shay slay flay fray tray okay stayed

oyster ahoy troy annoyed enjoyed alloys
soya yank yard yarn royal loyalty kayak

yoyo yore yokes yoga yolks layoff rayon
yes yet yea yeah yell yearn years yeast

only lyre rely holy idly lily ugly oily
rye airy fury jury salary artery theory

tyke tyro arty duty dusty frosty safety
deny tiny tony felony irony agony shiny

stodgy energy eulogy effigy tangy elegy
easy rosy nosy daisy lousy noisy heresy

dye lady tidy sturdy defy notify ratify
eyes greyer turkey donkey galley surrey

York Yale Yule Yalta Yeats Yuri Yonkers
Rely on a trendy lady to try your yoyo.

Ray says your dyed lily is really ugly.
It is good for us to try to get faster.
```

`. . . . 1 . . . . 2 . . . . 3 . . . . 4 . . . . 5 . . . . 6 . . . . 7 . . . . 8`

Send the following letter to Ms Holmes. You will find her address on page 207.

Dear Ms Holmes

<u>Office Equipment Demonstration</u>

We are grateful to you for giving us the opp. to visit you and discuss the range of office equipment that we have available. I would strongly rec. that you take up the offer made to you of putting on a two-day event on 17-18 July 19-- in order to demonstrate the wide range of software that we have on offer.

Your letter has been passed to me as I am responsible for organising two-day events of this nature.

A suggested programme for the 2-day event would be:

Day 1 ← (CAPS)

10.00	Welcome and Coffee
11.00	Demonstration of Word Processing Packages
1.00	LUNCH
2.00	Demonstration of Accounts Packages
4.00	" " Electronic Mail
5.00	Questions

(Line Space)

Day 2

10.00	Welcome and Coffee
11.00	Demonstration of Spreadsheets Packages
1.00	LUNCH
2.00	Demonstration of Databases
4.00	" " Integrated Packages
5.00	Close

It would be very useful if you could send a selection of the work you do in your company so that we can demonstrate the packages which would be most suitable for your needs. If you are unable to do this prior to the event staff could bring along a sample of their work on the day. *sk run on*

It is worth noting that we not only supply the software but we can also help with staff training and can provide a help line after the software has been installed.

the/s/ I am sure that you will be very impressed with our range of software and service that we offer and I do hope that we will be able to do bus. with you.

queries

✓ If you have any ~~questions~~ please do not hesitate to contact me.

Letter W

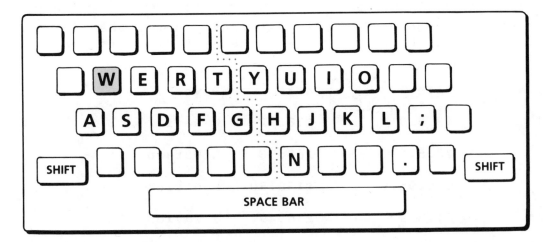

Locate **W–S** finger, upper row

Look at your hands – say and type sw sw sw sw
Look at the script – say and type sw sw sw sw
Watch the copy – say and type the drill below

Remember – flat wrists and a ballistic stroke

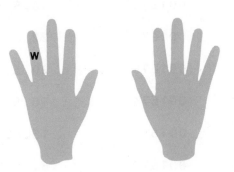

```
ew wr wa aw ow wo wi sw wn wl wh tw W W
we wet wed wee were well went west weld

ewe ewer stews grew drew flew slew anew
wry writ write written wrong wren wrest

war was wan wag way wad wash wall water
awl awe awed awful draw flaw slaw trawl

owe owed owl own grow show glow flowers
woe woes wolf wore worn work word world

win wig wits with wish wise wine winter
sway swat swan swag swig sweets sweater

town sown gown down dawn lawn fawn yawn
who why when whet what whit whirl where

two twin twit twitter twirl twist twine
howl fowl yowl yawl drawled lowly newly

Ward Will Welsh Windsor Wako Wendy Walt
We wish Howard were with us for awhile.

We will wait a week for the new flower.
This kind of work is going well for us.
```

. . . . 1 . . . . 2 . . . . 3 . . . . 4 . . . . 5 . . . . 6 . . . . 7 8

Send this memo to Jean Pullman, Finance Department. Mark it Private and Confidential.
Rearrange the list in chronological order according to the date of the cheques.

Further to your memo of (insert yesterday's date) the
following payments have been made to members of staff for
travel:

Cheque No	Date	*(this year)* Amt	Payee
001673	18.5.9-	£78.32	W Raji
001678	22.5.9-	£60.98	L Watson
001671	6.5.9-	£150.80	H Ulrich
001679	24.5.9-	£36.49	J Taylor
001675	18.5.9-	£78.98	D Williams
001677	22.5.9-	£45.98	H Wilson
001676	20.5.9-	£32.50	R Smith
001674	18.5.9-	£9.28	M Lunman
001672	15.5.9-	£18.24	J Finnegan
001670	6.5.9-	£42.50	P Doyle

Travel claims for staff who use their own cars ← 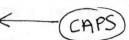 CAPS

The rate per mile at the moment depends on engine size. It is
expected that from 1 April all rates will be the same.

The ~~high~~ rate of 61.5p per mile is very high and does not *top*
truly reflect the cost of travel. The Board of Management has
looked into this problem and will be shortly informing staff
that the new rate will be 35.7%. This will be for all car
users. In addition petrol money will not be paid *now*
automatically. We will be looking at the cheapest method of
travel ie second class rail or bus fares or mileage.

COMPANY CARS

Providing company cars has been very expensive and I have been
looking at alternatives. We have been approached by ~~the~~
Freeman Garages. They are setting up a Car Lease Scheme and I
am going along on Tuesday (insert next Tuesday's date) to
discuss with them. It could be an alternative to purchasing
new cars for all our sales representatives. I believe that
the leasing period will be for three years after which
Freemans will take back the car and provide another new car.

the possibility of using leased cars

Using timings for skill building

Timings measure your progress from day to day but they are also very useful in identifying areas where special practice is needed.

Each timing below is for 15 seconds and targets a particular aspect of your skill. Concentrate as directed on each timing.

1 Type at a normal brisk pace. This timing will be used for comparison.

```
She wanted to thank you for all you did.
```
. . . . 1 . . . . 2 . . . . 3 . . . . 4 . . . . 5 . . . . 6 . . . . 7 8

2 Concentrate on ballistic stroking.

```
We all tried to get to know her friends.
```
. . . . 1 . . . . 2 . . . . 3 . . . . 4 . . . . 5 . . . . 6 . . . . 7 8

3 Concentrate on chaining.

```
I would like to find a new kind of work.
```
. . . . 1 . . . . 2 . . . . 3 . . . . 4 . . . . 5 . . . . 6 . . . . 7 8

4 Keep your hands close to the keyboard.

```
He did not like finding his work wasted.
```
. . . . 1 . . . . 2 . . . . 3 . . . . 4 . . . . 5 . . . . 6 . . . . 7 8

5 Slow down for keyboard control.

```
There is no other way for her to get in.
```
. . . . 1 . . . . 2 . . . . 3 . . . . 4 . . . . 5 . . . . 6 . . . . 7 8

6 Type fast to eliminate waste motions.

```
All the letters are filed in their desk.
```
. . . . 1 . . . . 2 . . . . 3 . . . . 4 . . . . 5 . . . . 6 . . . . 7 8

7 Relax and adopt a "who cares" attitude.

```
No one asked us to go to the new stores.
```
. . . . 1 . . . . 2 . . . . 3 . . . . 4 . . . . 5 . . . . 6 . . . . 7 8

8 Use the same pace as you did on timing 1.

```
See if there are any of your files here.
```
. . . . 1 . . . . 2 . . . . 3 . . . . 4 . . . . 5 . . . . 6 . . . . 7 8

Compare timings 1 and 8 for improvement in speed, keyboard control and fluency. Direct your practice to correcting any weaknesses that have surfaced. Type awkward words a few times.

Can you send the following letter to Miss Julie Thomas and Ms Ann Wilson. You have their addresses.

Thank you for your application for the position of Chief Administration Officer within our Sales and Marketing Section.

We are interviewing for this post on Friday (insert the first Friday of next month) at 2.00 pm and would like you to come along for interview

Please bring along with you all your examination certificates and any other documentation that you have which you feel is relevant to this post.

Letter C

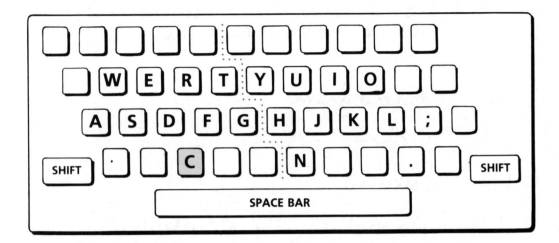

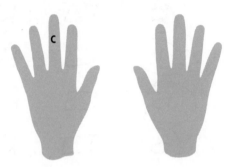

Locate **C–D** finger, lower row

Look at your hands – say and type dc dc dc dc
Look at the script – say and type dc dc dc dc
Watch the copy – say and type the drill below

Remember – flat wrists and a ballistic stroke

```
ch cl cr ce ca ci cu co ac oc cy ct C C
sc ck cc ic ice icy icicle chic chicory

chef char chow chug arch such inch each
cloy clot clod clad claw clay clef clue

crag craw crew crow crowd crude crucial
cell cent central decent face race once

card cart care cane case cake cafe cage
city cinders cider cigar circled circus

cut cute cure curt curd curry cuff cuss
colt cold cola coda code core cord coed

acre acne acid duct fiction fact tactic
scar scat scad scan scales scared scarf

tack lack sack sock lock rock rick tick
succeed success occur occult accidental

cyst cycle cynic lacy racy saucy agency
Carl Canada Carol Cindy Chad Cairo Cork

Cal can check coats on fancy occasions.
She will ask our agent to see us today.
```

. . . . 1 . . . . 2 . . . . 3 . . . . 4 . . . . 5 . . . . 6 . . . . 7 8

Please state your preference by putting ticks against 3 of the suggested venues. The conference will be held at the venue receiving the most votes.

(6) ☐ Birmingham
(13) ☐ Oxford
(11) ☐ Coventry
(10) ☐ Norwich
(2) ☐ Liverpool
(1) ☐ Brighton
(15) ☐ Blackpool
(3) ☐ Edinburgh
(5) ☐ Cardiff
(4) ☐ Swansea
(9) ☐ Plymouth
(8) ☐ Portsmouth
(7) ☐ Yarmouth
(12) ☐ Hastings
(14) ☐ York

(Re arrange order)

Name - - - - - - - -
Department - - - - - -
Ext - - - - - -
Remember this is your chance to have your say!
↓ (CAPS)

Letter V

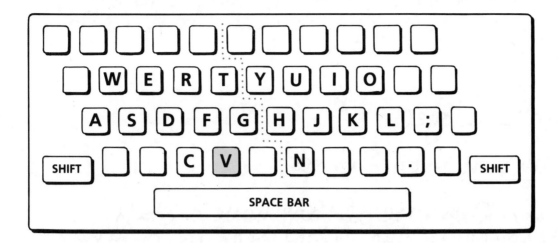

Locate **V–F** finger, lower row

Look at your hands – say and type   fv fv fv fv
Look at the script – say and type   fv fv fv fv
Watch the copy – say and type the drill below

Remember – flat wrists and a ballistic stroke

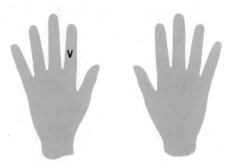

```
vo vi ov iv av va vy rv ve ev every V V
even event clever eleven elevate uneven

vote vogue volt vocal volunteer volcano
oval oven over overt grove gloves shove

vial vice visa vile villa vivid divided
ivy ivory trivet alive drivers shivered

veto very venture velvet live give have
avid avow avert avoid avail grave stave

vane vale vast value valet valid valise
envy levy navy wavy curve verve service

Volvo Vivaldi Venus Venice Virgo Virgil
Eva loved the velvet gloves I gave her.

Vincent invited Violet to visit Vienna.
Vivienne envied David his clever valet.

Vast vistas gave Val very lovely views.
Every vote for Victor is a valued vote.

Steven drove Vera and Oliver to Vernon.
This skill is getting very easy for us.
```

. . . . 1 . . . . 2 . . . . 3 . . . . 4 . . . . 5 . . . . 6 . . . . 7 8

Type this form letter which is to be copied and given to all staff with their next pay slips.

Dear Employee

Expansion into Europe

As you know we always have a Staff Conference in the first week in October and in the past it has been well attended. This year we are looking at our "Expansion into Europe" programme and the implications for this company. There will be many opportunities opening up for staff both in this country and abroad. Our "Expansion into America" programme will be the subject of another conference.

For the past 10 years we have met in London but last year it was suggested that we might change the venue. The following are suggested venues for our Staff Conference week. All staff are invited to indicate their preferences.

Yours

now add a tear-off portion as indicated on the next page. You should try and fit this page all on one sheet of paper.

Question mark

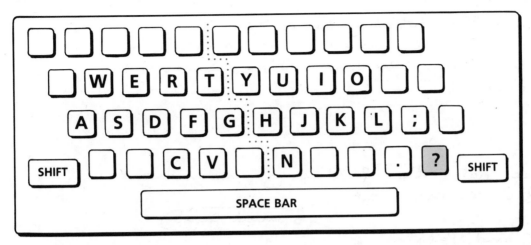

Locate **?** – **;** finger, lower row, upper case

Look at your hands – move both little fingers at the same time, the A finger to the shift key and the ; finger to the ? key.

Type ? ? ? ?
Look at the script – type ? ? ? ?

Remember – the ? is followed by 2 spaces

The ? may be located elsewhere on some keyboards but is nearly always an upper case character (on some electronic typewriters, the Code key must be pressed with the ? key). Use the appropriate finger.

Do not hesitate before a punctuation mark. Make it part of the word it follows.

```
Hello?  Ron?  How are you?  What?  Who?
When?  Where?  Why?  How?  On Saturday?

Is that so?  Did you know?  What is it?
How did I know?  Is it ready?  Why not?

Did I thank you?  How old?  On Tuesday?
How far?  To China?  With your friends?

Really?  Are you sure?  Who else?  Ken?
George?  Alan?  Are they going to tell?

Would they?  Should you?  Could anyone?
Which one?  How long?  Who told you so?

Is that for sure?  Anything else?  Now?
Who is that?  Is anyone there?  For Ed?

Do you?  Did they?  Does he?  Just you?
What day?  Today?  Tonight?  Wednesday?

Definitely?  Without fail?  For always?
I never knew I could learn this easily.
```

. . . . 1 . . . 2 . . . 3 . . . . 4 . . . 5 . . . 6 . . . . 7 . . . 8

Send the following memo to:
Susan McKenzie, Production Manager; with an extra copy for Linda Jones, Sales and Marketing.

Please note the following amendment to the current cat.

Post and Packing ← (Spaced Caps)

Cost of Goods ← — (Caps and underscore)

	£	ADD (£)	
not exceeding	10	1.50	}
not exceeding	20	2.50	Put in
" " "	30	3.00	descending
" " "	40	4.00	order
" " "	50	5.00	}

Orders over £50 are postage free. Payment can be made by credit card, switch card, cheque or postal order.

For delivery overseas add twenty per cent of the total order value.

One-minute timings

Start to type at any easy pace and let your speed build as you go along. Your speed is the total words to the last line you completed plus any extra words you typed.

Total words

Lots of these students enjoy travelling. 8
There are at least four fine days to go. 16
They are going to try to do good things. 24
This work is only just starting to grow. 32

. . . . 1 . . . . 2 . . . . 3 . . . . 4 . . . . 5 . . . . 6 . . . . 7 8

She can always find new things to learn. 8
Let us try to get this finished at once. 16
Thank you for your interest in our case. 24
He is all ready to start at entry level. 32

. . . . 1 . . . . 2 . . . . 3 . . . . 4 . . . . 5 . . . . 6 . . . . 7 8

The office of today has a lower level of 8
noise than the ones of even twenty years 16
ago. We do not hear the clatter of keys 24
nor the clicking of heels on the floors. 32

. . . . 1 . . . . 2 . . . . 3 . . . . 4 . . . . 5 . . . . 6 . . . . 7 8

Tasks for entry level staff will involve 8
a variety of diverse skills. Each of us 16
can use a wide general knowledge as well 24
an interest in learning all that we can. 32

. . . . 1 . . . . 2 . . . . 3 . . . . 4 . . . . 5 . . . . 6 . . . . 7 8

The rate of change has increased so that 8
now just to get started there is a great 16
deal of learning. Every year and a half 24
you face twice the new data and research 32
findings in every field. 37

. . . . 1 . . . . 2 . . . . 3 . . . . 4 . . . . 5 . . . . 6 . . . . 7 8

We cannot afford to stand still or these 8
new data will get far ahead of us and we 16
could find ourselves outdated. Everyone 24
will have to recognise that we can never 32
let ourselves ignore this very fast rate 40
of change. 42

. . . . 1 . . . . 2 . . . . 3 . . . . 4 . . . . 5 . . . . 6 . . . . 7 8

Every advance in any field affects other 8
areas rather like the way a stone tossed 16
into a lagoon sends out rings of growing 24
circles. As other stones are thrown the 32
rings start to touch so they affect each 40
other. 41

. . . . 1 . . . . 2 . . . . 3 . . . . 4 . . . . 5 . . . . 6 . . . . 7 8

Type/key in the following checklist. Please put the names in alphabetical order.

SWIFT STATIONERS PLC

CUSTOMERS' CHECKLIST

The following new members of the company will be attending the presentation on Sales Techniques and Marketing.

<u>Name</u>	<u>Responsibilities</u>
Peter Holmes	Financial control
Nik Wiles	Sales planning
Rajbir Sindhu	Production
George Ahmad	Customer relations
Jules Metcalf*	Market planning
Angela Tarrant	Accounts
Jean Fisher	Market research

* Special responsibility for overseas policy and expansion into Europe

---

Letter M

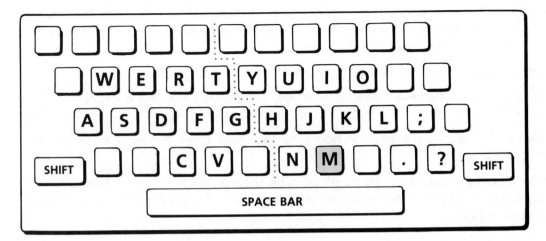

Locate **M–J** finger, lower row

Look at your hands – say and type jm jm jm jm
Look at the script – say and type jm jm jm jm
Watch the copy – say and type the drill below

Remember – flat wrists and a ballistic stroke

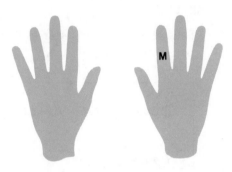

```
me em mi  im  am  ma  um  mu  mo  om  mm  rm  M  M
lm my myth myna mylar myrrh myself army

men met mere memo memory same tame time
emu emit emir emote them stem item ahem

milk mill mild mile mine mire mike mice
him grim trim swim slim shim skim image

amok amid amen clam cram dram gram tram
mall malt male mate mare mart mark mama

slum chum swum drum filmed calms salmon
mull mule mute muse mush musk must much

mode move more mold mock monk demo domo
from omit whom omen omni aromas economy

summit dimmer hammer common comma jimmy
firm form farm harm warm worm dorm norm

Maine Millie Mollie Melvin Mayan Munich
Most forms must come from some manager.

Many times my mama has come to my dorm.
Mail that letter to him today for sure.
```

ELEMENT 5.1

Produce text from oral and/or written material using an alphanumerical keyboard.

You are working for Frank Gerard, Personnel Director in charge of personnel and training. He has left you the following tasks to do. You will need to plan your work. Letterheaded paper must be used and envelopes are required.

The letters and files contain the following information needed for these tasks:

Mrs Brice's address is 64 Wykeham Avenue, Storkley, Oxford, OX4 5ER. She works for Beaverman PLC.

Ms Andrea Holmes' address is Westwood House, 89 The Vines, Otley, Oxford, OX4 9PQ. She works for Billings.

Application forms have been received from Miss Julie Thomas, 124 Northwood Avenue, Oxford, OX4 9OP, and Ms Ann Wilson, 6 Farley Drive, Oxford, OX4 6MA, for the post of Chief Administration Officer.

■ TASK 1

Send the following letter to Mrs Brenda Brice. You will be given the file of standard paragraphs you will need.

Dear Mrs Brice

(para 4)

(para 7)

We note that this is your first order placed /with us. and wonder if whether it might be possible for our rep to call on you and tell you more about our company. Many of our regular customers receive substantial discount on all orders and this could prove beneficial to you. If you are interested please ring Mr Kumar our Sales Manager on ext 239.

(para 8)

(para 10)

Letter X

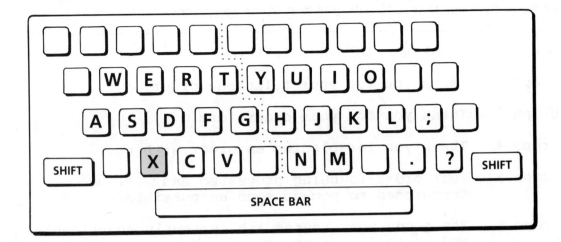

Locate **X–S** finger, lower row

Look at your hands – say and type sx sx sx sx
Look at the script – say and type sx sx sx sx
Watch the copy – say and type the drill below

Remember – flat wrists and a ballistic stroke

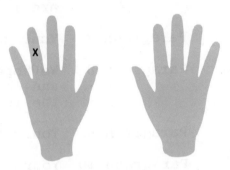

```
ex ix xt ax axe axle flax fax taxis X X
flex exit exude exult excel extra exist

fix six mixer elixir next textile twixt
ox oxen toxic sox lox fox noxious detox

Felix coaxed six of them to excellence.
Maxwell made an extra effort at Oxford.

Dex extended his tour to include Texas.
The tax on these fixtures is excessive.

I need an extra index for this extract.
Roxy knows excellent maxims and axioms.

The influx of Texans extended services.
This elixir is exactly sixty years old.

Alexis was fixing the auxiliary heater.
Axel was excited to excel in his exams.

A textured textile is extremely deluxe.
I took the Exeter exit after Middlesex.

Lex is studying taxidermy near Wexford.
We have learned this skill very easily.
```

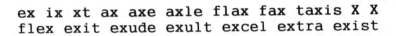

STANDARD PARAGRAPHS

File of standard paragraphs used by the company, which are being amended and will be available to be given out 15 minutes after the start of the assignment:

Paragraph 1	Thank you for your letter.
Paragraph 2	Thank you for your telephone order.
Paragraph 3	Thank you for your order form.
Paragraph 4	Thank you for placing an order with us.
Paragraph 5	Your order is being processed and will be despatched to you as soon as possible.
Paragraph 6	The goods you ordered are currently unavailable and we shall advise you as soon as these items are in stock.
Paragraph 7	Your goods will be despatched within 24 hours.
Paragraph 8	We hope you will be pleased with our service and look forward to doing business with you in the future.
Paragraph 9	Yours faithfully
Paragraph 10	Yours sincerely

Letter Q

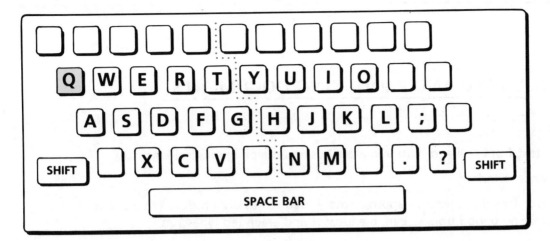

Locate **Q–A** finger, upper row

Look at your hands – say and type aq aq aq aq

Look at the script – say and type aq aq aq aq

Watch the copy – say and type the drill below

Remember – flat wrists and a ballistic stroke

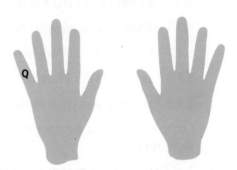

```
qua quack quart quality qualm quake Q Q
que queen queer quell queue query quest

qui quick quid quiet quite quill quilts
quo quoits quorum quota quoted quotient

enquiry vaquero liqueurs inquest acquit
sequel esquire liquid required requited

sequins sequoia liquefy request inquire
Quigley Quant Queensway Quiller Quixote

He cooks quail and squid in hot liquid.
Squire Quin is acquainted with croquet.

They acquired my cheques for the queen.
He requires a new marquee for the quay.

Quentin lacquered their antique chairs.
Was tequila called liquor or a liqueur?

Quincy quit when his query was quashed.
A quarter of his quota was quite small.

That quarrel was quickly quelled today.
Find the folders as quickly as you can.
```

National Vocational Qualification

Administration

Level 3

UNIT 5   PREPARING AND PRODUCING DOCUMENTS

Element 5.1

Produce text from oral and written material using an alphanumerical keyboard

Performance criteria

5.1.1   error-free documents of approximately 1500 words are produced in a 2.5 hour working period from screen, manuscript and amended typescript

5.1.5   presentation must conform to house style and/or accepted conventions

5.1.6   faults are dealt with or reported promptly

5.1.7   work schedules are arranged to accommodate changing priorities

5.1.8   safe working practices are always followed and implemented

5.1.9   security and confidentiality procedures are always followed and implemented

Competence must be demonstrated on a minimum of 3 separate occasions within a 2.5 hour working period.

A different set of materials must be produced on each occasion.

RSA subject examination certificates (pass or distinction) will constitute sufficient evidence for performance criteria 5.1.1, 5.1.5 and 5.1.7 when combined in either of the following formats:

1 Typewriting Skills III Part 1
   Word Processing III Part 2
   or
2 Typewriting Skills III Part 2
   Word Processing III Part 1

Instructions for the tutor

The list of standard paragraphs on the next page should be given to the students 15 minutes after they start the assignment.

Letter B

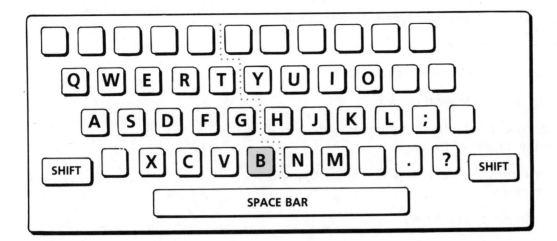

Locate **B**–**F** finger, lower row

Look at your hands – say and type fb fb fb fb
Look at the script – say and type fb fb fb fb
Watch the copy – say and type the drill below

Remember – flat wrists and a ballistic stroke

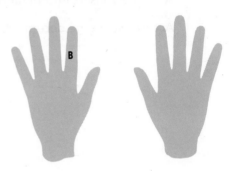

```
ab ba eb be bi ib bo ob bu ub bl lb B B
by mb rb bb br brag brad bred brew brow

abet abut able flab blab grab stab slab
bane band bank balk bask bark bare barn

bell belt best bent bend cube tube rube
bide bite bike bill bilk bird bind bias

glib crib snib bribe tribe ascribe ibid
body bode bone bore born both boll bolt

knob slob snob obey obituary oboe obese
bud bus but bun bugs buy busy bush busk

stub snub grub club flub scuba cherubim
blah blab blob blow blew bled blue blur

bomb comb tomb dumb numb limb lamb jamb
curb herb garb verb carbon forbid turbo

bubble babble rabble rubble cabby hobby
Ben Bob Bruce Betty Brian Blake Bermuda

I bought both boys a box of bubble gum.
Be sure to finish all the work on time.
```

Performance criteria	Date	Signature
Produce circular letter from typescript/manuscript	_____	_____
Correctly indicate date	_____	_____
Produce circular letter with tear-off form	_____	_____
Correctly design a tear-off portion	_____	_____
Correctly use the asterisk for footnotes in the text and at the bottom of the page	_____	_____
Allocate correctly space for insertion of photograph, diagram, plans	_____	_____
Produce form/standard letters	_____	_____
Accurately insert information on form letters	_____	_____
Accurately merge documents together	_____	_____

Letter P

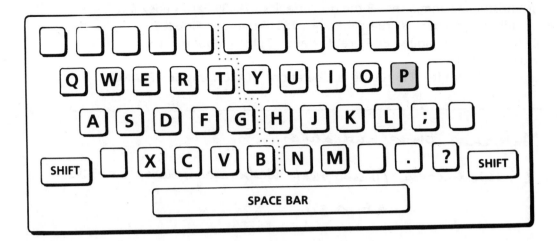

Locate **P – ;** finger, upper row

Look at your hands – say and type ;p ;p ;p ;p
Look at the script – say and type ;p ;p ;p ;p
Watch the copy – say and type the drill below

Remember – flat wrists and a ballistic stroke

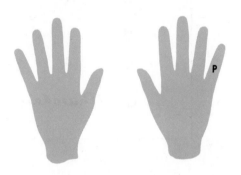

```
pa ap ep pe pi ip pu up op po pr rp P P
pl lp pt pp mp ramp camp lamp lump jump

pan pad pat pal par part pare pale pace
snap trap flap slap clap chap apt adapt

adept crepe crept inept swept step epic
pen per perk pert pest hope cope capers

pill pile pine pink ping pint pita pith
snip slip ship chip clip blip grip trip

punt punk puck puce pure purr purl pull
open opal opus chop shop slop flop clop

pole pose posh post port pork pore pone
prey pray pram prim copper pepper poppy

harp tarp warp carp help kelp yelp gulp
plop ploy play plan plea kept wept rapt

Pat Paul Peter Peggy Polly Pam Penelope
Pat plays a prominent part in politics.

Spicy paprika and pepper improve pasta.
All typed letters are to be signed now.
```

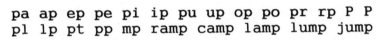

Address list of applicants to receive this letter:

1 Monsieur Jacques Goleo   24 rue de Aramand   46084 Longueil   FRANCE
2 Madame Juliette Mouchard   94 Boulevard de Martre   Paris Cedex 6   FRANCE
3 Monsieur Christophe Cannessant   8 rue de Versailles   76489 Paris Cedex 4
4 Monsieur Philippe Paumier   37 rue des Bains   78116 Dieppe   FRANCE
5 Monsieur Mathieu Dominique   84 Place de Galle   711818 Montigny Le
  Bretonneux   FRANCE
6 Monsieur Georg Metcalfe   115 rue de la Liberation   76480 Cleuville   FRANCE

Interview times and dates:

1   Wednesday (insert next Wednesday's date) at 9.30

2.   "   at 10.30

3   "   at 11.30

4   "   " 14.30

5   "   " 15.30

6   Thursday   "   9.30

Letter Z

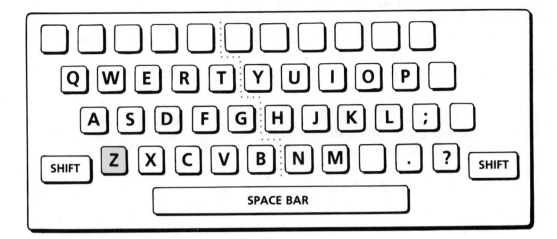

Locate **Z**–A finger, lower row

Look at your hands – say and type az az az az

Look at the script – say and type az az az az
Watch the copy – say and type the drill below

Remember – flat wrists and a ballistic stroke

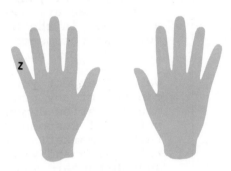

```
az za ez ze oz zo zz iz zi zip zinc Z Z
azaleas azure graze glazed blaze brazen

zap zag zany stanza wizard lizard plaza
fez trapeze zone zombie zodiac bozo zoo

zero zeta zest daze laze maze haze raze
fizz fuzz buzz jazz razz dazzled pizzas

Zulu Zaire Zanzibar Zorba Zachary Zeiss
A dizzy Lizzy nuzzled a puzzled vizier.

Ezra realized no one muzzles a buzzard.
Juarez and Lorenzo dozed in the gazebo.

Dozens of jazzmen lazily played kazoos.
Hazel gazed at a citizen in the piazza.

Mendoza wrote a snazzy stanza for Liza.
Fuzzy Wuzzy was a prized lionized bear.

The Wizard of Oz was lazier than Eliza.
A freezing grizzly sneezed and wheezed.

Suzanne from Brazil stayed at the Ritz.
This skill is growing faster every day.
```

. . . . 1 . . . . 2 . . . . 3 . . . . 4 . . . . 5 . . . . 6 . . . . 7 8

Now use an appropriate method to insert the names and addresses from the following address list. The letters will then be ready for signature when Frank Gerard returns.

1 Mr John Collins   6 Mount View Place   LONDON   SE6 4UJ
2 Mr Peter Sullivan   89 Downs Road   LONDON   NW3 5LM
3 Mrs Rajbir Sindhu   96 Cliftonville Avenue   LONDON   SE9 1UU
4 Mrs Kathleen Wright   Flat A   Mountbatten House   64 Abbey Road   LONDON   SE7 8JK
5 Mr Parminder Sarojini   3 Whitcombe Place   LONDON   SE14 9JL
6 Mr Michael Lamb   10 Queens Avenue   LONDON   W1 4MD

■ TASK 4

Prepare another standard letter which is also for Frank Gerard when he returns. Use tomorrow's date and the reference FG/your initials/F

Dear

Thank you for your application for the post of sales rep. in France. We are pleased to invite you for interview on (date) at (time) in the Board Room. Please bring with you all the relevant documents. The interviews will be conducted over a three-day period, a programme for which is enclosed.

We will expect you to do a fifteen minute presentation. You can select any product you choose and within the fifteen-minute period demonstrate how you would introduce this to a potential customer. Alternatively you could give a general talk on marketing and sales. An overhead projector, screen, television and video, film slide projector, magnetic board and whiteboard will all be available for your use. If there is anything else that you need, please do not hesitate to contact my secretary on extension 236 and she will make arrangements to ensure that everything will be ready for you.

Arrangements have been made for you to stay at the Hotel Plaza, 9 Dover Street, London EC1 5XY. You will be met at Victoria Station on Tuesday (insert next Tuesday's date). There will be two company cars waiting outside the station. They will have the company logo on the side and will be easily identifiable.

If you have any further queries please do not hesitate to contact my secretary.

Yours sincerely

Comma

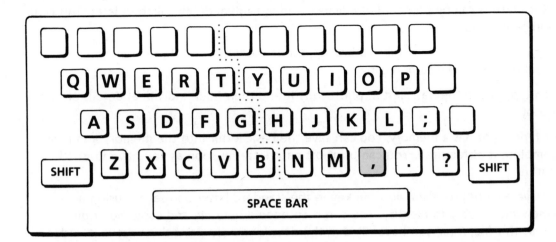

Locate , – **K** finger, lower row

Look at your hands – say and type k , k , k , k ,
Look at the script – say and type k , k , k , k ,
Watch the copy – say and type the drill below

Remember – flat wrists and a ballistic stroke

Do not hesitate before a punctuation mark. Make it part of the word it follows.

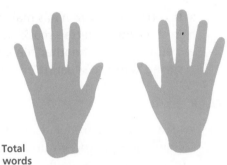

Total words

```
Thank you, Mr Harwood, for your letter.
No, we do not expect any rate increase.

Susan, Ed, Vera and Alec will be there.
Find him a chair, table, sofa and lamp.

Our group, of course, will offer funds.
This man, Leo Page, bought a new house.

Sharon, I have a copy of your new book.
The Greens, our friends, are in Norway.

The students, who were eager for lunch,      8
handed in all their papers, notes, pens      16
and rulers after the test.   By the time     24
they reached the lunchroom, most of the      32
seats were taken.   The teacher, Mr Lee,     40
arrived later, much later.                   45

Mr Lee joined Mr Harper, the new French      8
teacher, in the lounge for coffee, that      16
he found, to his disappointment, brewed      24
to a thick, inky blackness.   He decided     32
that, in future, he would bring his own      40
thermos.                                     42

No one seemed to want to drink any tea.
```

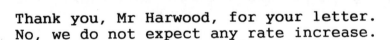

STANDARD/FORM LETTERS

Sometimes there is a need to send out the same or similar letters to a number of different people. Such letters can be prepared in advance and individual details filled in later. This can be done in several ways:

1 If using a typewriter, you can take carbon copies of the letter and then fill in the individual details on the carbon copy.

2 You can type/key in the basic letter, photocopy it and then fill in individual details on the photocopy.

3 If your typewriter has a memory, you can save the basic letter into the memory and recall and complete it as required. You can print off each letter as soon as you have finished filling it in.

4 If you have a word processor, you can key in the standard letter and save it using a filename which is easy to identify. You can then open a new file and copy the original letter into this file. Once you have filled in the details you can print this or save it under a different filename – all the time keeping the original letter.

5 If your WP program has mail merge facilities, you can use these. This means that you key in the original letter, marking the places for individual details, and save it as a letter file. You then open another file and key in all the data that will be filled in at various points, saving this as a separate file. The two files can then be merged.

■ TASK 3

As Frank Gerard from Personnel will be away today, I would like you to prepare the following letter and produce one copy of it. Use tomorrow's date and give it FG/(your initials)/app as a reference.

Dear

Thank you for your application for the post of sales rep. in the London area. You will be hearing from us shortly regarding this vacancy.

Yours sincerely

Two-minute timings

Type the following paragraphs. Divide the total words you typed by 2 to get your rate.

Total words

Learn the names of all the people around   8
you just as soon as you can. Very often   16
you will be referred to someone for some   24
information you need and knowing exactly   32
who you are looking for is a great saver   40
of your time and also that of the person   48
who is training you.   52

. . . . 1 . . . . 2 . . . . 3 . . . . 4 . . . . 5 . . . . 6 . . . . 7 8

You should keep all your reference books   8
within easy reach so that answers needed   16
are always close at hand. No one should   24
expect you to know everything but if you   32
are able to find out answers quickly you   40
will create a good impression. The most   48
useful of all may be your dictionary.   55

. . . . 1 . . . . 2 . . . . 3 . . . . 4 . . . . 5 . . . . 6 . . . . 7 8

Most of us are a little bit nervous when   8
we start a new job. The first day tends   16
to be the most worrisome but all of your   24
colleagues had first days so they really   32
do understand how you are feeling. They   40
will help you to find your way until you   48
can manage on your own. In a very short   56
time you will feel at home and as if you   64
had been there for years.   69

. . . . 1 . . . . 2 . . . . 3 . . . . 4 . . . . 5 . . . . 6 . . . . 7 8

Try to organise your time as efficiently   8
as you can. Put every one of your tasks   16
in priority order so you can do each one   24
according to its importance. Start each   32
morning with a list of jobs in the order   40
you must do them so they will be done as   48
they are needed. Cross out each task as   56
you complete it and put any of those not   64
done on the list for the next day.   71

. . . . 1 . . . . 2 . . . . 3 . . . . 4 . . . . 5 . . . . 6 . . . . 7 8

Every industry has its own vocabulary of   8
words that take on a special meaning for   16
that particular business. This specific   24
list will become very useful to you when   32
you must check on the definition or just   40
how to spell them. Start your list when   48
you begin your job and keep adding to it   56
as each new word comes up. Just writing   64
them down will help you to remember them   72
more easily.   74

. . . . 1 . . . . 2 . . . . 3 . . . . 4 . . . . 5 . . . . 6 . . . . 7 8

Name ‿ ‿ . . . . ‿ ‿ . . . .

Dept . . . . ‿ ‿ ‿ ‿ ‿ . . .

Tel Ext No . . . .

Other Courses I would be interested in ~ *attending*
‿ ‿ ‿ ‿ ‿ ‿ ‿ ‿ ‿ ‿
‿ ‿ ‿ ‿ ‿ ‿ ‿ ‿ .
‿ ‿ ‿ ‿ ‿ ‿ ‿ .

* Delete as applicable

Numbers 3 and 4

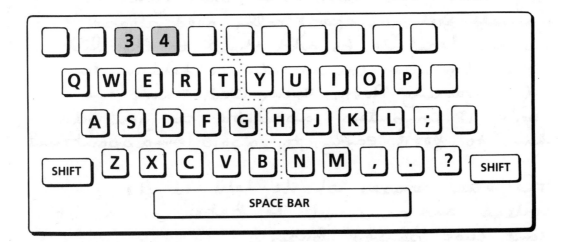

To type numbers, place your hands on the top row of keys so that your **F** finger is on **4** and your **J** finger is on **7**. Place the other fingers on the top row just as if it were the home row. Move your hands to this position whenever you type a number.

Now your **D and F** fingers are your **3 and 4** fingers.

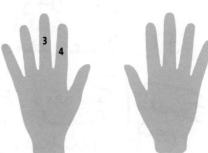

Look at your hands – say and type 34 34 34 34
Still watching your hands, say and type 43 43 43 43

Look at the script – say and type 34 34 34 34
Then say and type 43 43 43 43

Watch the copy – say and type this drill

34 34 43 43 44 44 33 33 4 3 4 33 34 33 4
34 34 43 43 4 4 3 33 43 44 43 44 34 33 3

Use chains to type long numbers quickly, accurately and easily. There are 100 number chains and you already know 4 of them – 33, 34, 43, 44.

33 34 43 44 44 44 33 33 3 4 3 4 34 33 44
34 33 44 43 4 4 3 3 43 44 43 44 34 33 34

433 344 343 333 343 434 444 334 433 4433
4433 4334 3443 3434 4343 3343 4434 33344

I suppose he must be 43 or 44 years old.
Call for me at 434 Pine between 3 and 4.

They were here until 3 minutes before 4.
Renewal for membership No 443 is 3 July.

Policy No 4433433 expires on 4 November.
I could not find size 3 or 4 shoes here.

Most of us are more skilled than she is.
I can type very well now and so can she.

. . . . 1 . . . . 2 . . . . 3 . . . . 4 . . . . 5 . . . . 6 . . . . 7 8

op) If there are any other ^topics that you ~~yourself~~ feel you specifically need please do not hesitate to add these to the list.

NP [The Computer Courses wl. be held in the Co. Training Room every Wed. There are only 18 computers available so you will have to book early to avoid disappointment.

The other courses wl. be held at the College and names wl. be taken on a 1st come first served basis.

At this point in time it is not known on wh. day the course wl. be held but if you could state your prefered day and time, that would be very helpful.

op)

Inset 1" (25mm) from both margins

[I need to have this info. before (insert next Friday's date) as the Marketing Manager of the College is coming to visit me & I wd. like to have the ^list ~~info.~~ ready /then ^by

Yours sincerely

Frank Gerard

Personnel & Training

– – – – – – – – – – – – – – – – – – – –

* I am/am not interested in Staff Dev. & training

I am available   * Mon/Tue/Wed/Thur/Fri

I would prefer   * mornings/afternoons/evenings

Numbers 7 and 8

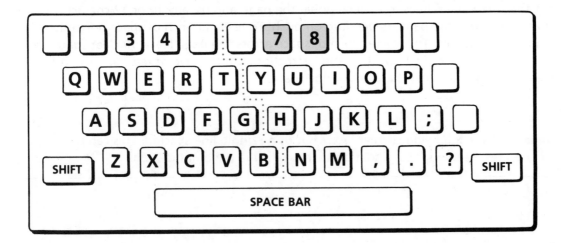

Place both hands on the number row with your **J and K** fingers becoming your **7 and 8** fingers.

Look at your hands – say and type 78 78 78 78
Look at the script – say and type 78 78 78 78
Look at your hands – say and type 87 87 87 87
Look at the script – say and type 87 87 87 87

Watch the copy – say and type the drill below

Remember – flat wrists and a ballistic stroke

```
87  78  88  87  77  77  88  88  8  7  8  7  87  88  77
78  87  77  87  7  7  8  8  78  77  87  77  87  88  78

47  48  84  83  38  37  73  33  34  43  44  7  8  3  4
8347  4748  8374  7344  7787  8843  7833  34387
```

The 747 from Chicago arrives about 7 pm.
There were 7 of them, 3 men and 4 women.

All 74 of us were there between 7 and 8.
They live at Flat 78, 738 Cypress Grove.

They sat in the 37th row, seats 7 and 8.
Be there at 7 for your 8 pm appointment.

Read section 3 on page 783 of your text.
The board measured 3.78 by 4.878 metres.

The journey took me 8 weeks plus 3 days.
There were 78 boys and 87 girls at home.

Everyone I know admires my typing skill.
I worked hard to type so well with ease.

. . . . 1 . . . . 2 . . . . 3 . . . . 4 . . . . 5 . . . . 6 . . . . 7 8

ALLOCATION OF SPACE

Sometimes you need to leave space for the insertion of photographs, diagrams, plans, etc. Remember that there are 6 lines to an inch down the page and usually 10 or 12 character spaces to an inch across the page, depending on pitch. To leave an inch of space down the page, turn up 7 line spaces. To leave an inch of space across the page leave 10 clear spaces in 10 pitch and 12 clear spaces in 12 pitch. If the instructions are to leave *at least* an inch, it is usual to leave 2 or 3 additional character or line spaces.

■ TASK 2

Prepare a draft of the following circular letter but using single line spacing. This can use more than 2 pages. Head your continuation sheets with the page number only.

January 19--

Dear Employee

STAFF TRAINING

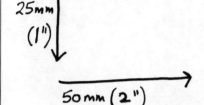
25mm (1")

50mm (2")

This company is looking very seriously at staff training and development and is ~~putting on~~ /organising a series of courses. We have approached the local college and they are very willing to provide the training that we need.

They have asked us to /~~come up with~~ provide a list of topics /which we would like covered. This will be up to you. At the moment the topics suggested include:

2 clear line spaces

- Customer Satisfaction and Care
- Managing your Time
- Marketing a Product
- Team Building
- Good Selling Techniques
- Computerised Accounts
- Word Processing
- Databases, Spreadsheets, Graphics
- Desk Top Publishing
- Shorthand
- Competence Based Assessment
- Assessing in the Work Place
- The European Market
- Language Courses
- NVQ Courses

} alphabetical order and double line spacing

2 clear line spaces

(Jenny Lutrec started to type this but can you do this again and add the following)

Numbers 1 and 2

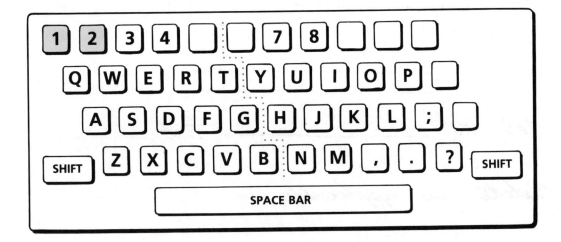

Place your hands on the number row with your **A and S** fingers becoming your **1 and 2** fingers.

Look at your hands – say and type 12 12 12 12
Look at the script – say and type 12 12 12 12
Look at your hands – say and type 21 21 21 21
Look at the script – say and type 21 21 21 21

Watch the copy – say and type the drill below

Remember – flat wrists and a ballistic stroke

```
21 12 21 12 11 22 13 14 18 78 23 1 2 1 2
17 23 24 27 28 12 21 22 11 22 11 1 2 1 2

71 81 41 31 32 42 82 72 11 22 12 21 22 1
12 21 42 32 31 41 71 81 82 18 17 14 11 2

111 222 121 323 424 727 828 818 717 4141
212 313 232 242 272 282 181 171 141 1313

1234 4321 7822 8711 2371 4282 2181 41141
13228 271242 322817 112724 141231 181232
```

There would be at least 11 or 12 people.
All your courses begin by 12 or 13 June.

We have all considered 1 or 2 new ideas.
It was 31 degrees on the 11th of August.

Add 12 cups of water to 1 cup of bleach.
He packed 2 shirts, 2 ties and 1 jacket.

I begin all my work as soon as I get it.
He finished all his work before he left.

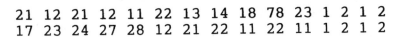

Name _____ Position _____

Co _____

Address _____

_____

Tel No _____ Ext _____

* Delete as applicable

Numbers 9 and 0

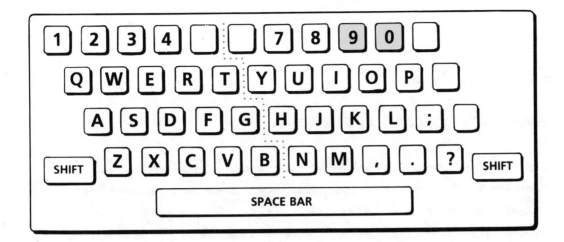

Place both hands on the number row with your **L and ;** fingers becoming your **9 and 0** fingers.

Look at your hands – say and type 90 90 90 90
Look at the script – say and type 90 90 90 90
Look at your hands – say and type 09 09 09 09
Look at the script – say and type 09 09 09 09

Watch the copy – say and type the drill below

Remember – flat wrists and a ballistic stroke

99 00 90 98 97 94 93 92 91 99 00 09 08 9
01 02 03 04 89 79 49 39 29 19 10 29 39 0

90 80 70 40 30 20 10 100 200 300 400 700
00 800 900 1000 2000 3000 4000 7000 8000

9193 2091 1099 0398 7940 9810 7008 90970
0490 9101 2939 8908 7993 1909930 1920407

I expect a 9 per cent increase in sales.
This year will be our 100th anniversary.

Buy 20 pens, 30 pencils and 40 notepads.
By 0900 at least 800 people had arrived.

We had 79 or 80 new orders before 10 am.
Deliver 40 boxes of 100 watt bulbs by 9.

In 1900 our company employed 200 people.
Sales were best in 1970, 1980, and 1990.

All the work I do now will pay off soon.
I see every drill leads to better skill.

. . . . 1 . . . . 2 . . . . 3 . . . . 4 . . . . 5 . . . . 6 . . . . 7 8

TASK 1

Prepare the following circular letter. Allow space for a name and address to be inserted later.

Date as Postmark

Dear Customer

MONTHLY SALES FIGURES

uc — We have just installed a new Customer Service Program on our computing system program 𝒹 which means we will be able to supply you with details of what each sector or division

had — within your Company have spent instead of just giving you the figures for the co. as

run on — a whole.

You will then be able to work out the exact cost of supplies for each dept. on a monthly basis. This will ~~be able to~~ 𝒹 help you with your costings and business

s/ NP — plans. [At the moment we are the only stationery co. in GB that is able to provide such a service & at no extra cost to you. This will be demonstrated

𝒹 — at our Open Evening on Mon.

If you are interested in coming along to our Open Evening — a programme is enclosed — please could you complete and return the slip below

so that we will have some idea of how many to expect.

- -

To: P Darmi, Sales Accts.

*I shall/shall not be able to attend the Open Evening on Mon. (insert next Mon's date) at 6.30 pm.

Numbers 5 and 6

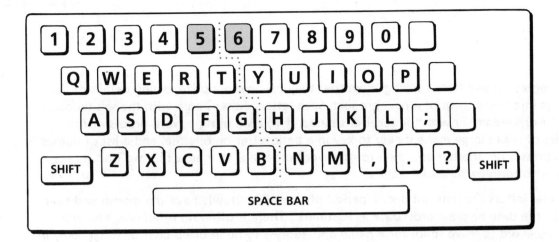

Place both hands on the number row and use the **4** finger to control **5** and the **7** finger to control **6**.

Look at your hands – say and type 56 56 56 56
Look at the script – say and type 56 56 56 56
Look at your hands – say and type 65 65 65 65
Look at the script – say and type 65 65 65 65

Watch the copy – say and type the drill below

Remember – flat wrists and a ballistic stroke

```
45 54 45 54 76 67 76 67 55 66 56 65 6 5
35 53 25 52 15 51 86 68 96 69 06 60 5 6

56 65 75 57 85 58 95 59 95 59 50 05 5 5
64 46 63 36 62 26 61 16 65 56 55 66 6 6

450 450 500 500 600 600 650 650 560 560
6475 5785 9558 5036 5963 4606 6176 6256

1626 3646 5666 7686 9606 1525 3545 4565
66565 45676 866836 876950 265345 765436
```

```
He used at least 50 or 60 A6 envelopes.
All 5 houses will be complete by 6 May.

Divide the sum of 8550 and 9675 by 590.
They moved to 66 Bluebird Lane in 1985.

Please reserve a table for 15 for 6 pm.
Sales had increased by 5 or 6 per cent.

This skill only has to be learned once.
I know and use the best of work habits.
```

. . . . 1 . . . . 2 . . . . 3 . . . . 4 . . . . 5 . . . . 6 . . . . 7 8

Section 9 Business correspondence

NVQ Level 3

CIRCULAR LETTERS

Many people receive letters telling them that they have won a prize, giving details of latest offers or informing them of a new product. Such letters either begin with the salutation 'Dear Sir or Madam' or with the receiver's name. If you are using a word processor the facilities of mail merge make it easy to key in a basic letter on one file, and a list of names and addresses on another and then for the word processor to merge the two documents together to form personalised letters.

As circular letters are sent out over a period of time they usually have the month and year only for the date or the words 'Date as Postmark'. There is often no reference. You will either be asked to leave space for a name and address to be inserted later or to type/key in eg 'Dear Sir or Madam' 2 line spaces below the date. You must always follow instructions.

Obviously not all letters will be personally signed. The master letter can be signed and then the rest copied. If several letters are to be mail merged then it will not be possible to sign a 'master' as every letter is unique. In this case you would put:

Yours sincerely

1 clear line space

Adriano Guillaim

1 clear line space

Sales Representative

Some circular letters also have a return slip at the bottom to be completed and returned to the company. If there is a continuation sheet, the tear-off slip is put at the bottom of the second page.

There are two ways of calculating where the tear-off portion of the letter should start:

1 Turn up 2 line spaces after the last line of the letter – usually the name of the signatory – and then type or key in a row of hyphens from edge to edge of the page, or from margin to margin if your word processor cannot do this. Turn up 2 line spaces and start the tear-off form. There must be at least one clear line space above and below the row of hyphens.

2 **Word processors**   Calculate where to place the row of hyphens by counting the number of lines the tear-off portion will occupy. Take this away from 54 or 58 (ie the last line on your word processing screen). Make a note of the line number where you want to key the hyphens in and watch your screen for when you reach this point.

   Typewriters   Calculate where to place the row of hyphens by counting the number of lines the tear-off portion will occupy plus a further 6 lines for the bottom margin. Mark this lightly with a pencil so that you will know when you reach this point. Erase the pencil mark later.

   Remember to leave a clear space before and after typing each group of leader dots on the tear-off slip.

Symbols

Many symbols do not have a standard place on the keyboard, as the comma and semi colon usually do, and you must learn their location on whichever keyboard you are using. Symbols may be either located as the upper case characters of numbers or of other symbols. You already know which finger to use.

Locate each one; the name, use and correct spacing are shown.

Type the examples 3 times.

:   The colon is used to introduce a list. (In some countries it is used after the salutation in a business letter.) There is no space before the colon but it is followed by 1 space in the UK (2 in the USA and Canada).

```
Buy: sugar, flour, milk.
```

/   The stroke (also known as the diagonal, oblique, solidus or slash) is used in numbers, in fractions not on your keyboard, which you create yourself, to represent an alternative and in computer commands. Leave no spaces before or after it.

```
Sign and return Endorsement 789/987.
Use 1/4 cup of sugar.
and/or
dir a:/w/p
```

–   Use the shift lock and the underscore to underline when you are using a typewriter. Word processors have a special command key for this.

Spaces between words may or may not be underlined.

```
We use 'The Secretary's Desk Book'.
```

```
_____
```
signature

%   Per cent – there is no space between the number and the percentage sign %.

```
All stock is reduced by 25%.
```

()   Brackets (parentheses) hug everything inside, with no spaces between them and the material enclosed.

```
John (he was Manager) resigned.
```

*   The asterisk (star) may be used for footnotes and is repeated at the bottom of the page with the explanation.

```
in Anmore*
```

```
* A small community near Vancouver.
```

The hash mark is in common use in the USA, Canada and other parts of the world but is not normally used in the UK. Before numbers it means 'number'; after numbers it means pounds (weight, not sterling). It can also mean sharp in a key of music. There are no spaces around the hash mark.

```
Sign and return form #81823.
He lifted two 50# weights.
Transpose this song to C#.
```

Performance criteria	Date	Signature
Produce a multi-page document correcting inconsistencies		
Correct spelling and keying in errors		
Correctly paginate a document		
Use the header facility		
Use the footer facility		

" Quotation marks are used for direct quotations and hug everything inside. There are no spaces between the marks and the material they enclose.

A quotation mark may be used to represent inches.

```
Tom asked, "What time is it?"
Harry is 3" taller than Peter.
```

' The apostrophe represents letters omitted in contractions such as can't and is used in possessives, such as Walter's son. There is no space before or after it unless it is being used as a plural possessive, as in girls' shoes.

```
I'll be home soon.
Tom's book is in the boys' locker room.
```

! The apostrophe is also used to form the exclamation mark on a typewriter if there is not one on the keyboard. Type ' then backspace and type . directly below it ! to form the exclamation mark. The exclamation mark is followed by 2 spaces but has no space before it.

The apostrophe may also represent feet.

```
The ceilings are 10' high.
```

Use apostrophes for a quote within a quote.

```
She said, "Did you see 'Moby Dick' on TV?"
```

£ There is no space between the symbol and the amount of money.
$

```
The total raised was £950.00.
```

When there is a column of amounts, the rule is that the decimal points are aligned and the £, $ or other currency indicator is typed in the column one space to the left of the longest amount. It is typed before the first amount and before the total.

```
£  9.50
  940.50
£950.00
```

- The hyphen joins words together and uses the space between them.

```
My son-in-law drove me home.
```

If a word is too long to finish on one line, type a hyphen then finish the word on the next line. Break a word only between syllables and have at least 3 letters on each line.

```
Every single piece of our new furni-
ture is teak.
```

In the UK the dash is 1 hyphen with a space before and after it.

```
Karen - she is our local expert - disagreed.
```

This is an acceptable alternative in the USA and Canada, where two hyphens side by side with no spaces normally constitute the dash.

& The ampersand has a space before and after it because it is a word on its own.

```
He works at Coopers & Billings.
```

@ This mark is sometimes used in extensions on statements and invoices.

```
5 hours @ £10.00 = £50.00
```

Créche ③

It has been agreed at the mtg of the Board of Dirs. that a créche fac. will be available on site from 1 April. but this is

NP   only for children over the age of 2. // We have applied for permission to run a créche for children under the age of 2 but this has not been granted yet. We are not expecting any problem with the application. We have appointed two fully trained nursery nurses and an

NP.   assistant. // The créche wl. be opend every day from 8 am - 6 pm. Lunch will be provided in the morning at 10 00 am and a drink will be provided in the afternoon at ~~TR~~ 1530hrs. ~~Beds will be provided~~ There wl. be beds for children who still need an afternoon sleep or who are not well.

run on   Linen will be provided.

who /   However, we wd. ask anyone / is sending a child to the créche to supply a small hand towel and face cloth

NP   clearly marked with the name. // If you wish to use this facility cd. you pl. let Mrs Nightingale know asap.

single line spacing   If you have any items of interest for the newsletter can you let the editor have them on the first Tuesday of the month.

Using numbers and symbols

Copy these examples exactly, beginning each at the left margin.

```
15 June 1983            3'                  0800 hours
8 August 1937           12 miles            1430 hours
10 January 1991         3/4"                2200 hours
4 March 1967            15 m                0745 hours

071 847 8332            2 cups              25%
081 324 1847            1/2 tsp             0.75
0932 324789             30 kg               3.95
0539 783205             12 oz               0.9%
```

```
Farley-Benson Motors            Eva Darnell
Georgia Park Row                304-2322 Pender Street
BRISTOL                         VANCOUVER
BS23 3GR                        British Columbia
                                Canada
Attention: Personnel Manager    V5R 7YH

Kelly's Key Kutters             C# Music (1985) Limited
114 Cabramatta Road             454 Elm Street
Dee Why                         MIDLAND
NSW 2098                        Ohio
AUSTRALIA                       USA
                                98354


Department 34/P654              Miss Elaine Coe
The Advertiser                  c/o Miss Linda Porter
Box 2322                        Flat 32
The Independent                 Belsize House
87 Gray's Inn Road              44 Ingersoll Terrace
LONDON                          BIRMINGHAM
WC1E 2ER                        B3 9HY

Herr Doktor W Braun             Mr Colin Holmes
5 Schulstrasse                  764 Rae Avenue
Hamburg                         ALEXANDER
GERMANY                         Middx
                                MH3T 3DR


12 October 1993                 7 July 1994

Le Department de Compte         Barnes & Belmont
Le Service de l'Ordinateur      894 Cypress Grove
12 rue de Bain                  INVERNESS
Paris Cedex 6                   Scotland
FRANCE                          IN5 2LK
```

Darts Team

(2)

Ic
quarterly /

Our darts team ~~is~~ is continuing to do well, having beaten <u>NOTTS</u> Riders in the / finals. The next match is to be played next Wed. We ~~wish~~ wish them the best of luck

) leave space
50 × 25mm
(2" × 1")
to insert
match
fixtures

Welcome Visitors

 (4)

leave
space
50mm × 25mm
for photo
of visitors

On 3 March we are having a party of 8 visitors from Milan coming to discuss the poss. of opening up a retail outlet in Italy.

run on

If there is any member of staff who can speak Italian & who is interested in going over to Milan can they please contact Patrick Dubuc on ext. 236

First Aid Course

(3) (5)

I have contacted the Red Cross with a view to running a basic first
training / aid / course for all staff who are interested. They can offer a 2-day training session & we are very happy to release staff for this. The course will be repeated on 4 separate occasions so that several members of staff can attend.
If you are interested contact Frank Gerard on ext 239

3 Keyboarding development

Work through this section to consolidate your keyboarding skills and prepare yourself for the examination coursework which follows.

Timings enable you to measure your progress and identify areas where specific practice is needed. The timings and drills in this section can also be used for further practice.

Longer timings and speed test pieces for employment are given. Advice and practice on punctuation, word division and paragraph numbering end the section, in preparation for Level 1 NVQ which follows.

Specific instructions are given for each of the drills which follow the timings.

```
        If anyone has any problems please contact me.


        Frank Gerard
        Personnel Director


        (Insert today's date)


        REMEMBER SAFETY AT ALL TIMES ON SITE
```

■ TASK 2

Prepare the following draft in double line spacing with an unjustified right margin. Number each page in the centre at the bottom and use the header SWIFT STAFF NEWSLETTER. Read through the whole task before you start.

SWIFT   MASTERMIND TEAM ①

Congrats. to our splendid team who won the Business Mastermind Trophy at the final ~~tast~~ heat held in Birmingham last week. This was a tremendous achievement and we are all very proud of the team.

We would like to thank you all for your support, help and encouragement. Particular thanks go to Michael Adams who came in early every ~~day~~ to put the team through ✓ their paces. The trophy wl have pride of place in our trophy cabinet in reception   u.c. Well done!

Leave ~~After~~ 10 lines to insert newspaper cutting.

Skill building drills

As soon as a problem surfaces, it can be corrected and these drills are aimed at specific areas of concern.

Moving at a faster rate than can be controlled results in accidents – in typing we call these errors. By slowing down, you can control the keyboard.

However, by typing at a controlled rate when you are trying to build skill, you do not know where practice is needed. Put another way, by practising slowly, you turn a worksheet into a finished product. Practice at a brisk, not panicky, rate so errors will identify themselves and you can correct them.

Speed and accuracy do not grow together; practise one and then the other. Build a lot of speed and then release it at a controlled rate. Build speed; build control to that speed; then build more speed, etc.

Substitution drills refine the response. Letters like B and V are often confused because the fingers are not sure where V ends and B begins.

Chaining drills will help you to shorten the pauses between strokes and type faster without feeling under pressure.

Shift key drills will overcome any lingering on the shift key.

As specific weaknesses arise, add them to your 'hit list' and cross them off as they are mastered.

MY HIT LIST

Substitutions	Chains	Shift
~~B/V~~	~~tr~~	~~A~~
M/N	~~at~~	~~G~~
U/Y	~~gt~~	M
	ro	

Other drills – common words, contractions and end-of-the-line drills – which you have already done will help you to type with confidence and fluency.

As you do these drills, you will notice that motions will 'click into place' and become automatic. Often these clicks will come in clusters and this is the reason progress in typing is not a smooth climb. There are leaps forward and plateaux in speed when errors will fall away quickly.

Timings will show your progress and will prepare you for employment tests. Apply the knowledge you have gained to find your best rate, fast but with control as needed.

The following draft has been prepared but there are several alterations to be made. Type/key in a final copy in double line spacing, making all the necessary amendments. Correct the errors which have been identified. Use the header HEALTH AND SAFETY IN THE OFFICE. Number each page in the bottom left-hand corner.

We have just had a review of the health and safety within this company and would like to draw your a(tenti)on to the following points.

*/ It is the duty of every employee (tobe)have in a way that will not endanger any(^)one on the premises = either visiting or working.

Employees/
δ) ~~They~~ / will at all times observe the code for safe working conditions.

WORKING (with) COMPUTOR(s)   ← SPACED CAPS

We do try to ensure that all the computers are positioned so that you have plenty of space around you.   However, / are quite   we/
concerned that computers are being moved and that safety conditions are not being observed.   Please note:

1   C(//)mputers should not be moved.

should   2 δ) ~~You should allow~~ (s)uf(fi)cient space /on your desk for the
be left/   computer workstation, the printer and for your work.

3   It is a regulation that (al) keyb(o)rd(s) should be detachable and therefore the old computers with an integrated keyboard should no longer be used.   ~~These have been writen off and should not be about.~~

chairs/ Λ 5   We have purchased /with (a)justable backs to give back support. If you have any problems with your chairs please notify maintenance imm(e)di(t)ely.

δ 4   We have purchased desks which have ducts built in for
2/   cabling.   It is therefore with regret that we notice that
2/   members of staff are adding further equipment/ ie audio
uc   machines/ and that wires are trailing across the floor.   If   2/
          you need to have add(@)itional power points/ speak to
          maintenance.

workstations/
6   The computer/should be (so positioned) that the screen is   trs
    away from glare A(l)though we have blinds at the (the) windows
    this will not completely block out the sunlight.

7   The ceiling has acoustic tiles to reduce noise level in the room and all floors have been carp(e)tt(e)d.

δ 9   All walls ha(s) been painted in pastel/matt colours which do not reflect the sunlight.

δ 8   Acoustic hoods have been fitted to all printe(r t)o reduce noise level.   These must not be removed.

⊘ 10   All equipment should be switched off overnight.

11   Eye tests are provided regularly for all members of staff.

Substitution grid

Copy the grid below on A4 paper, or use graph paper, and plot your substitution errors to direct your practice.

For example, if you typed:

dregs instead of	drags
clem	clam
dog	cog
swapt	swept
selt	salt
wall	well
cuties	duties
crake	drake
cesk	desk
nide	nice

the results would be plotted as shown, indicating that you should do the A/E and C/D substitution drills.

Certain squares will fill up and show at a glance which letters you are consistently confusing.

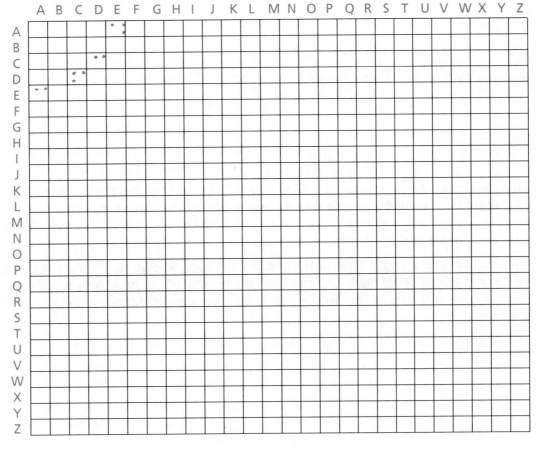

I typed:

I should have typed:

Section 8 Business documents

NVQ Level 3

You are working for Frank Gerard, Personnel Director at Swift Stationers PLC. Date all documents and use the reference FG/(your initials).

MULTI-PAGE DOCUMENTS

When producing a document that will go on more than one sheet you must make sure that you use paper of the same quality throughout. You should also ensure that all margins are the same and that the page number is in exactly the same position on each page. There are several positions for a page number:

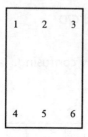

and you can use any of the following page number styles:

2   –2–   – 2 –   (2)

The important thing is to be consistent.

PAGINATION

On a typewriter leave a margin of 1″ (2.5 cm or 6 line spaces) at the top of the page before inserting the page number on the seventh line. A header (text repeated at the top of all pages in a multi-page document) can also be included. Leave at least one clear line space after the number and/or header.

If numbering and/or text is to be at the end of each page (known as a footer), it is a good idea to put a light pencil mark 2″ (5 cm) from the bottom of the page. You will then know there are only a few more lines to use. Leave one clear space before inserting the number and/or footer.

Your word processor automatically allows a 1″ space at the top and bottom of a page. These spaces are known as header and footer zones.

Page numbers and any text which is to be repeated on all pages should appear as a header or a footer. Many word processing programs allow the automatic printing of page numbers in a chosen position. To insert page numbers, headers and/or footers you will have to use the appropriate commands/menus. If you do not know how to use these, refer to your program manual or ask your tutor.

Substitution drills

The drills below will help correct confusion of letters. Do only those you need to do. Check your grid and hit list.

For each pair of letters that you confuse, type the corresponding drill 3 times.

A/C car arc acre cash taco talc call cap can clam scat cat
A/E are ate tea era agree gate beta area sea appear aerate
A/Q aqua squad quay quaff qualm quaver quart equals quotas

A/S sat sag lass ash fast star swan sashay as amass harass
A/Z bazaar haze topaz waltz plaza lazy jazz amaze zag czar
B/G bag bigger gob garb berg bungle brig gab bingo cabbage

B/N ban numb nab knob bond bunny nub banana snubbed bonbon
B/V bevel above behave viable obviously proverbs invisible
C/D disco cad cuddle clod cold decoy cheddar cider succeed

C/S cost discusses scent access soccer class cause science
C/V cave vacant curve vice vicar advice cove convict carve
C/X boxcar coax cortex convex excise execute excuse excess

D/E denied dead ended decades descend wedded deed defended
D/F fuddle daft deft fad faded doff daffodil differed find
D/K dunk desk dirk duke duck dusk kind drink kidded banked

D/S suds sold address dusty stead dash saddle seed dressed
E/I edit emit hire peril heir brief eligible indeed titled
E/R are era eerie there river career reed tree per terrier

E/S eyes chess ease seeks access assent vessel stress sent
E/T the letter then eat tea beet settee tent east item ten
E/W west went drew dew whenever weekend were few endow new

F/G fig forget frog gruff fugue finger fling fogged figure
F/R fur far from friar fore fear roof refer differ terrify
F/T staff fort fact fret fault flit fat turf toffee fitted

G/H sigh higher haggard hugged girth hag hog hoping sleigh
G/T gent toggle gogetter stag straight tiger tugging grant
I/K ski ilk skip kid kin link kick skin kind kirk tick kip

I/O trio join prior coil omission iota prison oozing onion
I/U undid united unique using furious futile unified fruit
K/L talk ankle lark keel luke folk lock skulk knoll likely

L/O lo loss jolt follow holly cold polo oleo look log lots
M/N men numb mine gnome animal human minimum minnow summon
O/P stop poll pod opt poppy tropic optic hop stoop popcorn

R/T try starter retort portrait regret tarot turret letter
R/U urge rug guru jury hurl ruby blur purr spur usurp rude
S/W stew sway west whose woes slew shows wits wassail laws

T/Y sty type troy entry dynasty forty tightly putty twenty
U/Y ruby injury you buy musty usury blurry rusty ugly bury
V/Y very variety vanity convey volley envoy ivy every bevy

Checklist of achievements in Section 7 – Business tabulations

Performance criteria	Date	Signature
Correctly produce a ruled tabulation with adequate spacing between the columns	_____	_____
Line text up in a ruled tabulation	_____	_____
Insert vertical lines in a ruled tab correctly and neatly ensuring that all lines meet	_____	_____
Look up information to go into tabulation	_____	_____
Correctly sort information into alphabetical order within a ruled tabulation	_____	_____
Use footnotes with a ruled tabulation	_____	_____
Correctly use multi-headings within a ruled tabulation	_____	_____
Use leader dots within a tabulation correctly	_____	_____

Corrective chaining drills

DIAGNOSTIC CHAINING INVENTORY

Type this drill fast to identify chains that are not fluent. Do not repeat any words and do not stop until you reach the end.

Note any incorrect chains and type the corresponding drill 3 times.

```
aged afar flax tidy cram brat auto avid inform finish pliant
muff slab gasp rage gild sign harp hind rotate babble blazer

true oval soya even twit work wrap joke funnel stolid pisces
bias aide draw quay belt bomb busk byte anoint closet votive

hurt whip iris jazz kink know walk wily friend phobia didn't
cake fare dock easy diet lacy curl cloy welded yeoman popped

ecru dues data item grew life gull acme cinema chapel sector
mitt molt null glob bloc oath sago prod record sleeve eulogy

smog ooze purr papa ripe viva turn swim ignore jiggle summon
jump oust hard land what ship rise it's advent sadden animal
```

CORRECTIVE CHAINING DRILLS

ab   about abut abacus abed abode abrupt abuse grab stab blab
ac   ace act acre actual acme tract grace exactly space brace

ad   adjoin adept advice adhere grade shade trade spade evade
af   afar after afraid afoot afloat crafts graft shaft drafty

ag   agent agile again agree drag image diagram usage tragedy
ai   air aim aid ail aide again stair train await trail avail

al   ale alm also alto oval dial vial qualm scald scale stalk
am   amp amok amid amen among clam wham edam exam amble drama

an   and ant any anti anchor ankle scan than bran plant piano
ap   ape apt apse apart apathy wrap snap chapel burlap grapes

ar   arm art arc are aria area ajar afar star scar char spark
as   ask aster aspic aside alas bias phase clasp chase plasma

at   ate atop atom atoll atone that what slat scat fiat state
au   auto aunt aura auction autumn flaunt clause fraud trauma

av   avow avail avoid aviary grave bravo travel aviate cravat
aw   awl awe away awake award crawl prawn brawn drawer awhile

ax   ax axe axle axis axiom flax klaxon maxims taxied maximum
ay   fray play quay okay gray clay shay hurray astray crayons

Type or key in the following tabulation. Make sure that you read the instructions at the bottom before you begin.

Correct Spellings ← (Spaced Caps)

Underline the word which you think is spelt correctly			
Ocassion	occassion	occasion	occation
Priviledge	privilige	privilidge	privilege
accomodation	accommodation	accomodation	accommodation
Sceenery	Scenery	Scenery	Sceenery
fulfil	fullfill	fullfil	fulfill
receeve	receive	recieve	reseeve
disappear	dissappear	dissappear	disapier
embarres	embarrass	embarress	embares

Prepare this as a test for prospective applicants. Then underline the correct one so that I will have a master. Also use double line spacing and put in alphabetical order.

az azure azalea gaze daze plaza razor brazen blazer brazier
ba bar bat bag ban bay bad ball tuba cobalt debated cabaret

bb babble rabble robbed fobbed dubbed wobbled cobble rubber
be be bet beg bed beta beau babe jibe cube rube tuber label

bi big bib bin bit bio robin cubic cabin habit orbit mobile
bl blab blah bloc table cable fable noble black blade blues

bo bob bow box born bowl bozo lobo hobo bebop elbows nobody
br break bread broke brace dobro cobra debris inbred embryo

bu bud bud bug bun burg burn debunk buck tabu debut buckled
by by bye byte byway byroads byword baby ruby hereby nearby

ca cam can car cat cad camp pica recap decal recall decades
ce cell cent cellar pace mace race face lace dice rice nice

ch chow chap chip chin chew chum rich etch inch ouch urchin
ci city cite cider cipher cinnamon foci loci lucid incident

ck nick kick back rick rack tick tock muck mock rock locket
cl clef clad clap clod cloy uncle declare included inclined

co cos come coma cork cove cola cone taco loco decor record
cr cray creel crust crush crepe decry microbe sacred dacron

ct pact sect fact tact duct select fiction picture lectured
cu cue cud cup curl curd cubic recur locust excused vacuous

cy cyst cynic cymbal cyclone chancy bicycle recycle infancy
da dab day dad dam data coda soda madam sedan sedate madame

dd wedding cuddle muddle sadden middle dodder fuddle coddle
de den deb dew deco deli demo tide side wide mode code jade

di die did ding dill dirk dish disc midi radio radium media
do doe dole dome dosage doge judo lido undoes redone dodger

dr dram drop drip drab dress padre cadre drum dreary driven
du dug dud duo dual duet duke module reduce endure deducted

dy dyke dyne dyer dynamic eddy tidy body lady brandy shandy
ea eat ease earn early eagle ideal cheat cream wheat steady

ec ecology eclipse ecstatic erect spectrum species election
ed edit edict edam edge educated lied coed used died credit

ee eel eerie glee green greed greet freed sweep sleep steer
ei eighty eider either their deceit receive receipt deceive

el ell elm elk elf else elan elbow shelf spelt dwelt svelte
em emu emir emit embed embark item diem poem ahem them stem

en end endow enrol ensue enter oven open event spent golden
ep epee epic epoch epsom step swept crepe adept slept crept

Our overseas sales representatives are receiving a great deal of literature from stores in Europe and are having difficulty in working out European sizes. Please prepare the following as a guide. As the columns are not very wide, please rearrange the table into 4 columns as shown:

British	European	British	European
1	33	7	41
2	34	8	42
3	36	9	43
4	37	10	44
5	38	11	45
6	39		

CLOTHING SIZES

Shoe Sizes

British	European
1	33
2	34
3	36
4	37
5	38
6	39
7	41
8	42
9	43
10	44
11	45

Dress Sizes

British	European
32 (10)	38
34 (12)	40
36 (14)	42
38 (16)	44
40 (18)	46
42 (20)	48

Suit Sizes

British	European
38	48
40	50
42	53
42	55

er	ergo erne erst dyer pier user ewer over aver where there
es	espy escorts esteem hues rues cues uses foes woes values

et	etc etna etude etched eternally poet diet suet duet fret
eu	eureka eulogies euphoria pseudo sleuth queues rheumatism

ev	eve evil ever even sieve clever eleven prevent prevalent
ew	ewe ewer anew chew drew grew stew flew blew crew brewing

fa	far fact fang fade fawn farce fatal infant deface defame
fe	fed fen fez felt fell fern rife fife defer defend strife

ff	muff cuff huffed gaffer duffle caffiene giraffe differed
fi	fir firm fish fight finger refined refit defile definite

fl	fly floe flan flag flee flea rifle influx inflow inflate
fo	folk fore forty folly focus forget inform reform enforce

fr	fro frog fray frau friar frisk defraud defrayed carefree
fu	fund fuse fugue future fulfil tofu awful careful wakeful

ga	gay gab gap gas gang gaze gala regal organ legacy regard
ge	gel gem geo general gentry genie cage angel anger legend

gg	reggae noggin jagged mugger rigged lagged jiggle jiggers
gi	gig gilt give giggle ginger engine edging regina legions

gl	glut glass gleam globe glint angle ingle unglued wrangle
gn	gnu gnaw gnome gnash gnarled signet resign signal magnet

go	goo gob goy gong gogo golfer gopher sago logo ergo ingot
gr	grey grog grit graph grace angry ingrate engross degrade

gu	guy gulp gully guide guess jaguar yogurt figure argument
gy	gyp gym gyro gypsy gyproc edgy logy clergy energy stingy

ha	hah halo half hang harm hack aghast behalf inhale behave
he	hem hen hew hey here herbs scheme beheld adhesive upheld

hi	hifi hive hick hiccup hiatus behind aching schism uphill
ho	holy hole hone horn howl hobo coho abhor cohort beholden

hu	hut hue hub hula hurl hutch hunch exhume unhurt inhumane
ia	trial phial briar friar pliant triage initial speciality

ic	ice icy icon icicle epic chic evict tropical slice price
id	idle idea ides idol acid arid avid ibid quid skids slide

ie	alien grief brief tries skies flies chief grieve friends
ig	ignite ignore igloo iguana frigid brigand brigade stigma

im	imp imbue imply image impair impasse slim whim grim trim
in	ink inch into inept inert incur twin shin chin skin akin

LEADER DOTS

If you have to put leader dots in a tabulation, allow one clear space after the last character before inserting the dots. Think of a group of leader dots as one word so that the last dot is the last character in the first column. If you are allowing 3 spaces between your columns you will leave 3 after the last leader dot.

Remember that the minimum number of leader dots to be used is 3.

■ TASK 3

All staff working for Swift Stationers PLC will have the opportunity of joining the Private Medical Plan at reduced cost. Prepare the following table to be included with all salary advices at the end of the month. There will also be a leaflet to go with this.

PMP — Private Medical Plan

Type of Cover *	Cost per month			
	Women Over 50	Women Under 50	Men Over 50	Men Under 50
	£	£	£	£
Complete Plan	21.50	17.50	25.50	22.50
Consultation plus hospitalisation ___	19.50	18.00	21.50	17.50
Hospitalisation only ------ ..	12.50	10.00	16.50	14.80

* Full details on PMP leaflet.

ip	quip skip drip flip trip slip chip snip whip grip sniper
ir	irk iris whir irony flirts spiral inspire thirty thirsty
is	isle island isthmus exist arise frisk wrist unison twist
it	its item itch italics skit flit twitch white spite quite
ja	jab jay jaguar jargon jangle jammed jalopy hijack pyjama
je	jet jest jerk jerry jenny object inject deject rejection
ji	jib jig jive jilt jinx jiffy jingo jigger jitney jujitsu
jo	jot joy job jowl jockey jocular dijon major enjoy cajole
ju	jut jug judo jumbo julep jumper adjust injured injustice
ke	key keg ken kelp kern keno kept mike hike like lake take
ki	kit kilo kiosk kimono kilter bikini taking unkind asking
kn	knit knob knew know knee knave knead knife knights knock
la	lax law lad lap lab lag late gala cola hula delay relate
ld	gold mold meld fold wild sold told weld bold cold mildew
le	let leg led lens levy less able file mile male dale sale
li	lie lid lit like lira lily line deli solid malign malice
lk	bulk calk folk walks polka talkie silken milkman walkout
ll	bell sell fell hill pill dill doll tall ball mall pallid
lo	lot log lop lob loll lord logic polo silo solo halo kilo
lt	salt malt bolt volt colt cult lilt belt melt silt filter
lu	ludo luke lurid lucid lunch values volume diluted deluxe
ly	lye lynx lyre lyric lying lynch wily idly rely only lily
ma	mask mash make mare magic major coma lima lama puma mama
mb	limbo limber timber tumble humble jumble lumber mumbling
me	meld menu mete medic media fame game lime lame tame home
mi	mid mink mice mini mien minx mica semi demi remiss mimic
mm	comma tummy gamma mummy dummy gummy lummox mammal summit
mo	mow moss mote motor mocha molar memo demo remote removal
mp	camper dumpster wimple dampen bumper rumple limpet lumpy
mu	mug mum muff mumps muddy demur femur gamut demure tumult
na	nab nabob native naval nanny nadir myna tuna ulna banana
nd	land hand rend pend tend kind send bond bind fond candle
ne	nettle nether nectar nerve pane wane lane mane cane bane
ni	nifty niche night ninny nipper mini senile ponies denies
nk	bank lank dank junk punk monk kink rink funk hunk hanker
nn	banned sinner canned tanner gunner manner nanny beginner

Prepare the following holiday rota. Look up the organisation chart on page 80 and include the divisions after each of the names.

SWIFT STATIONERS PLC

<u>Holidays</u> — Directors & Section Leaders

Name & Dept Division	Week 1	Wk 2	Wk 3	Wk4
H Kohl	X	X		
F Gerard		X	X	X
L Jones		X	X	
M Patel	X	X	X	
S McKenzie		X		
P Smythe		X	X	X
P Darmi	X	X		
L Scott		X	X	
C Major		X	X	X
J Bugden	X	X		
SJP Martin	X	X	X	
J Harrison	X	X		
JP Kumar			X	X
P Dubuc			X	X
S Peters			X	X
C Michaels *		X	X	X
C Watson *	X		X	X

* Can be contacted in an emergency.

Put C Michaels first, C Watson second and rest in alphabetical order.

no	now novel noble north notion mono keno minor donor manor
nt	tent bunt pant cent lint bent rents winter mantle mental

nu	nurse nutty nutmeg nuzzled menu bonus venue genus tenure
oa	oaf oak oar oat oath oases whoa broad gloat bloat aboard

ob	obey oboe obit oblige oblong obvious knob blob snob slob
oc	ocular octopus octagon stocked frock clock crock proctor

od	ode odious prod abode erode anode diode exploded cathode
og	ogle ogre ogee frog brogue stogie slogan shogun progress

oi	ointment choir stoic avoid spoils choices broiler anoint
ol	old oligarchy scold stolen whole stolid olympiad cholera

om	omit omen ominous omnibus from atom prom prompt promoted
on	on one once only anon neon iron icon ebony onions phoned

oo	shoo gloomy brook stoop stood shook scoop groove trooper
op	opt open opal option opera flop plop stop crop chop drop

or	orbit oriole orient orange flora score store sport scorn
os	ostler osprey ostrich osmosis frosty closet those chosen

ou	oust outer outlaw outfit cloud clout shout spout trouble
ov	oval oven overt overact overture stove shove grove trove

ow	scow owing owner stow glow brow meow flower glower scowl
oy	cloy buoy troy employ deploy convoy busboy cowboy tomboy

pa	pang pall pack pass pact papa repay expand repast impala
pe	pep pen peg per pet peso perm cope lope tape hyped caper

ph	phone phial phlox phobic physics pharmacy typhus epitaph
pi	pipe ping pith pity pica pixie rapid cupid coping hoping

pl	plea plod plot plum plug maple reply replay ample deploy
po	post pone pose pond posh posy depot import report depose

pp	puppy rapport ripple puppet topping supply hopper moppet
pr	prime prank prawn prepare improve depress supreme fabric

pu	pub put push purr putt pupil copula repute deputy impure
qu	quip quill quaff queue sequel acquired tequila requested

ra	rag ram rap raw ray rack rash aura lira okra sera tirade
rd	lord bard ward gird aboard curdled hurdles afford accord

re	rend resin recap recent reply rare tire lore lure surely
ri	rig rid rice rick rile rigid derive during wiring daring

rk	bark cork lark hark kirk murk perk market remark workers
rl	earl girl furl hurl purl burl early surly curled worldly

Patricia Smythe has some work that she wants you to prepare.

The following tabulation has to be ready for her to see before she leaves today. You will need to have it on her desk by 4.30 pm.

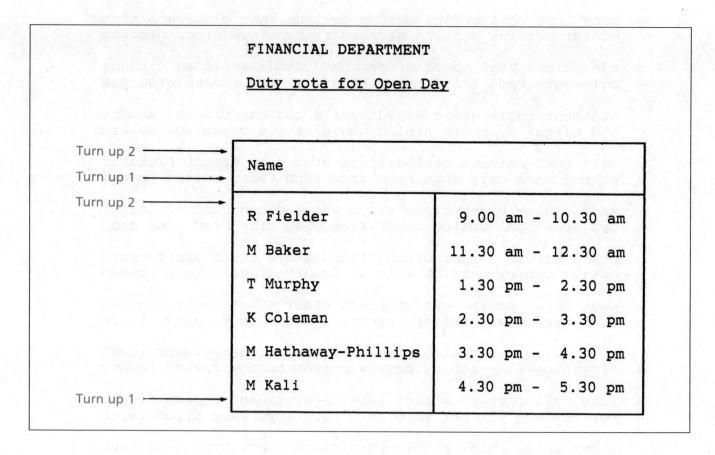

FINANCIAL DEPARTMENT

<u>**Duty rota for Open Day**</u>

Turn up 2 →
Turn up 1 →
Turn up 2 →

Name	
R Fielder	9.00 am – 10.30 am
M Baker	11.30 am – 12.30 am
T Murphy	1.30 pm – 2.30 pm
K Coleman	2.30 pm – 3.30 pm
M Hathaway-Phillips	3.30 pm – 4.30 pm
M Kali	4.30 pm – 5.30 pm

Turn up 1 →

rm	corm norm farmer inform dormant surmise carmine germaine
rn	corn tern turn kern lorn earnest warning infernal intern

ro	roc row rob rota rodeo carol taro biro moron apron tarot
rp	tarp carp corps purple corpus carpet serpent corporation

rr	burro furry curry carry sorry marry surrey borrow marrow
rt	party report certify martini mortal portal hurtle turtle

ru	rung rusk runt ruler rugby forum shrub syrup shrug ruddy
sa	saw sax say sank sari satin visa mesa pesa insane unsafe

sc	scowl scarf scald scalp disco discrete discover discount
se	set sewn sedan seven vase vise rose else fuse lose wiser

sh	shot shun shah shoo shoe shawl lash dash mash bush mushy
si	sick side silk silo sine since visit basic insist casino

sk	skate skein sketch skiff skull skulk cask busk mask dusk
sl	slag slap slob sloe slog slur aisle misled muslin mislay

sm	smart smelt smith smudge smooth dismay dismiss cosmetics
sn	snib snap snare snack sneak snide snuff ensnare misnomer

so	sow soy son sole sore sort sock sofa also peso ipso soso
sp	spa spy sped spur spry spud rasp lisp wisp hasp disputed

ss	boss lass suss sassy lesson passive recess excess access
st	stag stay stem stir stop just best east west last jester

su	suave suede sunny summer sully issue ensue result visual
sw	swig swirl swamp swarm swish swipe swatch answer unswept

sy	system syntax syllabus synthetic synoptic busy easy nosy
ta	tax tam tat tarp tabu tack tape taxi beta iota pita rota

te	tern telex temper teller tennis note date fate mate cite
th	thaw thin thud their moth oath pith father wither bother

ti	tire tine ting tile title tiger anti optic retire entice
to	tom top ton tock tort toff toga alto veto auto onto into

tr	trade trial track trait entry entreat detract untruthful
tt	mitt mutt watt tatty nutty ditto witty ditty kitty batty

tu	tuna tusk tutu tuber tunnel actual return quantum rotund
tw	twice tweak tweet twitch nitwit entwined between betwixt

ty	typo typhoid tyrant tyranny pity city duty acuity sporty
ue	ague glue moue cruet glued fluent truest cruelty bluejay

va	vale valve vapid valet valid lava java diva rival invade
ve	velum venom venue velvet wave gave cove hive dived river

vi	vim vicar vivid virus vigil saving revise advise revival
vo	vow vogue vowel votive havoc pivot revolt envoke devoted

ALTERNATIVE METHOD

You could also use the alternative method for ruled tabulations.

1 Remember that you calculated the longest line in each column and allowed 3 or 5 spaces between each column. You added these figures together, including the spaces between the columns.

2 This figure was subtracted from 80 (pica) or 100 (elite) – the number of character spaces across the page – and divided by 2. This gave you the point at which to start your left margin.

3 You work out ruled tabs in exactly the same way but allow an extra space at the beginning and end of the tab for the line extension if 3 spaces between columns (or 2 extra spaces if 5 spaces between columns).

Remember: **'Always turn up 2 after the line and 1 before.'**
This will help you centre your text between 2 horizontal lines.

VERTICAL LINES

If your typewriter or word processor has the facility for putting in vertical lines you can use this. If you are not sure, look in the program manual or ask your tutor.

If you do not have this facility, after typing, rule in the lines in black ball point pen or narrow felt tip pen, taking care to ensure that vertical lines do not extend above or below the horizontal lines. You need to use a pen that will not smudge.

Ruling lines with a typewriter

Before taking your work out of the typewriter, mark where you want the vertical lines to go. Do this by:

1 Moving to the first tab stop and backspacing 2 spaces if you have allowed 3 spaces between the columns (or 3 if you allowed 5 spaces). Put a light mark in pencil at this point if you are using a typewriter.

2 Move to the second tab stop, backspace 2 and make a mark for the next vertical line.

3 Continue until you have placed markers for all your vertical lines.

4 To ensure that lines are straight, mark both the top and bottom of your work.

```
wa   wax wave watt warn ward wasp warm reward onward cowardly
we   weft wept wend weld wedge jewel fewer lower tower newest

wh   whit whiz whoa what whom whim whey whew whet where whose
wi   win wick wife wile wily wine unwise rewire upwind sewing

wo   woe worry women worth wonder byword rework unworn reword
wr   wry writ wrack wrinkle wrangler rewrap rewrote rewritten

ya   yam yak yap yawn yarrow royal loyal kayak payable voyage
ye   yen yes yew yet yell yelp yellow buyer layer flyer slyer

ze   zen zeta zero zesty zenith gaze faze laze raze size ooze
zz   buzz jazz fizzy dizzy nuzzle razzle dazzle sizzle puzzle

's   Ed's 3's C's she's it's Don's how's why's what's where's
't   isn't can't don't won't didn't aren't wouldn't shouldn't
```

Number chains

Identify number chains that you are not quite sure of by typing at a brisk pace. When you come to an awkward number, type it 2 or 3 times and then continue the drill.

```
14 61 02 80 30 11 25 47 04 46 21 10 43 08 51
63 45 70 29 65 91 03 13 52 71 35 84 92 15 53

31 49 75 32 82 90 01 62 58 81 12 33 48 56 07
79 36 98 18 89 72 96 39 97 93 74 64 20 68 76

77 05 66 27 95 06 28 34 16 37 26 78 86 59 00
17 83 67 09 87 94 44 85 24 73 54 88 99 42 23

50 55 69 41 57 15 58 39 48 08 22 14 88 04 29
19 22 40 38 60 67 99 40 05 69 77 86 79 20 91

90 35 63 11 21 80 31 52 93 07 55 87 23 60 57
17 54 19 30 51 71 82 18 68 27 59 50 41 25 45

84 01 72 12 65 53 00 95 76 89 66 26 98 74 13
81 09 42 38 22 97 83 56 33 96 62 92 70 47 46

49 02 10 43 61 70 30 90 10 00 66 00 33 11 77
75 03 64 36 78 60 40 20 80 50 88 55 22 44 99
```

Section 7 Business tabulations

NVQ Level 3

So far the tabulations you have been doing have not involved any ruling. We are now going to add boxes. You can still work out the tabs in exactly the same way.

RULED TABULATION ON A TYPEWRITER

1 Move the typing point to the centre of the page. Identify the longest line in each column. From the centre point on the page backspace one for every 2 characters or spaces in the longest line, allowing either 3 or 5 spaces between the columns. Set your margin at this point.

2 You can set your tab stops in the usual way by pressing the space bar for each character in the longest line plus the spaces between the columns.

3 When you start to type, it is better to rule the horizontal lines as you go. At the left margin use your margin release key and backspace into the margin – 1 space if you are allowing 3 between the columns, or 2 spaces if you are allowing 5 between the columns. Now type your line extending 1 or 2 spaces into the margin. Note that no right margin stop is set.

4 Turn up 2 line spaces after your line and type the headings.

5 Turn up one line space and type the line below the headings, remembering to use the margin release key to extend into the margin for your lines.

6 Continue with the rest of the tabulation.

RULED TABULATION ON A WORD PROCESSOR

1 You will remember that to set tabs you went into tab mode and cleared all the preset tabs, and then set the tab stops where you wanted them to be.

2 You do exactly the same for ruled tabs but allow an extra space at the beginning and end of the tab for the line extension if you are using 3 spaces between the columns; allow an extra 2 spaces at each end if you are using 5 spaces between the columns.

CONTRACTIONS

Remember that the apostrophe in a contraction represents one or more missing letters and then you will find it much easier to spell them correctly. This extra practice will improve your fluency.

```
I'd I'll I'm I've he'll he'd he's she'll
she'd she's it's it'll it'd you've you'd

we're we've you'll you're they're they'd
they'll we'd we'll don't can't shouldn't

didn't won't isn't wasn't hasn't they've
hadn't haven't mustn't oughtn't there'll

wouldn't needn't mightn't daren't what's
who's where's there's why's how's who'll

ma'am how'd how'll what'll who'd weren't
when's there's A's B's 5's Sam's Donna's
```

END-OF-LINE DRILLS

Type each group of lines as a unit. Return and begin the next line as quickly as you can.

```
all right      jade ring      some boys      keep this
here goes      done well      like that      free time
going out      open door      quite new      user fees
your turn      this time      my friend      right now
west side      not clear      call home      her scarf

in a rush      east wing      pick them      back home
even then      over here      black tie      other guy
nice time      fire sale      years ago      go for it
very soon      many lost      at a stop      have hope
you tried      good work      on trains      any girls

come home      like them      art class      hard rock
just them      camp song      old times      called in
ash grove      paid work      good work      over paid
learn all      easy days      lights on      these men
trust him      your host      then what      night off
```

Checklist of achievements in Section 6 – Business meetings

Performance criteria	Date	Signature
Produce notices and agendas for meetings	———————	———————
Produce a chairperson's agenda	———————	———————
Correctly identify the order of items on an agenda	———————	———————
Produce minutes of a meeting using shoulder/side headings	———————	———————
Correctly identify the order of items on the minutes of a meeting	———————	———————
Expand abbreviations used for business meetings	———————	———————
Number sections and sub-divisions accurately	———————	———————

COMMON WORDS

In normal English prose, we use only a small fraction of the more than 500,000 words in the language. In fact, 25 per cent of our language uses the following 9 words: a, and, I, in, is, it, of, that, the, to.

The drill below includes about 75 per cent of the words you will type and, as you master these words, you will notice a quick jump in your skill.

Begin to type at a brisk rate. When you come to a word that is slow, awkward, or difficult for you, type it a few times (no more than 5 times and probably fewer) until the word is easy, and then continue the drill. Experiment with different chaining patterns on slow words.

```
if so to in up a I me or by an my do no
is us at am as it on be we he of go but
who she any out her all him our can his

the has was you and for not are now had
how off end its one why did may put old
went some than into very want know over

this time will from that more they when
been made only then with have were what
them your which their there would about

. . . . 1 . . . . 2 . . . . 3 . . . . 4 . . . . 5 . . . . 6 . . . . 7 . . . . 8
```

SPELLING

A hit list for spelling is very useful. When you make a spelling error, check the dictionary for the correct spelling and add the word to your hit list. Underline the tricky part of the word. When you have mastered the word, cross it off your list.

Each industry has its own specific vocabulary, often technical, which will provide you with other words to add.

Employers are sensitive about spelling and notice mistakes.

SPELLING HIT LIST

conceive

business

desperate

liaise

separate

acquire

convey

accommodation

5.00 pm   Talk on a single EUropean initiative

7.30 pm   Dinner at the Conference
                     Centre

WEDNESDAY

10.30 am Depart Paris
 2.30 pm   "   Calais
 3.45 pm Arrive Dover

1.30 pm Book in at Calais

Shift key drills

For each capital that is awkward or slow for you, type the corresponding drill 3 times.

A Ann Akron Avon Amos Alan Abe Aida Adam Asa Axel Ada Aaron
B Bob Bill Byron Ben Buddy Beau Bach Bruce Beth Brian Blake

C Carol Celia China Cindy Clare Cork Crete Cuba Cyprus Czar
D Dante Delhi Diana Donald Drake Duncan Dvorak Dwayne Dylan

E Ebert Ed Egypt Eli Emma Epsom Ernie Eastern Eton Eva Eyre
F Fay Fergus Fido Floyd Ford Fred Fuji Fyfe Fargo Fifi Foch

G Gail Gene Giles Gloria Godiva Grace Guy Gwen Gary Gillian
H Hal Henry Hilda Holly Hugo Hyatt Harry Helen Hilary Homer

I Ian Iberia Iceland Ida Igor Ike Ilsa India Iowa Iris Ivan
J Jane Jean Jim Joe June Java Jenny Jill John July Jack Jed

K Kathie Ken Khyber Kim Knox Kris Kurt Kyle Kent Kiev Kovac
L Lana Lewis Lily Lola Lulu Lyle Lagos Leon Liz London Lynn

M Mary Melba Mimi McMillan MacMann Mona Murray Myer May Mel
N Nat Ned Nina Nora Nan Newton Nigel Norman Naomi Neil Nile

O Oahu Oban Ocean Ogden Ohio Oil Olaf Oman Oregon Otis Oval
P Pat Pete Philip Pitman Plaza Polly Preston Putney Pyramid

Q Quay Quentin Quebec Queen Quan Quigley Quinn Quota Quincy
R Ralph Reno Rhine Rio Rod Ruth Ryan Ray Reg Rhone Rick Ron

S Saxon Scott Seth Sharon Silas Skye Sligo Smith Stan Sudan
T Tanya Terry Thomas Tina Toby Troy Turkey Twain Tyler Tzar

U Ubangi Uganda Ukraine Ulster Umberto United Upland Ursula
V Val Verna Victor Volkswagen Vulcan Vatican Verdun Vincent

W Wanda West White Willie Woods Wren Wyatt Way Wells Wilton
X Xavier Xenos Xmas Xerox Xanandu Xray Xyloma Xerxes Xanthe

Y Yale Yee Yonkers Yuma Yves Yalta Yemen York Yule Yarmouth
Z Zane Zeus Zippo Zorba Zulu Zaire Zenda Zola Zuider Zurich

Zelda and Roger are going to Las Vegas in July or August.
Mrs Bell got a puppy for Christmas and she named him Gus.

She invited Dawn and Fred to Quebec for dinner at Easter.
Polly sent Xmas cards to Ingrid in Oslo and Ken in Wales.

Tina and Ursula Hardy travelled from Yorkshire to Norway.
Jennifer gave Ross a ticket for the Dire Straits concert.

Prepare the following itinerary on A4 paper (see page 176) for Ranjit Singh who is attending a meeting in Paris. He will be driving over and will only need ferry times. Insert the dates for Monday, Tuesday and Wednesday of next week. As the 24-hr clock is used in France, convert all times to this.

On a postcard type/key in the following reminders which Mr Singh can keep with his itinerary.

Tell him that the rate of exchange on his £ sterling was Ff9.56. He has an allowance of Ff3,750 for the trip and he must keep all receipts of any expenditure. Also remind him that French time is one hour ahead.

Itinerary ← (Spaced Caps)

MONDAY (insert next Monday's Date)

(All times are local times)

9.30	am	Book in at Dover
10.30	am	Depart Dover
12.45	pm	Arrive Calais
3.45	pm	Arrive Paris – Hotel De La Republique, Rue St Honore, Paris Cedex 6 (Tel 40 30 28 90)
8.00	pm	Dinner with Monsieur Cartier

Tuesday (insert next Tuesday's date)

9.30	am	Leave for International Conference on the European Market to be held at the Exhibition Centre 34566 rue de Marche Paris Cedex 7
12.30	pm	Lunch with Monsieur Cartier, Monsieur Goland and Madame Lamarde
2.00	pm	Demonstration of language conversion software

Continued on next page

Progressive drills

These drills will bring a quick jump in your speed and will also give you the feeling of the higher typing rate.

If you finish the line before the call, begin the line again but return only on the call.

Find your present rate in the appropriate column according to the length of timing you will do. Begin with the NEXT group of lines.

Ignore any errors you make.

	Length of timing (seconds)	5	10	12	15
		Words per minute			

	5	10	12	15
horse and rider	36	18	15	12
enjoy your lunch	38	19	16	13
he sent me a memo	41	20	17	14
her work was right	43	22	18	14
there is no problem	46	23	19	15
find another process	48	24	20	16
my letter has arrived	50	25	21	17
use the proper methods	53	26	22	18
he went home on the bus	55	28	23	18
you know all these women	58	29	24	19
send me a job application	60	30	25	20
ask him for his references	62	31	26	21
this book is very expensive	65	32	27	22
he is taking a day off today	67	34	28	22
show him in and bring him tea	70	35	29	23
all the papers have been filed	72	36	30	24
turn off the lights and lock up	74	37	31	25
you can be sure it will be right	77	38	32	26
the tables are in all the offices	79	40	33	26
we need to order more file folders	82	41	34	27
make two copies of all your letters	84	42	35	28
adjust your station before you begin	86	43	36	29
you must always use a document holder	89	44	37	30
she moved those cartons to your office	91	46	38	30
she won by keeping her mind on the goal	94	47	39	31
send a covering letter with applications	96	48	40	32
your letter may be the first contact made	98	49	41	33
a company is judged by the people employed	101	50	42	34
your work should be an asset to the company	103	52	43	34
treat your work with the respect it deserves	106	53	44	35
formality is seldom out of place in an office	108	54	45	36
set high standards and take pride in your work	110	55	46	37
study the files to learn all about your company	113	56	47	38
a skilled confident operator is always in demand	115	58	48	38
you will use everything you learn sooner or later	118	50	49	39
courtesy is a way to show consideration for others	120	60	50	40

. . . . 1 . . . . 2 . . . . 3 . . . . 4 . . . . 5 . . . . 6 . . . . 7 . . . . 8 . . . . 9 10

POSTCARDS

Postcards are often used for short itineraries. This enables easy reference when travelling.

You will always need to leave margins of a minimum of half an inch, but if there is very little information then you can leave more.

Postcards may sometimes also be used to acknowledge receipt of items, for changes of address and other brief messages or notes. If there is a name and address, this can go on the reverse side of the card in the same way as you would type it on an envelope.

■ TASK 6

Prepare the following itinerary on a postcard. This is to be attached to the front of Angharad Lees' folder. Put the name and address of Swift Stationers PLC on the reverse side. If you have an electronic typewriter or printer which will not take a postcard, use A5 paper.

> **Itinerary**
>
> 9.00 am   Meet visitors in Reception Area
>
> 9.15 am   Coffee in the Cmttee. Rm.
>
> 9.30 am   Tour of the Factory
>
> 10.30 am   Talk by Production Man.
>
> 12.30 pm   Lunch
>
> 1.45 pm   Visitors depart for Oxford

■ TASK 7

Prepare the following invitation, which can be given to the visitors for the Grand Opening of the factory in Didcot.

> ```
>                    The Directors of
>                   Swift Stationers PLC
>
>         request the pleasure of the company of
>
>         ...........................................
>         at the Grand Opening of the New Factory
>         at 12 noon (insert next Tuesday's date)
>         to be held at 12 Foxgrove Road, Didcot
>
>
>   RSVP
>   The Factory Manager
>   Swift Stationers PLC
>   12 Foxgrove Road
>   Didcot
>   OX4 9LJ
> ```

Lines for speed building

To score these 8-word timings, calculate as follows according to the length of the timing.

For a 10-second timing, multiply the words you typed by 6
For a 15-second timing, multiply the words you typed by 4
For a 20-second timing, multiply the words you typed by 3
For a 30-second timing, multiply the words you typed by 2
For a 1-minute timing, your score is the total words typed

1   We mailed our last payment to you today.
2   Thank you for your interest in our plan.

3   She can provide references upon request.
4   Leave the completed report on your desk.

5   It will take two weeks for this project.
6   We were expecting your call before noon.

7   The terms of the contract are very fair.
8   Send copies of the memo to all sections.

9   Allow at least three weeks for delivery.
10   I draw your attention to the new ruling.

11   Please note these riders to your policy.
12   This new service will begin next spring.

13   Please send all your documents promptly.
14   Your enquiry was passed to my secretary.

15   That new system has just been installed.
16   Adjust your station to fit you properly.

17   We must not confuse process and product.
18   Your letters are all ready to be signed.

19   Your order has been filled and sent out.
20   Please initial and return this memo now.

21   The book you want is on the upper shelf.
22   Keep one extra copy in the pending file.

23   No one is quite ready to leave just yet.
24   I look forward to hearing from you soon.

25   Send me a copy of your most recent memo.
26   File these documents as soon as you can.

27   I expect at least two of them to attend.
28   That account with us is a month overdue.

. . . . 1 . . . . 2 . . . . 3 . . . . 4 . . . . 5 . . . . 6 . . . . 7 8

ITINERARIES

From time to time you will need to make arrangements for the executive(s) for whom you work when they are away from the office attending meetings, conferences or on other business. This may be in this country or overseas. You will need to book accommodation, make travel arrangements, organise necessary papers and plan an itinerary.

The itinerary should contain the following details:

- dates
- times of arrivals and departures
- times of trains, planes, ferry crossings, etc
- hotel accommodation
- names, addresses and telephone numbers of contacts
- dates, times and addresses of any meetings or conferences
- programme of events

Example

Here is an example of a one page itinerary which you can type/key in.

CONFERENCE IN LE TOUQUET 31 JULY - 2 AUGUST	
31 July	
0930 hours	**Check in at Lydd airport**
1030 hours	**Depart Lydd - Flight AF12 to Le Touquet**
1330 hours	**Arrive Le Touquet - met by Monsieur Le Maitre 12 Rue de la Mer, 76018, Le Touquet (Tel: 34 56 78 90)**
1400 hours	**Arrive Hotel Fantasia, 10 Rue de Parc, 76009, Le Touquet (Tel: 34 78 45 89)**
1630 hours	**Conference at Papier Plus, Maison de la Gens, Monteplasse (Tel: 34 67 78 12)**
2000 hours	**Dinner back at Hotel**
1 August	
0900 hours	**Check in at Le Touquet airport**
1000 hours	**Depart Le Touquet - Flight AF14 to Lydd**
1100 hours	**Arrive Lydd**

One-minute paragraphs for keyboard mastery

As soon as you complete the 25-word paragraph in one minute, without error, move on to the 30-word, and so on.

25 words These short passages will help you to gain control of the keyboard as you progress through each level. Relax and be at your best.

30 words Type briskly and finish the passage within a minute. Then slow down for control and complete it without error. It may take a few tries but keep at it.

35 words If a word or chain is awkward for you or you keep typing it wrong, practice it a few times till it is easy. Do not type rows and rows of the word; type it five times at the most.

40 words If you type a word over and over you will get faster but you will begin to transpose letters. Typing it just three or four times will solve the problem especially if you remember to read the word aloud.

45 words As you know, reading the drills aloud as you type helps you to chain because it prevents spelling. If you spell as you type then you will never be able to type any faster than you can spell. You will type everything slowly.

50 words Reading aloud has the added advantage that you triple the stimulus by having it come through your eyes, through your ears and by the use of your speaking apparatus. The stronger the stimulus, the quicker and stronger the response, that is, your stroking.

55 words When the situation makes it unwise for you to read aloud, then you must shout the words in your mind in order that you do not fall into a habit of spelling. Say them sharply to bring a fast response. By now, of course, your fingers remember for you; that is called touch typing.

60 words By the time you have reached this passage you are typing more than twice as fast as you can write by hand. You are able to get your thoughts on paper quickly and before an elusive idea can be forgotten. A fast scribble can often be illegible but even a first draft, if typed, can always be read easily.

65 words Corrections are very quick and easy if you are using a computer, and your first draft can easily become your final copy after you have edited it on screen. Not having to retype saves a great deal of time and many keystrokes, not to mention the tedium of repetition. Adding or deleting passages can be done with a stroke or two.

Outline planning permission had been granted. *↑Plans were*
with the local builder.

5 6 STAFF TRAINING

F Gerard outlined proposals for new training schemes and
read a paper on National Vocational Qualifications
(NVQs). All staff who wished to obtain this
qualification in Business Administration and Finance
would be encouraged to do so. Their line manager will
assess all the competencies and the local college will *of*
provide the underpinning knowledge needed on a day-
release basis. Accreditation will be given/prior *for*
knowledge and experience.

6 5 NEW GRADING AND PAY STRUCTURE

It was reported that new pay grades will come into effect
from the 1st of next month. It was agreed that a Staff
Appraisal Scheme will come into operation at the same
time. All staff will be involved in writing their own
action plans and will attend regular interviews with
their line managers to assess their performance.

7 AOB

There was no other business.

8 date of next meeting

6 May 19-- at 9.00 pm.

Chairperson ....

Date ....

When the next award comes in

Do not type in today's date as the date will be ~~the day~~ *that when* the
minutes are signed, ie at the next meeting.

Timings on numbers

Accuracy is the first priority in typing numbers because it is much more difficult to recognise mistakes in numbers than in words. Type with complete control and remember to chain.

```
27 21 56 07 80 51 91 65 32 70 19 55 135
57 40 81 43 77 03 67 38 60 92 76 06 201

11 75 87 85 00 93 04 52 94 10 82 28 613
74 98 62 96 44 59 42 88 22 95 08 36 830
....1....2....3....4....5....6....7....8

99 46 23 68 14 71 05 63 58 45 39 17 334
12 20 47 64 72 30 84 66 24 01 34 97 475

16 31 02 37 50 41 79 90 53 54 35 26 698
89 25 78 15 86 73 29 49 09 13 48 61 188
....1....2....3....4....5....6....7....8

204 019 245 308 495 136 326 530 410 609
617 527 508 020 579 703 458 662 791 866

805 382 430 031 124 313 826 715 914 687
159 974 740 632 362 046 831 426 923 193
....1....2....3....4....5....6....7....8

901 876 963 733 949 818 659 054 211 394
445 641 182 351 727 060 278 888 148 333

679 407 234 553 762 855 269 756 079 892
340 591 842 771 957 694 513 980 545 087
....1....2....3....4....5....6....7....8


9307 7498 8737 2666 0578 8677 2079 3664
5697 3948 3396 7212 7689 1868 7182 9035

7503 9132 8401 6292 1558 8153 3152 1349
4770 4525 1408 4361 1002 8021 4665 2904
....1....2....3....4....5....6....7....8

9002 0100 1163 5130 6804 8923 1702 8743
1001 2002 3003 4004 5005 6006 7007 8008

7 076 3 7660 770 95 3 1 134 92 2 51 807
87 100 7 0 4 03 1 58 00 328 56 97 31 69
....1....2....3....4....5....6....7....8

2 248 9 45 03 001 540954 45 9232 224386
9 747 07 5 382 35 6 5 3 4 483933 728128

1 63 924 1 59 8523 4 61 02 8 6 18 3 320
99 384 7 33 82 3 89098 43 3332 83 8 3 3
....1....2....3....4....5....6....7....8
```

■ **TASK 5**

Prepare the following minutes. Use whatever method you prefer to give emphasis to the headings.

Use a justified right margin.

S W I F T   S T A T I O N E R S   P L C

Minutes of a mtg. of the Board of Directors held in the Board Rm on Tue. (insert last Tuesday's date) at 9.00 am

Present   ← (CAPS)

C Michaels (Chairperson), M Patel, F Gerard, C Watson, B ←   Lh
Jones, H Kolz, S McKenzie, P Smythe, Your name (Secretary)

Names in alphabetical order

1   APOLOGIES FOR ABSENCE

     There were no apologies received.

2   MINS OF THE LAST MTG

     These were accepted as being a true record of the
     proceedings.

3   MATTERS ARISING

     3.1   It was confirmed by P Smythe that £45,000 had been
            transferred/to the Paris Office to cover the cost of
            refurbishment.
            on the 21st of each month.

     3.2   F Gerard had looked into the possibility of
            recruiting more sales reps for Russia and reported
            that 5 applications have been received. Interviews
            would be held in two weeks' time.   *hadh*

     3.3   M Patel reported that the additional software had
            been purchased and that staff training has taken
            place.   *develpmt*

            3.3.1

     *run
      on*   The Database package had been installed on all
            computers but was only used at present in the Sales
            Divisions. Minor modifications were needed for
            other Divisions.

            3.3.2

     *run
      on*   The Spreadsheet package had now been installed on
            all computers and is now widely used throughout the
            company.

4   CORRESPONDENCE

     The sec. read a letter from the local council regarding   *uc*
     an application to extend the Social Club building.

Employment tests

Employers usually give 5-minute timings to test typing skill. Scoring methods vary from one employer to another but errors will always be noted and considered in their assessment.

When you are being timed, start to type at an easy pace and allow your speed to build up. Don't rush, as you will only make mistakes. Slow down, and you will find you actually type faster. Your rate is the total words typed, divided by 5.

Apply the knowledge you gained in doing timings for skill building.

5-MINUTE TIMINGS

	Word count
Your attitude to time and your ability to manage it will have a	13
very significant effect upon your success in your career. It is	26
important that you are able to keep your eye on the time without	39
being a clock watcher.	41
Have a general idea of how long a task will take and expect to	54
complete it within the target time. This will help you to avoid	67
dawdling because, as Parkinson's Law states, work will expand to	80
fill the time available for its completion. If you work at a	92
slow and lazy pace, you will not have a sense of having done a	105
good day's work.	108

. . . . 1 . . . . 2 . . . . 3 . . . . 4 . . . . 5 . . . 6 . . . 7 . . . . 8 . . . . 9 . . . .10. . . .11. . . .12. . . .13

Punctuality, the courtesy of kings, sends a message to your	12
employer and everyone else that you respect your commitments.	24
One who is late is sending the message that the other person	36
does not matter very much. It says that the time of the one	48
who is tardy is more valuable and that others should wait for	60
him/her.	62
Giving that extra five minutes at the beginning or the end of	74
your day shows that you are above the pettiness of being paid	86
by the minute. Be at your work station a few moments early and	98
finish a task though it may keep you just a little late. Your	111
attitude of responsibility will be well rewarded.	121

. . . . 1 . . . . 2 . . . . 3 . . . . 4 . . . . 5 . . . 6 . . . 7 . . . . 8 . . . . 9 . . . .10. . . .11. . . .12. . . .13

Set a high standard for your work. Recognise that doing work	12
that is good enough is not good enough. Go beyond the minimum	25
requirement that what you produce is correct. Make your letters	38
attractive by careful spacing and layout so the recipient will	50
be impressed with the calibre of the company with which he or	62
she is dealing. The flawless appearance of the letter will give	75
confidence in the staff.	80
Make it a practice to be accurate with numbers. Double check	82
and cross balance for accuracy, which will establish and enhance	95
your reputation within the office as being one who does things	107
right. Everyone makes mistakes but if you find your own, no one	120
but you will know about them.	126

. . . . 1 . . . . 2 . . . . 3 . . . . 4 . . . . 5 . . . 6 . . . 7 . . . . 8 . . . . 9 . . . .10. . . .11. . . .12. . . .13

Now prepare a notice of meeting and Chairperson's agenda using the notes you had for Task 3.

MINUTES OF MEETINGS

You will be required to take notes at meetings you attend and from these notes you will have to produce the minutes of the meetings. Minutes are a concise and accurate record of the business discussed and the conclusions reached. They will include proposals, resolutions or motions passed together with the names of the proposers and seconders. All the main points of the arguments will need to be recorded, while at the same time keeping the notes as brief as possible. You should always write the minutes in the third person.

As soon as the meeting is over you should prepare your draft minutes and check these with the agenda for the meeting to ensure that you have not left anything out. The draft will then be approved by the Chairperson before you finally produce the minutes and circulate them to all members of the committee or board.

You will note that the items are in the same order as in the agenda, with the addition of a list of those present at the meeting. The Chairperson is at the top of the list with those in attendance listed in alphabetical order. The Secretary's name comes at the end of the list.

At entry level, when you are at the beginning of your career,   12
most of your expertise will be technical but, as you are promoted   25
to a supervisory level, you will find that your ability to deal   38
with people will become more and more important. That means that   51
if you intend to progress within the company then you must become   64
expert in dealing with people. Tact, diplomacy and courtesy will   77
take you a whole lot further than will a voice that can be heard   90
barking orders from out on the street.   98

When you first start a job, dress like the others but, as you   110
aspire to promotion, try to look like the person holding the   122
kind of job you want. Good grooming is assumed but notice how   134
trendy the supervisor is in dress and take your cue from that.   146
In general, supervisors dress more formally than entry level   158
personnel.   160

. . . . 1 . . . . 2 . . . . 3 . . . . 4 . . . . 5 . . . . 6 . . . . 7 . . . . 8 . . . . 9 . . . . 10 . . . . 11 . . . . 12 13

An education is the lightest bundle of tools you will ever have   13
to carry so learn as much as you possibly can. Having a broad   25
general knowledge demonstrates your ability to learn as well as   38
your appreciation of knowledge for its own sake. It prevents   50
you becoming a one dimensional person and allows you to have   62
conversations with a wide variety of people.   71

Being known as a great conversationalist is quite frequently the   84
result of being a good listener. We have one mouth and two ears   98
and they should be used in that proportion. Bear in mind, too,   110
that when the mouth is moving, the ears don't seem to work very   123
well. Even a fish would stay out of trouble if he knew when to   136
keep his mouth shut.   140

. . . . 1 . . . . 2 . . . . 3 . . . . 4 . . . . 5 . . . . 6 . . . . 7 . . . . 8 . . . . 9 . . . . 10 . . . . 11 . . . . 12 13

More people lose their jobs through poor personal relations than   13
because of incompetence. A common mistake is bringing troubles   26
to work. Try to imagine that your problems are all in a carrier   39
bag and leave that bag outside the door to be collected on your   51
way home. Do not bring your own personal worries inside with   63
you; nobody wants to hear about them and you don't want to have   76
the reputation of being a moaner.   83

Try, instead, for a cheerful, alert disposition that will make   95
people glad to see you instead of inwardly groaning at the time   108
you will waste with your morning recital of woe. Smile at your   120
colleagues and when you answer the telephone. You will find that   133
smiling improves your state of mind and it can be heard in your   146
voice on the telephone.   150

. . . . 1 . . . . 2 . . . . 3 . . . . 4 . . . . 5 . . . . 6 . . . . 7 . . . . 8 . . . . 9 . . . . 10 . . . . 11 . . . . 12 13

CHAIRPERSON'S AGENDA

The Chairperson's agenda is very like an ordinary agenda. The only difference is that the agenda is on the left of the page and the right side of the page is left blank for notes. Additional space (2 or 3 lines) is usually left between items allowing room for the Chairperson's notes. The numbers of items are repeated on the right of the page with the heading 'NOTES' over them.

If we take the agenda in Task 2, it would look like this for the Chairperson:

Meeting of the Social Committee to be held at 2 pm on Tuesday _____ in the Board Room

C H A I R P E R S O N ' S   A G E N D A

		NOTES
1	Apologies for absence	1
2	Minutes of the last meeting	2
3	Matters arising	3
4	Correspondence	4
5	Election of Secretary	5
6	Election of Treasurer	6
7	Finance Report	7
8	Forthcoming events	8
9	Plans for extending the premises	9
10	AOB	10
11	Date and time of next meeting	11

Paul Abbott

Try to see your place in the company and where your duties fit 12
into its overall performance. When you realise the value of 24
your job, you will experience satisfaction in it. High pay is 36
not nearly as important to an interest in the job as is seeing 49
its place in the total picture. Even though your tasks may be 61
simple ones when you are a beginner, they do matter or you would 74
not be there at all. No one will assign you more complex ones 86
if you do not do the elementary ones properly. 95

Make an effort to learn other jobs in your department. This is 108
free training and experience when you apply for promotion or if 120
you should change to a different company. Holidays, illness, 132
conferences and training all require that other staff be absent 145
and that gives you a chance to learn. Your willingness to learn 158
will be appreciated and you will do yourself a good turn. 169

. . . . 1 . . . . 2 . . . . 3 . . . 4 . . . . 5 . . . 6 . . . 7 . . . 8 . . . 9 . . . . 10 . . . . 11 . . . . 12 13

Take advantage of any training your company offers. There could 13
be in-house demonstrations, seminars, workshops, brain storming 26
sessions, courses, lectures or conferences. They may be put on 38
during working hours or they may be held in the evenings or on 50
weekends. They may be paid for or you may have to pay part or 62
all of the fee. But even if you do have to pay, take anything 75
you can, even if it does not seem relevant to your present job. 88
Employers are aware of just who wants to learn and you could be 101
training for your promotion when it comes. 110

Be aware of the importance of using proper English. This is the 123
information age and the ability to communicate has never been of 136
more importance. Perhaps you will find it necessary to take some 149
courses but be sure that you learn how to write reports. Even if 162
you have no other reference books, be sure that you have at least 175
a dictionary and use it. 180

. . . . 1 . . . . 2 . . . . 3 . . . . 4 . . . . 5 . . . 6 . . . 7 . . . 8 . . . 9 . . . . 10 . . . . 11 . . . . 12 13

Try to develop innovative ways of doing things. Your firm may 12
have an incentive programme that will reward you for your ideas. 25
Keep asking yourself if there is a faster, easier, cheaper, more 38
accurate way to do any tasks. Any ideas that can save time and 50
money for the company will always be welcome. In addition to this 63
type of thinking, the ability to see things from such different 75
perspectives prepares you for moving up to other jobs and other 88
departments. 91

Your ability to see the issues from the point of view of your 103
company makes you part of the team. Cultivate an openness of 113
mind that allows you to think about the good of your employer 127
alongside your own priorities. 133

. . . . 1 . . . . 2 . . . . 3 . . . . 4 . . . . 5 . . . 6 . . . 7 . . . 8 . . . 9 . . . . 10 . . . . 11 . . . . 12 13

■ **TASK 3**

Prepare a combined notice and agenda. Include AOB.

SWIFT STATIONERS PLC

AGM

NOTICE IS HEREBY GIVEN that the Fifth AGM of Swift Stationers PLC wl. be held in the Board Rm. on Mon. (put in the date for the first Monday of next month).

1   Chairperson's Report

2   Finance Director's Report and Statement of Accounts

3   Auditor's Report

4   Shareholder's Report

5   Announcement of Dividends

6   Report on Company performance

7   Changes in the constitution

8   Election of Chairperson

By Order of the Board

Claire Watson

Managing Director

(Insert today's date)

NOTE: Every employee and shareholder is entitled to attend and to vote at the AGM or to appoint a proxy to attend and vote if s/he is not able to attend. Anyone appointing a proxy must notify this office at least 24 hours before the meeting. Failure to do so will result in loss of vote.

Style and usage

Punctuation

Open punctuation is the preferred style of most businesses. Punctuation marks are used for clarity only and are omitted after abbreviations and at the end of display lines in letters. Closed punctuation uses marks which are often felt to be redundant. Type these examples of open punctuation:

```
Mr L Hanson left on BA flight 085 at 6 am.
Policy No 67833 expires 5 June at 1200 hrs.
```

Measurement

A number is a word on its own and has a space before and after it. In a unit of measurement there is no 's' after a plural nor a full stop after the abbreviation unless it ends a sentence. 'By' may be replaced by 'x' in dimensions. Type the examples:

```
We were at least 60 km from home at 6 am.
The new dining room is about 10 m x 12 m.
```

Numbers and figures

Use figures for all numbers except when a number begins a sentence or is the number one on its own in the text.

```
Two more women showed up just before 2 pm.
I will try one more time to find your hat.
There should be 6 or 7 copies in the file.
```

Money

Be consistent within the work, words with words and figures with figures. The rules apply to pounds, dollars and other currencies.

Round numbers of pounds – £10, £10.00 or ten pounds.
Round numbers of dollars – $10, $10.00 or ten dollars.
Less than £1 – £0.20, 20p, 20 pence or twenty pence.
Less than $1 – $ 0.20, 20c, 20 cents or twenty cents.
Mixed pounds and pence – £35.75.
Mixed dollars and cents – $35.75.
Millions of pounds – £60,000,000 or sixty million pounds.
Millions of dollars – $60,000,000 or sixty million dollars.

```
Pay the sum of £162 (One hundred and sixty-two pounds).
He needs more than £75 for his car repair.
The new chairs cost £150.75 plus VAT each.
The cost of the building was $250 million.
```

Prepare the following Agenda for the Social Club meeting which is to be held next Friday. Keep to the order indicated and note item 11 – the date, time and place of the next meeting is always arranged at the current meeting to ensure that a suitable date has been chosen. It is much easier to arrange this when everyone is present.

See page 168.

Meeting of the Social Committee
to be held at 2.00 pm next
Tuesday (insert date) in the Board
Room

Agenda ← (Spaced Capitals)

1 Apologies for absence

2 Minutes of l̶ last Meeting ᴸthe

3 Matters arising

4 Correspondance ᴸe

trs { 5 Election of Treasurer
      6   "   "   Secretary

7 Finance Report

8 Forthcoming events

9 Plans for extending/premises ᴸthe

10 AOB

11 Date and time of next mtg.

Paul Abbott
Hon. Sec.

Word division

Avoid breaking a word if possible, but sometimes it is necessary to maintain an even right margin.

The hyphen appears on the first line only. Break the word between syllables and leave at least 3 letters on each line. Some words can be broken in several places, eg phil/o/soph/i/cal. Any of these breaks would be acceptable but try to break the word near the middle.

Break words with double consonants between the consonants (slip-ping), unless the root has a double consonant (fall-ing). Break a compound word between its components (heart-felt), and a hyphenated word only at the hyphen (blue-eyed).

Do not break very short words (idea), words with one syllable (school), numbers (6000), abbreviations (RNIB), or proper nouns (Cleopatra).

Do not break the last word on a page or the last line in a paragraph.

Type only those of the following words which can be divided, showing where they should be hyphenated:

pleasant	Darlene	appendix
basic	ambiguous	insecurity
forty-one	typewriter	extra
consonant	ogre	regulation
scheme	imaginative	stopping
willing	oven	furniture
teacher	preconceived	momentarily
Leonard	cringe	unnecessary
easy	freight	unilaterally
breeze	pencil	argumentative

Numbering

Numbers (or letters) for paragraphs are typed at the left margin and followed by 2 or more spaces. If you are using a manual machine, set the left margin for the paragraphs and use the margin release to type the numbers.

Type this passage.

SALAD

1   Choose firm, fresh vegetables without flaws or
    bruises.

2   Wash all ingredients thoroughly in cold running
    water. A collander is useful.

3   Dry the vegetables.

4   Cut the vegetables into bite-sized pieces and
    store in the refrigerator until it is time to serve.

5   Serve with a selection of dressings.

Prepare the following notice of a meeting to be sent out today.

Swift Stationers PLC ← (spaced capitals)

The next mtg of the Social Club wl. be held in the Club Room on Friday (insert next Friday's date) at 6.00 pm. The agenda wl. be circulated later. At the mtg. voting wl. take place for the pos. of Secretary of the Club and also ~~be of~~ treasurer. If you ~~are unable to~~ _cannot_ attend, voting by proxy wl. be allowed provided you have the rec. forms. There can be obtained from Ms Mary Dawkins on ext 230.

Paul Abbott
Hon. Sec.

Composing

Composing at the keyboard is one of the most useful applications of your typing skill. The exercises that follow are designed to help you to draw the copy from your mind instead of from the page. There are no 'right' answers. Do not ponder, just respond. You do not have to have an answer for every question – just do your best.

With these short answers, you may make corrections as you go along but remember that the purpose of these exercises is to stimulate, not to create a finished product.

1 Type 5 girls' names and 5 boys' names beginning with each of the following letters: **J, D, M, L, S.**

2 Type an opposite of each of the following words: **right, careful, beautiful, difficult, serious, work, sunny, accept, agree, dependable, neat, sharp, boring, brave, early.**

3 Change any letter in each of the following words to make a new word: **race, fail, date, full, rent, sole, dice, take.** For example, 'cast' could become last, card, case or cost.

4 Change one letter at a time in the following words to make new words: **will, sort, gate.** You may add a letter or drop one each time but the order must not change. For example, for 'cold' your list might have been: bold bolt dolt dot rot not note nose rose rise risk, etc.

5 Type 5 words using each of these double letter chains: **dd, tt, ss, ll, mm, ff, pp, rr.** For example, 'bb' words could be bubble, lobby, rabble, pebble, dribble.

6 Type 8 words with each of the following chains: **re, st, cl, wh, le, tr, nk, do.** The chain can appear anywhere in the word. For example, the chain 'te' could include tell, temper, tent, fate, detest, dote, intend, bite.

7 List at least 10 pairs of words, such as salt and pepper, table and chair, Romeo and Juliet.

8 Type at least 5 words that rhyme with each of the following: **green, late, well, coal, sled.** For example, rhymes for 'tense' might be rents, Hortense, sentence, fence, dense.

9 Fill in the blanks. For example, '_____ table' could be work table, dining table, water table or unstable.

_____ heart	_____ case	_____ nail
_____ pan	_____ shoes	_____ paper
_____ book	_____ berry	_____ attendant
_____ carpet	_____ days	_____ brush
_____ money	_____ work	_____ chocolate
_____ door	_____ break	_____ teacher
_____ pie	_____ board	_____ oil
_____ powder	_____ tree	_____ trap

Section 6 Business meetings

NVQ Level 3

You have just been promoted to Personal Assistant to Ms Claire Watson, the Managing Director of Swift Stationers PLC. One of your first major tasks is to make arrangements for various meetings. You did not produce any documents for business meetings in your previous position and therefore need to refer to the company's house book on meetings. It identifies:

- the notice of meeting
- the agenda
- the minutes of the meeting

NOTICE OF MEETING

This is sent to everyone who is entitled to attend the meeting or to vote. It will state the day, time, place and purpose of the meeting. The agenda may be included with the notice of meeting.

AGENDA

An agenda is prepared by the Company Secretary and the Chairperson of the meeting. This is circulated to everyone who has a right to attend the meeting. It is a list of numbered items to be discussed and usually appears in the following order:

---

1   Apologies for absence

2   Minutes of the last meeting - these are circulated in
     advance of the meeting, usually with the agenda, and have
     to be read by those present at the meeting and agreed as
     a true record of what took place

3   Matters arising from the minutes of the last meeting -
     items on which those present at the last meeting were
     asked to take action

4   Correspondence

5   Specified item(s) to be discussed at the meeting - see
     Task 3

6   Any other business - known as AOB

7   Date of the next meeting

Abbreviations must always be typed in full, eg:

AGM   Annual General Meeting
AOB   Any other business
Hon Sec   Honorary Secretary

10 Fill in more blanks. Complete familiar expressions or make up your own. Use any number of words.

copy _____   paper _____   ring _____

table _____   chicken _____   car _____

apple _____   drum _____   sharp _____

as quick as _____   as big as _____   as pretty as _____

as happy as _____   as dark as _____   as easy as _____

as warm as _____   as bright as _____   as red as _____

11 Make up a sentence using words beginning with the letters in each of these groups: **ABC DEF GHI JKL MNO PQR STU VWYZ**. For example, ABC might be Alice bought cake.

12 Finish each sentence:

He thought that _____

I am going _____

Will there be _____

We may be able to _____

Bring your _____

Write a letter _____

Please lend me _____

Fill the bag _____

Be here _____

Could I _____

13 Type a sentence of any length using the letter **A** at least 10 times. Continue with a sentence for each other letter of the alphabet.

14 Answer each of the following questions in a sentence or short paragraph. It is more important to get your ideas down on paper than it is to produce a perfect copy on your first draft, so make any corrections after you have completed your answer.

a   What do you usually have for breakfast?
b   What would you wear to an employment interview?
c   Where would you take a visitor for an outing?
d   How would you describe your progress in typing so far?
e   What kind of first job would you like to have?
f   What career goals have you set so far?
g   How would you spend an unexpected free afternoon?
h   Describe the shoes you are wearing.
i   Describe the hair style of anyone you choose.
j   You have won 2 tickets for a concert and may choose any artist you like. Who would you choose and who would you ask as your guest?
k   Plan the menu for a birthday party for a 10 year old.
l   Write instructions for a friend to get to your home.
m   Do you think driving lessons should be included in the school curriculum? Give reasons for your answer.
n   Do you think public transport should be free? Your reasons?
o   What do you consider in accepting or refusing an invitation?

6 National Vocational Qualification
Administration
Level 3

Section 6 Business meetings

When you have completed this section you should know how to lay out correctly and present an agenda and minutes of a meeting. This element will be tested as part of NVQ Business Administration Unit 8 – Servicing Meetings.

Section 7 Business tabulations

When you have completed this section you should have the knowledge and skills to present data in tabular form. This element will be tested as part of NVQ Business Administration Unit 5 – Preparing and Producing Documents.

Section 8 Business documents

Section 9 Business correspondence

When you have completed these sections you should have the underpinning knowledge and skills to take the NVQ Business Administration Unit 5 – Preparing and Producing Documents:

Elements of competence

5.1 Produce text from oral and written material using an alphanumerical keyboard

5.2 Present narrative, graphic and tabular information using an alphanumeric keyboard

5.3 Organise and arrange the copying, collating and binding of documents

Please type the following in double line spacing. Make your own line endings.

The average home contains at least ten doors, most of which have various functions and therefore different locking devices.

The front door is usually the most vulnerable. Twenty-eight per cent of all break-ins occur from the front of private houses. It is advisable to ensure that adequate locking devices are fitted to a front door. A security chain will guard against an unexpected intrusion if you secure it before opening the door to strangers. A door viewer will allow visitors to be identified before the door is opened and thus adds further security.

Back and side doors are also a security risk and locking devices should be fitted to these doors as well - sixty-two per cent of break-ins occur at the back of the house.

Over sixty per cent of house break-ins occur through windows, Burglars use this route because an unsecured window can be quickly opened from the outside - it would take an experienced burglar not much longer than fifteen seconds. Window Security Devices (WSDs) should be fitted properly to all windows to prevent intrusion by strangers. It is worth fitting WSDs to all windows, even those above ground level, because an agile burglar could easily scale a drainpipe or use a ladder that has been carelessly left out.

NOMINEES   ← Spaced Caps

(1) <u>Chairperson</u>

    L Johnson
    P Smitherman
    L Lumark
    R Singh

(3) <u>Secretary</u>

    P Watkins
    M Stephens
    L Luttenberg
    P Dietrech
    R Bannerman
    P Abbott

(2) <u>Treasurer</u>

    P Lewis
    R Watson
    M Attwater

Please put names in alphabetical order within lists

	Strokes to line end
Fax machines combine a scanner for memorising documents, a modem	66
for transmitting data and a printer to print out messages received.	134
To operate a fax machine all you have to do is place your document	202
in the feeder, dial the target fax number and press the sender	265
button. The cost of sending a fax message is exactly the same as	332
making a telephone call of identical length.	378
The mobile fax machine should be a very useful piece of equipment.	446
It is intended to aid the businessman who is always on the move and	515
needs to keep in touch with the office or with clients either at	580
home or abroad. The mobility of the machine has been restricted by	649
the need for access to a telephone by the use of an interface, which	718
was difficult if there was not a telephone.	763
Several suppliers now market interfaces which allow the fax machine	832
to be connected to a car phone. This is achieved by adding another	901
socket to the base unit so that the machine can be plugged in, as	967
well as the phone. The fax is powered either through the car	1030
cigarette lighter or via a wire run directly into the car battery.	1097
The machine can be situated either in the front or on the	1156
back seat and in most cases can be easily removed. For a small	1221
extra cost it is possible to have installed a portable phone combining	1292
all the necessary cables to allow direct connection of a fax machine.	1362
Anyone who has used a mobile fax machine will know that there is a	1430
problem with quality. To overcome this difficulty a system has been	1500
developed to monitor lines and to correct any affected print.	1562
This increases costs because the rate of transmission is slowed	1627
down as it may take several attempts to achieve a good copy.	1688
A further problem affects printing and scanning heads of a fax	1752
machine, so even when the data is received the accuracy of the	1815
printout may still be doubtful.	1848
Strictly speaking a faxed document is a copy of the original.	1911
The transmission report is not proof that the document has been	1976
sent or received. Therefore, whichever fax machine you use, if	2041
you want your fax to have legal status, you should arrange this	2105
beforehand with the other party and draw up a legal document to that	2174
effect.	2181

Memo

From   Martin Johnson

To   Social Club Members

Date   (Insert today's date)

I am enclosing a list of the nominees
for Chairperson, Secretary and Treasurer.
They are all well known and need no
introduction // Voting will take place on
(Insert next friday's date)

Rules. ← (Caps)

2 1 Each member is entitled to one vote.
3 2. Proxy forms are available if you
        are unable to attend
4 3 After voting has finished the votes
        will be counted by 3 volunteers.
5 4. All members will be notified of the
        results by post
1 5 Office will be for three years.

National Vocational Qualification
Business Administration
Level 1

Section 1 Business documents

Section 2 Business correspondence

When you have completed these sections you should have the underpinning knowledge and skills to take the National Vocational Qualification Business Administration Unit 3 – Data Processing competency:

Element 3.1   Producing alpha/numerical information in typewritten form

Please type this notice in double-line spacing

Car Parking

headings in block capitals and underlined

⌐ There is a serious problem and this is being looked into. Please do not park immediately outside the gates. There has been several complaints have ⌐ from local residents about this and the police ✓ are now going to have double single yellow lines put in. //

car ⌐ Temporary ⌐ parking space has been allocated at the back of the social club. This will be only for members of the staff. Visitors will now have their own car park. If you have any ideas on a long-term basis please put them in the suggestion box. // There are

(SKIING) still vacancies for our skiing holiday so if anyone is interested please contact Ann Collins on extension 1619.

Staff Outing

Our next trip will be on December March ⌐ ⌐ 24 14. We will be taking the 8 am ferry from Dover and returning on the 1830 hrs ⌐ from Calais. You can either meet the coach at Dover or catch the coach outside the main gate at 5.30 am. Names on list please.

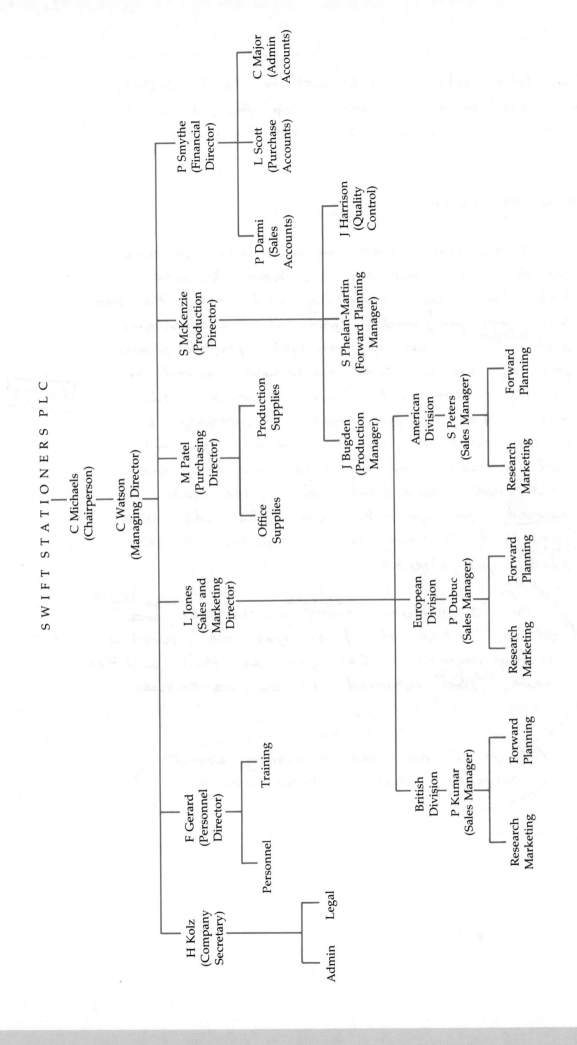

The letter below is to be sent to Mr J Walker, 21 Ravensbourne Crescent, Orpington, Kent BR10 4ER using Our Ref PD/Soy/44

Dear Mr Walker

I am sorry that you have had so much trouble with your van. I have decided that this needs replacing and would therefore like it you ~~could~~ to look at the enclosed ~~list~~ catalogue. There are several you can choose from as we are now no longer limited to leasing from Batts Garage services. This will take a few weeks to arrange so in the meantime our rep. from Newport will be away on an American trip and will not need his ~~van~~ car. He has agreed for you to have this when you ~~need~~ want/requires it. // I have another matter which requires your attention.

BATTS

NP

Mr J Matheson would like ~~needs~~ you to call ~~out~~ urgently to collect a box of files that are surplus to requirements. Can you do this and then have the files ~~them~~ returned to our warehouse.

There is no need to worry about insurance - that is taken care of.

Section 1 Business documents

NVQ Level 1

At the start of this section you will need to know:
- how to change margins (see pages 2–5 and page 14)
- how to adjust line spacing (see pages 2–5 and page 14)
- how to underline (underscore)
- how to embolden (commanding the printer or using the typewriter to go over the same piece of text two or three times to make it darker)

For each machine or system these are different, so you will need to know how they work on the equipment you are using. Some of these have already been covered in the keyboarding sections, but here is a reminder. First, you should know the most common international paper sizes.

Paper sizes

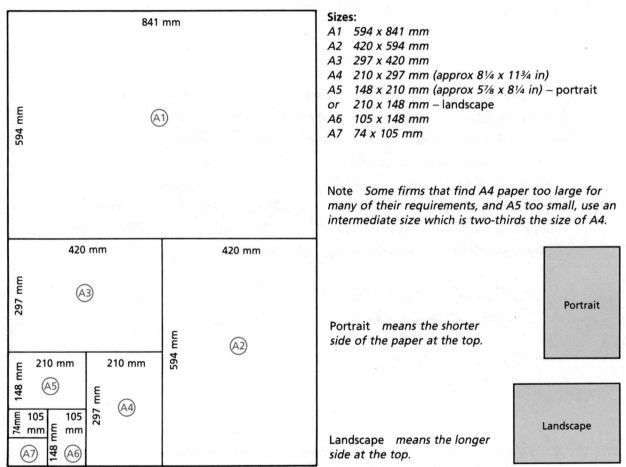

Sizes:
A1   594 x 841 mm
A2   420 x 594 mm
A3   297 x 420 mm
A4   210 x 297 mm (approx 8¼ x 11¾ in)
A5   148 x 210 mm (approx 5⅞ x 8¼ in) – portrait
or   210 x 148 mm – landscape
A6   105 x 148 mm
A7   74 x 105 mm

Note *Some firms that find A4 paper too large for many of their requirements, and A5 too small, use an intermediate size which is two-thirds the size of A4.*

Portrait *means the shorter side of the paper at the top.*

Landscape *means the longer side at the top.*

Pitch (size of type)

Pica type has 10 characters to the inch (25 mm)
Elite type has 12 characters to the inch (25 mm)

Proportional spacing (PS) spaces letters to look like typesetting found in books, newspapers, etc – eg M takes more space than I. This can enhance the appearance of typewritten work but makes correction more difficult.

SWIFT STATIONERS LIMITED ← *Centre and underline*

of This company has ~~now~~ been in operation for ten years and since its
beginnings in London has now expanded/ and has sales reps. all over *considerably*/
of Britain ~~and~~ Europe and America. We are now seeking new markets and are
NP looking into the possibility of increasing our sales market into Russia. // We
have just purchased a new warehouse in the Docklands and this will mean
a/ that we can store/ greater quantity of goods. As a result of this we can
purchase in bulk and our main suppliers ~~has~~ increased our discount. *have*/

We can now pass this over to you – so our products will be highly
competitive.

We aim to please. Our policy is to supply whatever your company
run on requires. ⟶

⎨ Our aim is to provide a swift, efficient service for our customers.

As soon as we receive your order we
guarantee delivery next day. If we do
not have the product in stock we will
order immediately. If it is not
available we will contact you
immediately and either offer an
alternative or let you know the new
expected delivery date.

Patrick Pubur
Sales Manager

(Today's Date)

*Make all necessary amendments.
Embolden Britain, Europe and
America. Print one copy justified
and in double line spacing*

Margins and Spacing

For all work that you are going to produce, use a minimum top and bottom margin of 25 mm (one inch) as well as both a left and right margin of 25 mm (one inch). You can use your own judgement on display.

There are 6 single line spaces to 25 mm (one inch) vertically.

HEADINGS

There are five different kinds of heading – **main, sub, shoulder, side** and **paragraph** – used within documents or files and you need to be familiar with the differences between them.

MAIN HEADING

This will tell the reader what the work is about. The heading is usually blocked at the margin although it can sometimes be centred over the work. One clear line space is usually left between the heading and the paragraph when using single line spacing or 1 or 2 line spaces when using double line spacing. You can type this for practise.

Headings can be typed in several ways:

1   S P A C E D   C A P I T A L S   with one space between each letter and three spaces between each word.

2   CLOSED CAPITALS with or without underscore (underlining). There are no spaces between the letters and only one space between each word.

3   <u>Lower case with initial capital(s)</u> which must be underscored.

4   **Emboldened** if your machine has this facility.

When using the underscore you must start under the first letter and finish under the last letter. Never underline punctuation at the end of the heading.

After a main heading, leave either 1 or 2 single line spaces, ie turn up 2 or 3 times before starting your work.

<u>Sub-headings</u>

These are used with the main heading and contain additional information. They are typed in a different format from the main heading, eg if the main heading is in block capitals, the sub-headings may be typed with initial capital(s) and underscored. They may be bold or italics, or a different size, if your machine has these facilities. They are always consistent in their position on the page.

SHOULDER HEADINGS

These are used to indicate different topics within a document and are typed at the left margin. You can use either block capitals or initial capital(s) and underscore.

---

for the whole week. // We note that you need reception staff. I would suggest that you contact the local college. Many students are studying for their National vocational qualification and as part of their Reception module they do have to carry out reception duties in a "real life" situation. Although this can be carried out on work experience some students might not have the opportunity to meet several members of the public. This would be an ideal opportunity. If you offered a nominal fee they might be only too happy to help.

I would very much like to join you in your advertisement. This is a copy of our logo which I would like included.

Please leave at least 2" here for logo

I have noted your fee and a cheque is enclosed with this letter. // I would very much appreciate having a list of exhibitors competitors and also a list of companies whom you have invited to attend.

Yours sincerely

```
SIDE HEADINGS          These are also used to indicate different
                       topics or separate items.  If you are
                       keying in side headings on a word
                       processor you can use the indent facility
                       to block the paragraphs away from the
                       headings.  If you are using a typewriter
                       you can set the margin for the paragraphs
                       and press the margin release to backspace
                       into the margin and type the headings.
                       There must always be a minimum of 2 clear
                       character spaces between the heading and
                       the paragraph of text.  Shoulder headings
                       can be in block capitals, or initial
                       capital(s) and underscored.

PARAGRAPH HEADINGS     These are part of the paragraph.   They can
                       be:

1   CLOSED CAPITALS with or without underscore

2   Initial Capitals or Initial capital with underscore

3   run into the first sentence and therefore have no
    punctuation mark after them, eg Paragraph headings   These

4   followed by a full stop or colon, eg
    Paragraph headings.   These
```

■ TASK 1

For this section you are working for Mr Parminder Kumar who is the Sales Manager for the British Division of Swift Stationers PLC. He wants you to prepare the information sheet on page 84 using shoulder headings and with double line spacing. You can alter the spacing on your typewriter or word processor.

When using double line spacing, you must always turn up 2 double line spaces between the paragraphs. Turn up only one double line space after the shoulder heading, to leave only one clear line space.

Wherever you see '(your initials)' in the material put in your own initials. Where you see '(insert today's date)' put in the date on which you are typing/keying in the document.

Please type/key in the following letter. You do not need to do this on letterheaded paper as it is only a draft. Drafts should be in double line spacing (here only the body of the letter needs to be in double line spacing). I might want to make some amendments later. It will need to go on two pages. Produce one extra copy. This can be a photocopy.

Ref PD/Your initials/EX

Mr Peter Adams
98 Western Avenue
Birmingham
B7 8LK

Dear Mr ————————

Business Exhibition - April

Thank you for your letter of (yesterday's date). // I was [NP] most interested to hear of this exhibition and would certainly like to take part. We have our own exhibition stands and would not need any additional tables.

←———— We would like to have an area approx. 10' x 6' and would need access to power points. We always take with us a range of computer hardware that we have in our cat. and need this to demonstrate the software that we also offer.

←———— We also sell photocopiers, fax machines, collators, electric staplers and so on. At [this moment the] in time we are not sure exactly what we will be taking with us but we do need at least 4 power points. We do not like the idea of having trailing wires across the floor and would therefore like a position close to the wall. // We can provide three reps. to be at the exhibition

Turn up 7 single line spaces

PARTS OF A STAND ALONE WORD PROCESSOR

Turn up 2 double line spaces

The Keyboard

Turn up 1 double line space

This is a device which enables you to key in text or data. It is based on the QWERTY keyboard - that is the letter and figure keys are in the same position as they are on the typewriter keyboard. There are also some additional keys known as the function keys. These are used to perform specific operations.

Turn up 2 double line spaces

The Central Processing Unit - CPU

Turn up 1 double line space

This is the central part of the computer through which the devices are connected. It is usually based on a computer chip which links the keyboard, the screen, the printer and the storage media. These links are known as interfaces.

Turn up 2 double line spaces

The Printer

Turn up 1 double line space

The printer is the device which enables you to produce a hard copy (ie paper copy) of all the data you have keyed in.

Turn up 2 double line spaces

Visual Display Unit - VDU

Turn up 1 double line space

This enables you to see the text that you have keyed in on a screen before it is printed out. Any amendments or alterations can then be made.

Turn up 2 double line spaces

Parminder Kumar
PK/(your initials)/Comp
(Today's Date)

EUROPEAN SALES ← (Centre)

	1988	1989	1990	1991	1992 *
France	21,674	18,964	26,149	32,429	33,649
Germany	11,961	12,798	17,891	21,487	24,981
Italy	9,864	10,189	11,167	12,764	15,649
Spain	9,812	10,987	13,678	14,898	18,912
Holland	12,614	12,987	14,987	13,614	12,641

* Please note the Sales figures are different to ~~than~~ those on your spreadsheet. We have had more receipts and these have now been added to the total.

Patrick Dubuc
Sales Manager
(Insert today's date)
PD / (your initials) / ES

TABULATION AND INDENTING

The TAB key or bar is used to indent text a particular number of spaces from the left margin at the beginning of a line or to move from column to column in a table.

If you are using a typewriter, you will have a TAB SET or TAB+ key which sets tabs, a TAB CLEAR or TAB- key which clears existing tabs, and a TAB key or bar which you press to indent or move from column to column. This key may be marked TAB or with two arrows. You will need to identify all your tabulator (TAB) keys and their different functions.

When you wish to set a tab, move the carriage to the point where you want the tab and press the TAB+ key to set. If you are using a word processor, you will need to find out how to tabulate and indent on your system. You will already have default (preset) tabs set at 5 character intervals from your margins. You also have a paragraph indent facility. Call up the correct menu required to alter these settings.

Make sure you locate the Tab keys on your typewriter and the Indent key if you are using a word processor, and practise using them before you begin Task 2.

■ TASK 2

Type/key in the following notice using the side headings indicated.

1 Type/key in the headings and set a tab at 26 if you are using a typewriter or 16 if you are using a word processor. Then use the Tab key (typewriter) or Indent key (word processor) for each line of text.
   or
2 Set a margin at 26 (16) – the point at which the text starts – and press the margin release key to backspace into the margin for each of the headings.

FILING SYSTEMS USED WITHIN THE COMPANY

ALPHABETICAL   This is used for 90% of all company filing. A named folder is allocated for every company that does business with us. If you are not sure of the rules for alphabetical filing, consult the company handbook.

CHRONOLOGICAL   This is used when files need to be stored in date order. The most recent date goes to the front and the work can then be dealt with in date order.

SUBJECT   Files are arranged in alphabetical order according to subject.

GEOGRAPHICAL   Files are arranged in alphabetical order according to the country, county and town.

PK/(your initials)/Comp
(today's date)

THE SWIFT STATIONERS SOCIAL CLUB — *Spaced capitals*
Centre

FACT SHEET — *Centre and Underline*

UL   The social club started in 1987 and has been very popular with
all members of staff. We started off with only 33 members but
we now have 247 members on our books. // The social club is open   NP
every evening from 6.30 pm - 11.30 pm and offers a variety of   ✓
activities.

	6.30-7.30	7.30-8.30	9.00-10.00
MONDAY	Table Tennis	Snooker	Snooker
TUESDAY	Aerobics	Table Tennis	Indoor Football
WEDNESDAY	Snooker	Darts	Bridge
THURSDAY	Aerobics	Snooker	darts
FRIDAY	DISCO	DISCO	DISCO
SATURDAY	Social night	Social night	Social night
SUNDAY	Closed	Closed	Closed

Table Tennis ⌐

Inset ½" from both margins

Once a month the club arranges an outing which will either be   *Social* ⌐
on Saturday or Sunday. There is a Ramblers Association which
meets regularly every Sunday and will walk about 6-10 miles.
The darts team competes against other clubs and has won   ⊃
several trophies. The Bridge group has also been very
successful in the past year. At the moment the table tennis   # ⌐
team has only just entered the competitive field and we are
hoping for great things from them.

Leave at least 1" here

MEMBERSHIP IS ABSOLUTELY FREE

If you are interested do come along and see for yourself how
much fun we have!!!

Patrick Dubuc
(Insert today's date)

*Please check for consistency.
Make all amendments.*

■ **TASK 3**

The following extract should be typed/keyed in double line spacing using the paragraph headings indicated.

You can embolden the main heading for emphasis. If emboldening, do not underline.

STAFF VACANCIES

<u>ADMINISTRATION ASSISTANT</u> This position will be in the Advertising Section and has arisen because the present assistant has been promoted and is now working for Linda Jones, the Sales and Marketing Director.

<u>ACCOUNTANT</u> You will need to have a recognised qualification and have had a minimum of one year's appropriate experience.

<u>SECRETARY</u> You will need to have a minimum typing speed of 40 wpm, shorthand at 80 wpm, and word processing experience. There will be an opportunity for you to attend the local college one day a week to improve your skills and obtain a National Vocational Qualification.

PK/(your initials)/Comp
(Today's Date)

Numbered/lettered items or paragraphs

There are several ways to number or letter items or paragraphs. Whichever method you choose, you should be consistent within a document. You must always allow at least *2 character spaces* between the number or letter and the text. On the word processor you can use the paragraph tab or indent facility. This will automatically start the text at point 5.

Roman numerals can either be blocked to the left or the right. It is best to follow the style used in the draft. For example:

     i or i
     ii   ii
     iii   iii
     iv   iv
     v   v

INSTRUCTIONS FOR STUDENTS

Before you begin the assignment you have 10 minutes to:

- select the stationery, carbon paper, correcting fluid, pencils, pens, rulers, etc, that you need;

- ensure that you have the dictionaries, calendar and reference books that you might need;

- plan the order of your work. The European Sales Figures are urgently needed for a Sales Conference.

You have two-and-a-half hours to complete the following tasks. If you have a fault with your typewriter you will be allowed extra time. After the two-and-a-half hours you must present the work for signature.

For all exercises you are Secretary to Mr Patrick Dubuc, Sales Manager.

Envelopes will be required for all letters.

■ TASK 4

Please prepare the following lists of instructions for all new employees on the care of disks. Emphasise the word 'disk' throughout, using whichever method you prefer.

CARE OF DISKS

1   Although disks are fairly robust you need to look after them so that the work you have stored is not lost because a disk has been corrupted. To prevent this from happening a few essential rules should be observed.

   a   Keep disks away from electrical equipment, particularly telephones, as these generate magnetic fields which can erase text off a disk.

   b   Do not touch the exposed surface of the disk.

   c   Do not write on the disk with a biro as this can cause damage. Use a soft felt tip pen.

   d   Keep disks away from sunlight and heat.

   e   Keep disks away from dust.

   f   Do not eat, smoke or drink near a computer disk drive.

   g   Do not bend or twist the disk.

   h   Always put disks back into their sleeves when you have finished with them.

   i   Store disks upright in a box. Never lay them flat on your desk where they can pick up dust.

   j   Never leave disks in the computer as they can be corrupted when the computer is switched off and you will lose your work.

2   Boxes of disks must be stored and it is wise to fill in an index and attach this to the front of the box so that you know what is in each box. This could contain the following information:

   i   The name of the operator(s).

   ii   The name(s) of the originator of the work on disk.

   iii   The dates of the files, eg September '92 to February '93.

   iv   The first and last file number on each disk.

National Vocational Qualification
Business Administration

Level 2

UNIT 16   TEXT PROCESSING

Element 16.1

Produce a variety of business documents from handwritten/typewritten drafts.

Performance criteria

16.1.1.   you must be able to produce mailable copy of approximately 1200 words in a two-and-a-half hour working period

16.1.2   you must make sure files (backup and/or hard copy) are always produced and stored safely*

16.1.3   you must amend documents accurately as directed

16.1.4   you must ensure that layout conforms to house style and acceptable typewriting conventions

16.1.5   you must ensure that all corrections are made and that these corrections are not visible

16.1.6   you must collate and distribute correctly copies and originals as appropriate

16.1.7   you must ensure that security and confidentiality of information is always maintained

16.1.8   if you have any faults with the equipment these must be reported promptly

16.1.9   you must maintain procedures for the security/confidentiality of materials and follow operating, safety and maintenance procedures at all times

Competence must be demonstrated on a minimum of three separate occasions within a 2.5 hour working period.

A different set of materials must be produced on each occasion.

Possession of a pass or distinction in both Parts I and II of: Typewriting Skills Stage II or III or Word Processing Stage II or III will constitute sufficient evidence for the accreditation of this Element, provided that performance criteria 16.1.7, 16.1.8 and 16.1.9 are otherwise assessed.

You may use either manual/electric/electronic typewriters or word processing equipment.

---

* 16.1.2 requires production of carbon copies or photocopies or backup computer disks for all your work (hard copy means a copy printed out on paper).

TYPING FROM MANUSCRIPT

Sometimes you have to prepare work from manuscript (handwriting). The author may use abbreviations which you will have to expand and write in full.

The initial of a word may be used only, followed by a line. This indicates that the word should be typed in full – the word will always have appeared in full earlier in the document (*see* Task 5).

The ampersand (&) meaning 'and' is usually typed in full. There are, however, certain occasions when it can be left as an ampersand (&). These are:

- in the names of companies, eg Watts & Peters PLC
- in the names of partnerships, eg Robbins & Bradley
- in certain standard abbreviations, eg M & D Depot

Here is a list of abbreviations which you should be able to recognise.

accommodation	accom.	inconvenient/ence	incon.
account(s)	a/c(s)	manufacturer(s)	mfr(s).
acknowledge	ack.	miscellaneous	misc.
advertisement(s)	advert(s).	necessary	necy.
appointment(s)	appt(s).	opportunity/ies	opp(s).
approximately	approx.	receipt(s)	rec(s).
believe	bel.	receive	rec.
business	bus.	received	recd.
catalogue(s)	cat(s).	recommend	recom.
committee(s)	cttee(s).	reference(s)	ref(s).
company/ies	co(s).	referred	refd.
definitely	def.	responsible	resp.
develop	dev.	secretary/ies	sec(s).
exercise	ex.	separate	sep.
expense	exp(s).	signature(s)	sig(s).
experience	exp.	sufficient	suff.
governments	gov(s).	temporary	temp.
guarantee(s)	gntee(s).	through	thro'.
immediately	immed.		

as soon as possible	a.s.a.p.	would	wd.
dear	dr.	with	w.
shall	sh.	will	wl.
should	shd.	year(s)	yr(s).
which	wh.	your(s)	yr(s).

days of the week	eg Mon, Tues, Wed
months of the year	eg Jan, Feb, Mar, Apr
words in addresses	eg Rd, Cres, St, Ave, Dr

Make sure you can spell all the words in the above list.

Checklist of achievements in Section 5 – Business and personal correspondence

Performance criteria	Date	Signature
Produce a variety of business correspondence from typescript/manuscript ready for signature	_____	_____
Check work against original for errors in spelling, punctuation, grammar, layout and omission	_____	_____
Correctly indicate enclosures	_____	_____
Compose a letter	_____	_____
Place address on envelope/label accurately	_____	_____
Identify continuation sheets and correctly place information	_____	_____
Produce copies and correctly route these	_____	_____

The following can be retained as abbreviations:

eg	exempli gratia	for example
etc	et cetera	and others
ie	id est	that is
NB	nota bene	note well
am	ante meridiem	before noon
pm	post meridiem	after noon
Messrs	Messieurs	courtesy title
Mr	Mister	courtesy title
Ms		courtesy title
Mrs		courtesy title
Miss		courtesy title

Abbreviations are retained if used with figures:

m	metre(s)
mm	millimetre(s)
cm	centimetre(s)
g	gram(s)
kg	kilogram(s)

The following 3 notices should be typed or keyed in on separate sheets of paper. All abbreviations must be typed/keyed in full. Refer to the list of abbreviations if necessary.

■ TASK 5

> CHRISTMAS PARTY
>
> A C——— p——— will be held on our last day. This wl. be in the conference hall at 7.30 pm. Entry is free, but there will be a raffle to raise money for the local children's home
>
> You will need a ticket to attend as we have to know how many to cater for. Can you, therefore, collect this from the reception desk a.s.a.p.

Worldwide Travel
47 Kentish Street
London WC1 4XY) ← (Centre)

The contact name is Ms Lucy Jones.

2/ 3. We did need to have an invitation from Russia in order to go over ~~and~~ to try to secure new sales customers. This has been obtained and sent on to Ms Lucy Jones. A copy of this letter will also be sent to her so that she knows what information you have been given.

4. You will need to take American dollars with you as all payments at the hotel are in dollars. You cannot obtain roubles outside Russia. <u>Under no circumstances ~~can~~ must you buy roubles on the black market.</u>

I hope I have satisfactorily answered all your queries. (run on)

If you need to know anything else do not hesitate to get in touch.

I will see you at the meeting on the/14th of next month.

Yours sincerely

Make this last sentence a PS after Sales Man

Patrick Dubuc, Sales Man

cc Ms Lucy Jones

STAFF INTERVIEWS

Staff who wish to make appts. to see the accom. officer shd. contact the receptionist as she holds the appts. book.

This co. has a policy of using local properties and will do all it can to help anyone who has just moved into the area. It acks. the problems and has done its best to dev. good relationships with local property owners who have flats/rooms to rent! We bel. that in all circumstances we can help.

If you do have a problem we will need to know immed. If you request a specific appt. time and this is incon., another sh. be made a.s.a.p.

Staff Security ← (Blocked capitals and underline)

There has been a spate of thefts recently from offices. In particular handbags have been taken. All necy. action will be taken to tighten up on security. In the meantime do not leave bags or valuables lying around. There have been several sep. incidents and we will def. prosecute anyone who is caught leaving the premises with property wh. does not belong to them.

<u>The Police will be notified</u> ← (Spaced Caps)

Type/key in the following letter to Mr Peter Jefferies, 29 Hollybank Hill, Bromley, BY4 6QT. Use the reference PD/(your initials)/369 and today's date.

Use headed paper. This will need to go on to two pages so make sure that the second sheet is plain bond paper and not headed paper. A copy of the letter will be sent to Ms Lucy Jones.

Dear Mr J———

VISAS FOR AMERICA AND RUSSIA ← (embolden)

Thank you for your letter (insert last Monday's date). I am sorry that you have not yet received your application forms for the Canadian, Russian and American visits. All forms were sent out ~~and~~ at the beginning of last month. However, there is still plenty of time as you do not need to apply until 8 weeks // In answer ↑before you [NP] to your questions: travel.

of

1. ~~In answer to~~ You were right when you said that British citizens do not need a visa when travelling to America. However, if you are entering America from ~~Canada~~ Britain you will need a visa, and if you do not have one you will be refused entry.

(Inset numbered items by 1" both sides) ✓

~~2.~~3 There is an English translation of your visa application form for Russia. You will need to know the address of your Russian hotel. It is:

Hotel Aeromat
10 Leningradsky Prospekt
Korpus 7
125 198 Moscow
Russia

← (Centre)

You will also need to put the name and address of the Travel Agency. It is:

CORRECTION SIGNS

Any corrections or amendments that have to be made in a document are usually indicated in the margin with the proof correction, or printers' correction signs, as they are sometimes called. The most frequently used are shown below.

Mark in the margin	Meaning	Mark in the text	
l.c.	Lower case – small letter, not capital, required	S̲ ⌿	Under or through letter to be changed
u.c. or CAPS	Upper case – capital letter(s) required	c̲ ⌽	Under or through letter to be changed
∂	Delete	~~word~~	Through letter(s) or word(s)
NP or //	New paragraph	// or ⌐	Placed before the first word of a new paragraph
stet or ✓	Keep in the word(s) with the dotted line underneath	~~word~~	Under word(s) crossed out
run on	A new paragraph is not needed – continue on from previous sentence	⌒	Joining 2 paragraphs
⋀	Caret mark – insert letter, word, punctuation mark, etc, shown in the margin	⋀	Where the omission occurs
⌣	Close up – delete space	⌣	Between letters or words
trs or ⎍	Transpose – change the order of words or letters indicated	⎍	Between letters/ words, sometimes numbered
#	Insert a character space	⋀	
‖	Keep margin straight	——	Underscore (underline)
ital.	Put into italic print	——	Underscore
bold	Put into bold print	——	Underscore

Type/key in the following letter to Mr Alan Yetman, Hillcrest, Lower Road, FARTHING, Kent, ME6 4TH. Use the reference PD/(your initials)/34 and today's date.

A copy will need to be sent to Mr Roger Lambe.

Dear Mr Y_____

I was very sorry to hear about the trouble you have been having with your telephone/answering machine / which you purchased from us. This is the first complaint we have recd.

// I am arranging for our rep. in your area, Mr Roger Lambe to call to /and collect your machine. He will bring a replacement with him and a new gntee.

He will call first thing on / Mon. morning (insert next Monday's date). A copy of your letter will be Sent / forwarded to him as well as a copy of this letter. *(A)

∂/ I can only apologize and again for any inconvenience caused.

Yours sincerely

(Insert at A)
* If you wish to contact Mr Lambe him / before Mon. his /number is / telephone / 679827.

Prepare the following 3 documents, making *all* the corrections.
Check for spelling errors. There will be one spelling error in each task. Proofread against the document underneath each task.

■ TASK 8

WORD PROCESSORS

Word processors allows work to be manipulated. Text once stored on a disk can be recalled, edited and amended. This can include altering margins, spacing, changing the order of text, and inserting additional text. Work of a repetitive nature such as multiple or letters and standard paragraphs for contracts & reports are ideally suited to word processing. Standard paragraphs can be taken from one file and transferred to another to form another completely new document. Letters from one file can be merged w. the names and addresses from another and sent out as personalised, individual letters. WPs. allow all typed text to be stored and reproduced automatically as many times as it is required. Each copy is an originally printed docement.

Many w.p. packages now contain a spell check which will check the spelling of all your work and a thesaurus. This means that if you have been using a particular word in a document you can look at the thesaurus and find a similar word that can be used in its place.

Corrected version, Task 8

WORD PROCESSORS

Word processors allow work to be manipulated. Text once stored on a disk can be recalled, edited and amended. This can include spacing, altering margins, changing the order of text, and inserting additional text.

Work of a repetitive nature such as multiple letters and standard paragraphs for contracts and reports are ideally suited to word processing.

Standard paragraphs can be taken from one file and transferred to another to form a completely new document. Letters from one file can be merged with the names and addresses from another and sent out as personalised, individual letters. Word processors allow all typed text to be stored and reproduced automatically as many times as it is required. Each copy is an originally printed document.

Many word processing packages now contain a spell check, which will check the spelling of all your work, and a thesaurus. If you have been using a particular word in a document, you can look at the thesaurus and find a similar word to use in its place.

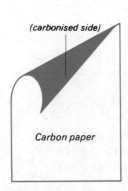

(carbonised side)

Carbon paper

Carbon paper has a dull side and a glossy side. It is the carbon side which makes the impression on the paper.

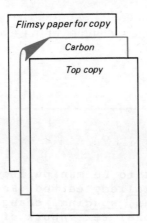

Flimsy paper for copy

Carbon

Top copy

The carbon side is put against the paper on which you wish to make a copy.

Check that the paper is straight and that the carbon paper is the right way round.

CORRECTING ERRORS ON THE CARBON COPY

Always read through the whole document when you have finished typing/keying in, as it is much easier to correct the work in the typewriter or on the word processor screen before printing. If you know you have made a mistake, it is better to correct this immediately. If you are using a typewriter you can correct the error on the top copy by using correction paper, correction fluid, or self-correcting ribbon.

Remember that, with a carbon copy, when you are correcting the top copy it is easy to mark the bottom copy. Insert a piece of protecting scrap paper between the carbon paper and the copy to prevent this. The carbon copy can be corrected using correction paper, correction fluid or typewriting eraser. Whichever method you choose, it is important that the error should hardly show. Always remember to take out the piece of protecting paper before you start typing again.

ROUTING OF COPIES

If you have been asked to send a copy of a letter to someone other than the addressee, ensure its correct distribution or routing. Insert the name(s) of the person(s) receiving the copy/copies either at the top or bottom of the copy/copies. Sometimes these will appear on the top copy also. If you have been asked to send a blind copy you will omit cc from the top copy (sometimes this is shown by putting bcc instead of just cc).

Example

1st carbon copy   3rd carbon copy

cc <u>Mr D Evans</u>   cc Mr D Evans   cc Mr D Evans
   Mr M Whittaker   <u>Mr M Whittaker</u>   Mr M Whittaker
   File   File   <u>File</u>

cc stands for carbon copy.

Tick, highlight or underline one of the names on each copy so that you know where to send it.

■ TASK 9

ADDITIONAL FEATURES OF A WORD PROCESSOR!

Desk Top Publishing Desk top publishing allows graphics of a
very high quality. Text can be boxed and articles laid out
like a newspaper page.

to be produced

Different sizes and styles can be used for emphasising
particular words. Letter headed paper can be designed.

Graphics This is the production of an image on screen under
the control of the computer. Examples can be seen with bar
charts, pie charts, line graphs and so on.

Database A database contains a collection of information wh.
can be organised very easily, and from wh. information can be
extracted. It operates like a central filing depart. where,
data is controlled, organised and maintained.

Spreadsheet A spreadsheet is a program to enable a set of
calculations and the layout of the results to be specified.
It is often used in financial analysis, budget forecasting,
estimating and general accountancy.

to be made

It is essentially a large sheet of paper on which there are
rows and columns which contain tables of information.

run on You can carry out calculations (additions, subtractions,
multiplication and divisions) and forecasts can be made from
these calculations.

Corrected version, Task 9

ADDITIONAL FEATURES OF A WORD PROCESSOR!

Desk Top Publishing Desk top publishing allows graphics of a
very high quality to be produced. Text can be boxed and
articles laid out like a newspaper page.

Different sizes and styles can be used to emphasise particular
words. Alternative letter headed paper can be designed.

Graphics This is the production of an image on screen under
the control of the computer. Information can be bar charts,
pie charts, line graphs and so on.

Database A database contains a collection of information
which can be organised very easily, and from which information
can be extracted. It operates like a central filing
department where data is controlled, organised and maintained.

Spreadsheet A spreadsheet is a program to enable a set of
calculations to be made and the layout of the results to be
specified. It is often used in budget forecasting, financial
analysis, estimating and general accountancy.

It is essentially like a large sheet of paper on which there
are rows and columns which contain figures and other
information. You can carry out calculations (addition,
subtraction, multiplication and division) and forecasts can be
made from these calculations.

BUSINESS LETTERS WITH CONTINUATION SHEETS

All the letters you produced for Level 1 fitted on one sheet of paper. Sometimes long letters need to have a second sheet. The first page only should be on headed paper and any additional pages must be on plain paper.

Leave a top and bottom margin of 6 clear line spaces (1 inch) on the second sheet. If you are using a word processor, these are the default margins. You must make sure that you do not just carry one or two lines over to a second sheet. You should take over at least the last paragraph of the letter together with the complimentary close and name of the sender. There is no need to type PTO or Continued at the bottom of the first sheet.

At the top left-hand margin of the second sheet type/key in the page number, the date, and the name of the person to whom the letter is being sent:

Turn up 4 lines (3 clear line spaces)

2

Turn up 2 lines (1 clear line space)

14 February 199–

Turn up 2 lines (1 clear line space)

Mr R Frazer

This is the format for block letters, which is the style used by Swift Stationers. Should the pages of the letter become separated, the continuation sheets can then be easily identified.

CARBON COPIES FOR DISTRIBUTION

It is necessary for businesses to keep on file an exact copy of all the documents they send out. Although copies of documents are often made on the photocopier, carbon copies are still taken by some organisations.

To take a carbon copy:

1 Place the sheet of paper on which the copy is to be made on a flat surface.

2 Place a sheet of carbon paper with the carbon (dull) side down on top of the sheet of paper. (The glossy side of the carbon paper will be facing you – to help you, this is often printed with a design by the manufacturers.)

3 Now place your top sheet of paper (eg letterhead) on top of the carbon paper and pick them all up.

4 Insert all sheets into the typewriter or printer so that the glossy side of the carbon paper is facing you and you are at the point you want to start typing or printing (allowing for the fact that the printer will automatically turn up six clear line spaces).

5 Realign the paper if necessary.

■ TASK 10

WORD PROCESSING WITHIN AN ORGANISATION

The Author

The author is the originator of the work. They will need to know the capabilities and limitations of word processors so that ~~they will know exactly what the machine is capable of and~~ operators will not be expected to do the impossible.

The Operator

The operator ~~will~~ receive work from the author ~~either~~ from longhand, audio dictation, shorthand dictation, typescript, or on disk. It is esential that the operator has good keyboarding skills, good language skills, is able to follow instructions, present and display work and has a thorough knowledge of the word processing package used.

The Word Processing Supervisor

If work goes to a central processing dept. the supervisor will organise and co-ordinate the distribution of the work of the dept. The supervisor will need good communications skills, good organisation skills and must be completely up to date. Responsibility for staff development is very important.

Corrected version, Task 10

WORD PROCESSING WITHIN AN ORGANISATION

The Author

The author, the originator of the work, will need to know the capabilities and limitations of word processors so that operators will not be expected to do the impossible.

The Operator

The operator receives work from the author from longhand, audio dictation, shorthand dictation, typescript, or on disk. It is essential that the operator has good keyboarding skills, good language skills, is able to follow instructions, present and display work, and has a thorough knowledge of the word processing package used.

The Word Processing Supervisor

If work goes to a central processing department, the supervisor will organise and co-ordinate the distribution of the work of the department. The supervisor will need good communications skills, good organisation skills and must be completely up to date. Responsibility for staff development is very important.

Section 5 Business and personal correspondence

NVQ Level 2

In Level 1 you covered business letters. You also need to know about other kinds of letters:

PERSONAL BUSINESS LETTERS

A personal business letter is sent to a person or organisation about a personal business matter. You will use the same layout as that for a business letter but include your home address at the left margin 2 single line spaces above the name and address of the addressee. An alternative is to place your home address at the right margin. Use the right justification facility or, if this is not available on your machine, backspace each line from the right margin so that the right-hand margin is justified.

PERSONAL LETTERS

These are letters to personal friends. Your name and address can be exactly the same as in a personal business letter but you do not include the name and address of the addressee. You always use first names.

■ **TASK 1**

Compose on your typewriter or word processor a letter to a friend inviting her/him for dinner on Saturday evening. Dinner will be at 7 pm but you would like everyone there by 6.30 pm. You will have two other friends at this dinner (give their names).

■ **TASK 2**

Compose on your typewriter or word processor a personal letter to a different friend. You can write and tell her/him of your progress on your course and when your examinations will be. You can also say what you hope to achieve when you finish the course and what sort of career you would like.

■ **TASK 3**

Compose on your typewriter or word processor a personal business letter to a bank, addressing it to The Manager. As the subject heading give your name and Account No 123456. Ask for a statement of your account to be sent to you.

STAFF INFORMATION SHEET ← *Underline and embolden*

A group of 4 reps. will be going to Russia for 1 week. They will be visiting Moscow in an effort to gain orders. Moscow is full of many companies/including those from Germany, Canada, America and France/who are ~~now~~ sending reps. to Moscow as there are now many opportunities for business over there.

All companies need stationery and we would like to be one of the first to approach the new markets. We have 3 major competitors/the French,/and the Norwegians. As ~~far as~~ we see it t̶h̶e̶ French stationery is very expensive but transport costs are not as great as they are from the U.K. Stationery - paper in particular - is very cheap in Norway, but the cost of freight is very high. All stationery has to be shipped to Leningrad and then transported overland across Russia.

if the Danes/

We can offer a cheaper system of transport. We can either send part or full loads via Ramsgate/Dunkirk and from there the goods will be transported overland across France, Germany, Poland and into Russia. The maximum delivery time will be ~~10~~ *15* days.

15

We can use this as a selling point. Furthermore we will allow 6 weeks before payment is made from the date of receipt of goods not from the date of despatch. A generous discount of 3Ø%/will be offered. ~~on all goods supplied in the catalogue.~~ Payment will only be accepted for goods in American dollars and not Russian roubles.

5% on all goods in the Cat.

The hotel you will be staying at is Hotel Aeromat, 10 Leningradsky Prospekt, Korpus 7, 125198 Moscow, RUSSIA. It is a Soviet/French venture and therefore all cuisine will be in French. It is located 12 minutes from the Kremlin and 30 minutes from Sheremetievo 2 International Airport. // The hotel offers several amenities including a business centre, a shuttle bus to the Kremlin, ~~concierge~~, room service, long distance pay telephones, laundry ~~and pressing~~ service. All rooms will have private bath, individual temperature control, private telephone and colour t.v. with satellite reception and movies.

NP

An agenda for the week will be following shortly. At the moment my secretary is very busy trying to arrange appointments but it is sometimes very difficult to get through to Moscow during the day.

Checklist of achievements in Section 4 – Business forms

Performance criteria	Date	Signature
Correctly prepare forms from manuscript	_____	_____
Complete forms with leader dots accurately	_____	_____
Complete boxed forms accurately	_____	_____
Perform simple calculations using a calculator	_____	_____
Pass on messages accurately	_____	_____
Compose a job application form	_____	_____
Compose a CV	_____	_____
Extract relevant information	_____	_____
Record relevant information	_____	_____
Transfer relevant information	_____	_____
Compose messages	_____	_____

ALLOCATING SPACE

Vertical space   There are 6 lines to an inch (25 mm) down the page. If you have to leave 1″ down the page you must turn up 7 line spaces, as you will start typing/keying in on the seventh line. This is because an *exact* 1″ must be left. If you are told to leave *at least* 1″, then you can start your work on any line over 7.

Your machine will usually have 10, 12 or 15 character spaces to an inch (cpi) across the page, depending on the size of your typeface or pitch (*see* page 81).

If you are told to leave 1″ clear across the page and your pitch is 10, you will start your work on point 11.

If your pitch is 12, you will start your work at point 13.

Horizontal space   If you are told to leave at least 1″ across the page, then you can start your work at any point after 11 (10 pitch) or 13 (12 pitch). If you are unsure about the pitch you are using, check this.

JUSTIFICATION

```
Sometimes your work will need to be justified, if that is the
instruction given, and your typewriter or word processor has this
facility.   Justification means that both your left and right
margins are straight.   In order to achieve a straight right
margin, the words and spaces are spread out on the line.   This
is an example of a justified paragraph.
```

If your typewriter does not have this facility, then you cannot justify work, but you should try to keep your right margin as even as possible. This improves the look of your finished document. Some word processing programs default to print text justified.

CORRECTING ERRORS

In an office you will frequently have to amend documents that contain errors which have not been marked. You, therefore, do not know the exact nature of the error. It could be a spelling error, a keying-in error, a punctuation mark or character missing, or an error of agreement, eg six boys *was (were)* sent to do research for their projects.

Retype the following tasks on separate sheets of plain A4 paper, correcting the ringed errors. Justify the text if you have the facility. Use single line spacing and a left margin of 2″.
A correct copy is included on page 98 against which to check your work.

Additional Experience September 1987– June 1990	Saturday job with local newsagents for 3 years. This involved using the cash till, counting the day's takings, checking the stock books, entering payments into the newspaper delivery book.
Interests and Hobbies	Swimming, Reading, Listening to Music, Driving, Canoeing, Sailing, Wind Surfing.
References	The Principal West London Secretarial College Parsons Green LONDON SW4 9NM Mr Peter Hines 20 Waterbank Road BROMLEY Kent BR5 6ER

■ TASK 12

You are now working in the Sales Department. this department
is concerned with the selling of goods and services. It is
conserned with selling foods and goods to supermarkets and
they they sell directly over the counter. Payment is made by
cheque, cash or credit card. A seperate form is used for each
transaction. A company who would be interested in marketing a
new product would be like to rent space in the local papers.

■ TASK 13

You are now working in the Reception Office. This is one of
the most important area of any organisation as this is usually
the first place that a visitor will see. it is therefore
important to creat a good impression. The apearance of the
area is very very important and essential to creating this
impression You must remember that the receptionist should
allways be friendly, pleasent, courteous, polite, helpfull
and tactful. In adition you should note that the
receptionist should be well-spoken, patient, well groomed,
have a sense of responsibility, and and finally have a good
knowledge of the company.

■ TASK 14

You are now working in the Accounts Department and have only
just started as a trainee. Your first task will be to help
prepare the wage for all full-time and part time staff. this
will be done on the computor and a particular package has been
purchased for for this. You will need all the detail of
overtime before you can start We have also agreed to pay
accomodation costs for staff who has just moved into the area.
If you do not have the details i shall be happy to supply
them.

CURRICULUM VITAE

Name	Amanda Parkinson (Miss)
Address	14 Beckenham Way BECKENHAM Kent BK4 6LY
Telephone Number	081 678 6587
Date of Birth	18 October 1973
Education (1984-1989)	Swalelands Comprehensive School BECKENHAM Kent BK4 9PQ
(1989-1990)	West London Secretarial College Parsons Green LONDON SW4 9NM
Qualifications June 1989	GCSE English Language (C) English Literature (C) History (D) French (E) Maths (E) Combined Science (E) French (C)
Secretarial **Qualifications** June 1990	PEI Elementary Word Processing PEI Shorthand at 80 wpm RSA Stages I, II Typewriting PEI Advanced Typewriting PEI Audio Typewriting NVQ Level II Business Administration
Work Experience October 1989- May 1990	One day a week during College course at Hills & Peters, Solicitors, 16 Dover Street, LONDON, W1 6ML During this time I operated a computerised switchboard, used the telex and fax machines, took shorthand dictation, went on the reception desk, and used WordPerfect and WordStar.
Foreign Languages	French up to GCSE and German for 2 years at school. German lessons continuing at evening classes.

■ TASK 15

To see how many of the following abbreviations you have remembered, type/key in the full word. Check your accuracy against the list on page 88.

accom.	dev.	opps.	suff.
a/c(s)	dr.	recs.	sh.
ack.	ex.	rec.	shd.
advert(s).	exp(s).	recd.	temp.
appt(s).	exp.	recom.	thro'.
approx.	gov(s).	refs.	yr(s).
bel.	gntee(s).	refd.	wh.
bus.	immed.	resp.	wd.
cat(s).	incon.	secs.	w.
cttee(s).	mfrs.	sep.	wl.
co(s).	misc.	sig.	yr(s).
def.	necy.		

Corrected versions

Corrected copies of tasks on page 97:

■ TASK 12

You are now working in the Sales Department. This Department is concerned with the selling of goods and services. It is concerned with selling foods and goods to supermarkets and they sell directly over the counter. Payment is made by cheque, cash or credit card. A separate form is used for each transaction. A company who would be interested in marketing a new product would be likely to rent space in the local papers.

■ TASK 13

You are now working in the Reception Office. This is one of the most important areas of any organisation as this is usually the first place that a visitor will see. It is therefore important to create a good impression. The appearance of the area is very important and essential to creating this impression. You must remember that the receptionist should always be friendly, pleasant, courteous, polite, helpful and tactful. In addition you should note that the receptionist should be well-spoken, patient, well groomed, have a sense of responsibility, and finally have a good knowledge of the company.

■ TASK 14

You are now working in the Accounts Department and have only just started as a trainee. Your first task will be to help prepare the wages for all full-time and part-time staff. This will be done on the computer and a particular package has been purchased for this. You will need all the details of overtime before you can start. We have also agreed to pay accommodation costs for staff who have just moved into the area. If you do not have the details I shall be happy to supply them.

■ TASKS 7 AND 8

There have been two telephone messages for Mr Paramjit Darmi. The first was from Mr Andrew Smith, of Wicks, Henderson and Jones, telephone no 0468 78908, who is returning his call and would like him to phone back. Mr Smith will be in his office after 3 pm. The second was from Dr Daz, 10 Park Avenue, Blackheath, London, SE3 10NB, telephone no 081-697 4343, who would like to receive a copy of the catalogue. Complete a separate form for each message.

When you apply for a job you will usually be sent an application form to complete and return. This should be returned with a letter of application. The application form must always be typed but the letter of application can either be typed or handwritten (often a handwritten letter is requested).

You may be asked to send in your letter together with a Curriculum Vitae (CV). A CV is different from an application form in that it is more detailed and you choose exactly how much information you wish to include. You may wish to alter your CV for particular requirements when applying for different jobs. You will always want to draw attention to your qualifications and the personal qualities you consider important for the particular post for which you are applying.

It is a good idea to store your CV on a word processor. You can then print an original to accompany each job application. It is also easy to make changes and update the CV when necessary.

■ TASK 9

Type or key in the following CV for Amanda Parkinson.

After you have done this, you might like to give some thought to what you would put in your own CV and to prepare one for yourself. You will need to plan your CV and to insert your details in chronological order, ie moving from the earliest dates to the latest dates for qualifications, and the other way around for work experience, etc, so that your most recent work is shown first.

When preparing the CV, use side headings so that the information on the CV is very clear and easy to read. It may require 2 pages, so number the second page in the top left-hand corner.

WORDS AND FIGURES

When you have to prepare a document that contains words and figures, it is always best to read through it first. In this way you can make a decision as to whether you will use words or figures throughout the document. Whichever you choose, you must be consistent. In other words, numbers must be represented in a document either by words all the way through or by figures all the way through. Never use a mixture of both.

However, although consistency is essential, there are a few rules to remember:

1   A sentence should never start with a figure – always a word, no matter what format is used in the document. For example:

    "Seven boys went to see the play."

2   The figure one should be typed as a word unless it appears in a list. For example:

    "It happened one fine day."

3   In measurements, and the day and year in dates, you should always use figures.
4   Money can be expressed in figures or words.

TIME

One of the most important things to remember when typing/keying in the time is that you must be consistent. Within a document you must either use the 12-hour clock or the 24-hour clock. You cannot use a mixture of both. You will either use:

0900 hours to 1245 hours (note no full stop) or 9.00 am to 12.45 pm

MEASUREMENTS

You must also be consistent when using measurements. You will either use words, symbols or letters. For example:

5 cm x 5 m or
5 centimetres x 5 metres

9' 4" x 3' 6" or
9 ft 4 in x 3 ft 6 in

6 kg of sugar and 5 kg of flour or
6 kilograms of sugar and 5 kilograms of flour

7 kms or
7 kilometres

You will notice that there is one space left after the number and before the unit of measurement. For example 5 cm, 6 kg, 9 ft 4 in. There is also no full stop when using abbreviations such as cm, kg, m, and so on.

Prepare the following job application form, and then fill it in with your own details. You could look in the local press to find a suitable position for which to apply.

```
APPLICATION FOR EMPLOYMENT
Position applied for .......................................
Name ......................................................
Address ...................................................
       ....................................................
       ....................................................
Telephone No ................. Date of birth ..............
Last school attended ......................................
       ....................................................
Qualifications obtained ...................................
       ....................................................
       ....................................................
       ....................................................
       ....................................................
Previous employment .......................................
       ....................................................
       ....................................................
Hobbies and interests .....................................
       ....................................................
References
(1) ........................   (2) ........................
       ...................        ........................
       ...................        ........................
       ...................        ........................
       ...................        ........................
Signature ................... Date .......................
```

FRACTIONS

You may find that you have some fractions on your keyboard. If you have none, then you will have to use ordinary figures with the oblique. For example:

1/2, 1/4, 2/3

or if you have whole figures with fractions:

3 1/2, 4 1/4, 4 7/8

You will see that there is a space between the whole figure and the fraction.

ACCENTS

If you have a keyboard which includes accents you simply have to key in the accent and backspace once to key in the character over which the accent is placed. However, you may find your machine gives another character in place of the accent, or does not have accents at all. If this happens, you will have to insert the accent afterwards with a black pen or biro.

Additional accents

FRENCH	
acute accent	é á
grave accent	è à
circumflex	â ê î ô û
cedilla	ç (makes the c soft like s)
GERMAN	
umlaut	ä ö ü
SPANISH	
acute accent	á é í ó ú
tilde	õ
ITALIAN	
grave accent	à è ì ò ù

You have taken a telephone message for Christine Major, from Mr Paul Redding of Tenko Supplies. He has received an invoice which should be for £464 and not £4640. He wants a phone call as soon as possible. Although telephone message forms are usually handwritten, Christine Major likes all hers typed for clarity. Can you therefore complete a telephone message form, making sure that you put the date and time of the message which is urgent. If you do not have a form, prepare the following form and then fill it in.

```
TELEPHONE MESSAGE FORM

To ...................................................

Department .........................................

Message from .......................................

of .................................................

Telephone No ....................... Fax No.............


ACTION

Tick one of the following:


Please call back .....

Urgent            .....

Will ring back    .....

No action needed .....


Message ............................................
...................................................
...................................................
...................................................



Message taken by ..................................

Date .................... Time ....................
```

Prepare the following 3 notices. There is a mixture of styles and you will have to make sure that there is consistency throughout. Use a separate sheet for each task. Read through each passage before typing it and make a note of the alterations to be made. A correct copy is included on pages 102–3 for you to check your work.

■ TASK 16

```
RECEPTION AREA

We are in the process of completely restructuring the
reception area.  This will now be extended and will measure
10 m x 24 m.  It will be manned from 9.15 am to 1730 hours
each day.  The switchboard will also be in the reception area
but this will close at 5.30 pm.  After that the answering
machine will be switched on.  Work will commence on (put next
Monday's date).

We have placed an order for a new carpet 8 metres by 22 metres
and a new oak table 400 mm x 200 mm.  This should be arriving
very shortly.  We feel that it is very important to have a
reception area that reflects the company image.

Parminder Kumar
Sales Manager
British Division
(insert today's date)
PK/(your initials)/47
```

■ TASK 17

```
TRAVEL CLAIMS

There will be new rates in operation for claiming travel
expenses from the beginning of next month.  For cars above
1600 cc the rate will be 44.6p per mile.  For cars below
sixteen hundred cc the rate will be 30.5p per mile.  This will
be for the first 2,000 miles.  If you are travelling more than
two thousand miles in a month then you will receive a reduced
rate.  This will be 10 p per mile less.  Payment is for whole
miles.  We do not calculate for a 1/4 or a 1/2 mile.  If your
journey is 25 1/2 miles you can round it up to 26.

Parminder Kumar
Sales Manager
British Division
(insert today's date)
PK/(your initials)/47
```

■ TASK 4

You want to apply for leave of absence as you are having your driving test and have used up all your holiday entitlement. Complete the form below by inserting your name and address and saying that you are in Accounts Department on extension 249. Your immediate line manager is Mrs Sally Everton. Remember to sign and date the form.

```
S W I F T   S T A T I O N E R S   P L C

APPLICATION FOR LEAVE OF ABSENCE

SURNAME (Mr/Ms/Mrs/Miss) ....................................

FIRST NAME ..................................................

ADDRESS .....................................................

............................................................

............................................................

............................................................

DEPARTMENT ..................................................

LINE MANAGER ......................... EXT NO ..............

REASON FOR REQUEST ..........................................

............................................................

............................................................

............................................................

DATE OF ABSENCE .............................................

SIGNATURE ........................ DATE ..................

PERMISSION GIVEN .................. DATE ..................
```

■ TASK 18

SALES MEETING

The AGM will be held on Wednesday 14 November (insert current year) at 9.30 am and is expected to last until 1630 hours. At 12.30 pm we will break for lunch. We will have two special guests, Monsieur Rènè Marnièr and Herr Heinrich Müncher, both of whom are working for the European Commission.

The meeting will be in the Committee Room. If you have any items for the agenda I must have these by 5 November.

Parminder Kumar
Sales Manager
British Division
(insert today's date)
PK/(your initials)/47

Corrected versions

Corrected copies of tasks on pages 101–2.

■ TASK 16

RECEPTION AREA

We are in the process of completely restructuring the reception area. This will now be extended and will measure 10 m x 24 m. It will be manned from 9.15 am to 5.30 pm each day. The switchboard will also be in the reception area but this will close at 5.30 pm. After that the answering machine will be switched on. Work will commence on (next Monday's date).

We have placed an order for a new carpet 8 m x 22 m and a new oak table 400 mm x 200 mm. This should be arriving very shortly. We feel that it is very important to have a reception area that reflects the company image.

Parminder Kumar
Sales Manager
British Division
(today's date)
PK/(your initials)/47

■ **TASK 3**

A credit note needs to be sent to Le Department de Compte, Le Service de l'Ordinateur, 12 rue de Bain, Paris Cedex 6, FRANCE. The credit is for 10 boxes of fax paper damaged in transit. The cost per box is Ff77.50, making a total of Ff775.00 that has to be credited.

PRINTED FORMS WITH LEADER DOTS

Forms may be prepared for later completion. Lines on which information will be typed/keyed in may be shown as a dotted line (using the full stop) or as a straight line (using the underscore). Prepare for yourself the 'Leave of Absence' form (page 142) and the 'Telephone Message' form (page 143). You will note that:

1 The forms with leader dots are in double line spacing so that there is space to fill in the information.

2 There is one clear character space before and after the leader dots or underscore line.

3 All dots or lines for completion finish at the same point.

If you have to complete a form by inserting information on dotted (or straight) lines, ensure you type/key in the information positioned so that the hanging letters such as q, y, p, j and g just clear the line and do not touch it.

If you are using a typewriter, release the platen by pushing in the cylinder knob, and move the platen up slightly before inserting the information. This needs practice. Filling in this kind of form is usually done on a typewriter unless the form is already on your computer.

There are a few points to watch for:

1 Do not type an address all on one line if several lines have been provided for it. The second and subsequent lines of the address can be blocked underneath each other.

2 It is best to leave 1 character space before inserting any information on the form.

3 If you have to delete any information on the form, as for example in Mr/Ms/Mrs/Miss, you can do this by using a capital X.

4 If you have to tick any boxes, this can be done with a black pen or biro afterwards.

For this section you will be working for Mr Paramjit Darmi, Sales Accounts, and Mrs Christine Major, Administration Accounts.

TRAVEL CLAIMS

There will be new rates in operation for claiming travel
expenses from the beginning of next month. For cars above
1600 cc the rate will be 44.6p per mile. For cars below
1600 cc the rate will be 30.5p per mile. This will be for the
first 2,000 miles. If you are travelling more than 2,000
miles in a month then you will receive a reduced rate. This
will be 10p per mile less. Payment is for whole miles. We do
not calculate for a 1/4 or a 1/2 mile. If your journey is
25 1/2 miles you can round it up to 26.

Parminder Kumar
Sales Manager
British Division
(today's date)
PK/(your initials)/47

■ TASK 18 (alternative versions – 12-hour or 24-hour clock)

SALES MEETING

The AGM will be held on Wednesday 14 November (current year)
at 9.30 am and is expected to last until 4.30 pm. At 12.30 pm
we will break for lunch. We will have two special guests,
Monsieur Rènè Marnièr and Herr Heinrich Müncher, both of whom
are working for the European Commission.

The meeting will be in the Committee Room. If you have any
items for the agenda I must have these by 5 November.

Parminder Kumar
Sales Manager
British Division
(today's date)
PK/(your initials)/47

SALES MEETING

The AGM will be held on Wednesday 14 November (current year)
at 0930 hours and is expected to last until 1630 hours. At
1230 hours we will break for lunch. We will have two special
guests, Monsieur Rènè Marnièr and Herr Heinrich Müncher, both
of whom are working for the European Commission.

The meeting will be in the Committee Room. If you have any
items for the agenda I must have these by 5 November.

Parminder Kumar
Sales Manager
British Division
(today's date)
PK/(your initials)/47

CREDIT NOTE – EXAMPLE

The following is an example of a credit note, which you might like to complete. If you do not have a credit note on your word processor, use a typewriter and a blank credit note form. At the back of this book, you will find a credit note form which you can copy.

CREDIT NOTE NO: C124

SWIFT STATIONERS PLC
DRURY HOUSE
10 KNIGHTS PLACE
OXFORD
OX1 4MC

Telephone: 0689 543545
Fax: 0689 657890
Telex: 789678278

To: Ross & Co
City Road
BIRMINGHAM
BM3 5JK

VAT Registered No: 47985678

Date: 7 July 19--
Invoice No: RC45679

Reason for Credit	Quantity and Description	Total Credit £
Goods damaged in transit	12 Boxes A4 paper (Bond)	129.95
	12 Boxes Listing Paper	164.65
E & OE	**TOTAL**	294.60

CHECKLIST

As well as fulfilling elements in your National Vocational Qualification, if you successfully work through each section of the book you will also have achieved other performance criteria. Type or key in the checklists and ask your tutor or supervisor to sign and date them so that you can keep a copy in your record of achievement.

Checklist of achievements in Section 1 – Business documents

Performance criteria	Date	Signature
Alter margins accurately	————	————
Embolden or underline text	————	————
Use a variety of headings within a document, including main headings, sub headings, shoulder headings, side headings and paragraph headings	————	————
Use spaced capitals, blocked capitals and initial capitals with underscore when instructed to do so	————	————
Allocate correct spacing when changing from single to double line spacing	————	————
Correctly produce documents from manuscript	————	————
Correctly expand longhand abbreviations	————	————
Correctly use correction signs	————	————
Allocate accurately space within text	————	————
Locate ringed errors and correct	————	————
Key in measurements correctly	————	————
Use the 12-hour and 24-hour clock	————	————
Use the keyboard for fractions	————	————
Use accents and the umlaut for foreign names	————	————
Use the indent facility	————	————
Justify text	————	————

The second invoice is to go to Ms Sue Jarrett, Overseas Travel Ltd, 78 High Street, Luton, LT8 9HB re their Order No C678. Their VAT rate is 17.5%. The goods they ordered are:

Cat No.	Quantity and Description	Price £	Total Price £
01 624	10 Reams White A4 Bond (Recycled)	2.70 per Ream	27 - 00
01 498	10 Boxes Computer Listing Paper A4 (Recycled)	12.00 per Box	120 - 00
01 947	10 Reams Dry Copier Paper	5.20 per Ream	52 - 00
01 957	5 Boxes Overhead Transparencies	15.00 per Box	75 - 00
		Sub Total	274 - 00
		VAT Total	
		TOTAL	

Section 2 Business correspondence

NVQ Level 1

This section includes business letters, memos, envelopes and labels. For Section 2 you will be working for Mr Patrick Dubuc, who is the Sales Manager in the European Division (refer to the organisation chart on page 80).

■ **TASK 1**

The following is an example of a business letter for you to type/key in on plain A4 paper. You will notice that there are no punctuation marks inserted in the reference, date, name and address of addressee, the salutation, or complimentary close when using abbreviations in the body of the letter. This is referred to as **open punctuation**. The letter also uses the **fully blocked style**, with all headings and paragraphs starting at the margin. Use 1" (25 mm) margins.

	turn up 13 single line spaces
1 Reference	**Our ref PD/(your initials)/ED345**
	single line space (turn up 2)
2 Date	**(Insert today's date)**
	single line space (turn up 2)
3 Special mark	**FOR THE ATTENTION OF Mrs M J Johnson**
	single line space (turn up 2)
4 Name and address of addressee	**Computer Plus PLC** **169 Rock Avenue** **Lewisham** **LONDON** **SE13 4TP**
	single line space (turn up 2)
5 Salutation	**Dear Madam**
	single line space (turn up 2)
6 Subject heading	**NEW ORDERS**
	single line space (turn up 2)
7 Body of letter	**Thank you very much for your letter of (insert yesterday's date). I should be most pleased to arrange for a representative to call on you to discuss your requirements. Our representative will be in your area on Monday of next week, (insert next Monday's date) at 2.30 pm, and will call to see you then. If this is not convenient for you, please let me know and an alternative date and time can be arranged.**
	single line space (turn up 2)
	In the meantime I am enclosing a copy of our latest catalogue.
	single line space (turn up 2)
8 Complimentary close	**Yours faithfully**
	4 single line spaces (turn up 5)
9 Signatory	**Patrick Dubuc** **Sales Manager**
	single line space (turn up 2)
10 Enclosure	**Enc**

■ **TASK 1**

Complete an invoice to go to Guaranteed Builders Ltd, 45 Homeward Avenue, London, SW7 9JK, regarding their Order No 04598. Their VAT rate is 17.5% The goods they ordered are:

Cat No	Quantity and Description	Price £	Total Cost £
03 816	3 Portable Drawing Boards	20.00 each	60.00
16 419	Hycron Gloves 30 pairs size L " " " M	1.99 per pair	119.40
14 614	Mens Overalls 15 pairs size L " " " M	7 per pair	210.00
	Sub total		£ 389.40
	VAT total		68.14
	TOTAL		457.54

Remember that all letters you produce must be of a mailable standard, ie error free, as letters must give a good impression of the company. At the same time you should try to get the letter right first time as it wastes both time and paper if you have to keep retyping or reprinting a letter.

Parts of a business letter

1   References

These are used on letters to identify the sender/recipient and file. Leave at least one clear space after 'Your ref' or 'Our ref' before keying in the reference. The reference usually consists of the initials of the originator of the document and also your initials with a file reference number. However, follow the house style of the organisation for which you work.

2   Date

All letters must be dated in full, eg 1 January 1994. Abbreviated dates such as 1/1/94, 1.1.94 or 1 Jan 1994 are not acceptable.

3   Special marks

You may have to use special marks such as PRIVATE, PERSONAL, CONFIDENTIAL, URGENT, RECORDED DELIVERY, SPECIAL DELIVERY, BY HAND, AIRMAIL or FOR THE ATTENTION OF. Leave 1 clear line space below the date and type/key in these special marks at the left margin, using block capitals with no underscore. The same format is used on the envelope accompanying the letter, unless you are using window envelopes.

4   Inside name and address

This is typed in single line spacing, leaving 1 clear line space below the date or special mark, with a separate line for each part of the address. The town (or country if the letter is going abroad) should be in capital letters, and the postcode must always be on a separate line.

5   Salutation

This is the greeting that begins the letter and will usually be in the form of Dear Sir (to an individual) or Dear Sirs (to an organisation). If you know the name of the addressee, their courtesy title and surname should be used (eg Dear Mr Smith). Leave 1 clear line space after the address and then at the left margin type/key in the salutation.

6   Subject heading

If there is to be a subject heading, this is typed/keyed in after the salutation in single line spacing and at the left margin in block capitals with no underscore. (Although if you are working for Mr S Foster of the American Division he favours initial capitals and underscore and you would have to adapt as this is acceptable also.)

7   Body of the letter

Leave 1 clear line space, ie turn up 2 single line spaces, after the salutation or subject heading, if there is one. Begin typing at the left margin. Use single line spacing with double line spacing (to give 1 clear line space) between the paragraphs.

PRINTED FORMS WITH BOXES

Printed forms may have lines or boxes where information is to be typed/keyed in. If the box has a printed heading, insert the information on the next line. If the box is large, you can leave 1 clear line space between the printed heading and inserted material.

If you have to present the information in vertical ruled columns, leave 1 clear character space each side of the vertical ruled lines. Leave 1 clear line space before and after each horizontal line. It is always best to block headings and text within columns.

■ INVOICE – EXAMPLE OF COMPLETED FORM

The following is an example of an invoice which you can type/key in. If you do not have an invoice form on your word processor, use a typewriter and a blank invoice form (see between pages 121 and 122 at the back of this book).

INVOICE NO: 264

SWIFT STATIONERS PLC
DRURY HOUSE
10 KNIGHTS PLACE
OXFORD
OX1 4MC

Telephone: 0689 543545
Fax: 0689 657890
Telex: 789678278

VAT Registered No: 47985678

To: Wyman Ltd
12-16 The Grove
OXFORD
OX1 4NB

Date: 18 May 19--

Your Order No:

Terms: Nett 30 days

Cat No	Quantity and Description	Price £	Total £
		£	£
SC129	12 Boxes Window Envelopes	2.25	27.50
SC67	1 Set of 50 Suspension Files	11.50	11.50
ST645	6 Filing Cabinets	54.00	324.00
ST6	9 VDU Desks	149.00	1341.00
	Sub Total	216.75	1704.00
	VAT Total at 17.5%		298.20
E & OE	TOTAL		2002.20

8 Complimentary close

You will need to leave 1 clear line space (ie turn up 2 single line spaces) after the body of the letter. Type the complimentary close at the left margin.

- If the letter opens with Dear Sirs, Dear Sir or Dear Madam, you should end the letter with **Yours faithfully**.

- If you use the person's name, eg Dear Ms Adams or Dear Mr Peters, then you should end the letter with **Yours sincerely**.

Note that 'faithfully' and 'sincerely' are in lower case.

You will receive some letters with the name of the organisation immediately below the complimentary close. This should always be in block capitals, eg:

```
Yours sincerely
TYLER STATIONERS PLC




Mr S Poster
American Division
```

However, Swift Stationers does not require its company name to be under the complimentary close.

9 Name of the signatory

This is typed/keyed in at the left margin 5 single line spaces (4 clear line spaces) below the complimentary close to allow sufficient space for a signature. If the designation (position within the organisation) is to be used, this is typed/keyed in on the line immediately following the signatory's name.

10 Enclosures

These are usually indicated by typing/keying in **Enc** for one enclosure, or **Encs** for more than one enclosure. Leave 1 clear line space below the signatory's name and designation, and type this at the left margin. If there is any mention of an enclosure within the body of the letter, you must type Enc, even if you are not specifically asked to do so. This will draw the attention of the mailroom and recipient to the fact that there is an enclosure. Some organisations like --- or ... placed in the left margin of the body of the letter on the line where the enclosure is mentioned.

11 Signing on behalf of the writer

Sometimes you have to sign a letter on behalf of the writer because he/she is not available and the letter has to go in the mail. You will still type/key in the writer's name but sign your own name, writing **pp** (for *per pro* meaning 'on behalf of') before your signature. Sometimes you will be asked to type/key in:

```
Dictated by (the name of the writer) and signed in his (her)
absence.
```

12 Postscript

A postscript (PS) may have to be included because the writer has left something out or wishes to draw attention to a particular point. The postscript starts 2 single line spaces (1 clear line space) below the last line of the letter (eg after Enc). Type/key in PS at the left margin and leave 2 character spaces before the text of the postscript, eg:

```
PS  I have just received the rest of the brochures.
```

Section 4 Business forms

NVQ Level 2

A wide variety of forms is used in business. When you first apply for a job you will fill in an application form. Telephone messages are written on telephone message forms. There are many forms such as quotations, invoices, advice notes and goods received notes which you may be required to complete.

FORMS FOR PURCHASING GOODS

Quotation

An organisation wishing to purchase any item will normally ask for quotations from several possible suppliers. The suppliers often send quotations giving special discounts (price reductions) to induce purchasers to buy their goods.

Order

The organisation will then send a Purchase Order to the chosen supplier.

Delivery note

When goods are despatched from the supplier's warehouse, a delivery note, advice note or goods received note is enclosed specifying the contents. This is signed by the purchaser when the goods are received.

Invoice

An invoice is sent by the supplier to the purchaser to request payment for the goods supplied. Invoices give details of the name and address of the supplier and purchaser, the order number, the invoice number, the VAT registration number, payment and discount terms, the quantity and description of the goods, and the total amount owing.

The purchaser then checks against the original order and the delivery note to ensure that the invoice is accurate. The initials E & OE (meaning errors and omissions excepted) are included at the bottom of many business forms. These initials show that the supplier reserves the right to correct any errors and omissions that are discovered later. (However, these no longer have legal validity.)

Once an invoice has been issued it cannot be changed. Any alterations are made by issuing a debit note, if the amount payable is to be increased, or a credit note, if the amount shown on the invoice is more than the final amount payable, eg if goods have to be returned as faulty.

Debit note

This includes a description of the goods and additional and total costs, quoting the invoice number and date.

Credit note

Usually printed in red, this will cancel all or part of an invoice, or give credit for goods that have been returned. It will quote the invoice's number and date.

■ **TASK 2**

Type or key in the following letter on letterheaded paper to Mr J L Peterson, 84 Wilton Road, BATCHING, Bath, BT7 8RY. Use the same fully blocked layout as in the previous letter (page 105). The ref is PD/(your initials)/ED/cn. All abbreviations must be in full. As Mr Dubuc will not be back until tomorrow, can you sign the letter on his behalf.

> Thank you for your letter recd. this morning. I was very pleased to hear that you have been so satisfied with our service and that you are going to recom. us to HK Supplies Plc. We shall be delighted to send our rep. round and will offer the same gntees. that we give you.
>
> In the meantime I am sending you 5 copies of our cat. as requested.

■ **TASK 3**

Type or key in the following on letterheaded paper to Guaranteed Supplies Ltd, 64 Godstone Rd, CARDIFF, CD6 8RT. Mark it for the attention of The Marketing Manager. Use the same fully blocked layout as in the previous letters. The ref is PD/(your initials)/ED/Ord. All abbreviations must be in full.

> Further to your letter of (put yesterday's date) I am sending you a copy of our latest cat. For one month only we have special price reductions on all our fax rolls, A4 bond paper, envelopes, labels, notepads, telephone message pads and ribbons for typewriters and printers. These price reductions are listed on a separate price list sheet which is also enclosed.
>
> I would like to point out that we have a policy of "delivery next day". After we rec. your order this is immed. processed and entered into our computer. We gntee. next day delivery. You will be invoiced immed. and we allow a four-week period from the date of rec. of goods for payment. If you pay within this four-week period we allow a discount of 37%, on all goods. We pride ourselves on being able to reply promptly to your orders and on the generous discounts that we are able to offer our customers. However, you will appreciate that in order to have such a quick response rate and to offer such a generous discount we do need to receive payment for goods within the time allowed. If we do not receive payment within this time, no further orders will be accepted.
>
> We look forward to doing bus. with you and receiving your first order. If you have any queries, please do not hesitate to contact this office.

Checklist of achievements in Section 3 – Business display and tabular work

Performance criteria	Date	Signature
Display work effectively using horizontal and vertical centring	———————	—————————
Correctly put figures in columns	———————	—————————
Correctly line up units under units, tens under tens and hundreds under hundreds	———————	—————————
Correctly align the decimal points in sums of money	———————	—————————
Correctly total sums of money	———————	—————————
Correctly align to the left or right	———————	—————————
Use footnotes	———————	—————————
Create new tabs/delete existing tabs	———————	—————————
Allocate equal spacing between columns	———————	—————————

ENVELOPES

Envelope sizes in most common business use are:

C5 162 mm × 229 mm (6⅜″ × 9″)
    Takes A4 folded once

C6 114 mm × 162 mm (4½″ × 6⅜″)
    Takes A4 folded twice

DL 110 mm × 220 mm (4¼″ × 8⅝″)
    Takes A4 folded equally into three

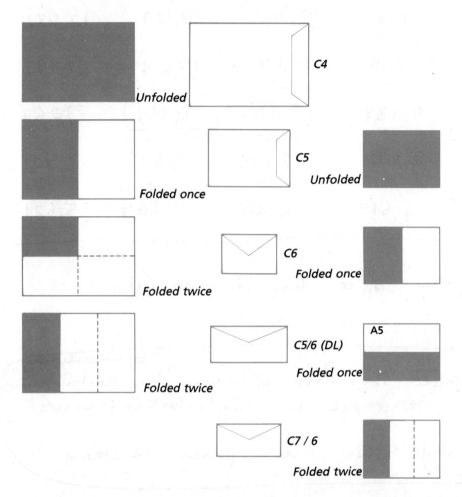

For every letter you will either type an envelope or use a window envelope, ie envelopes which have an opening through which the address on the letter can be seen. A guideline on the letterheaded paper will indicate where the address should finish so that it shows in the window of the envelope.

Departmental expenditure[1] - (block capitals)

	Jan-Mar	Apr-Jun	July-Sept	Oct-Dec
Purchasing	£12,694	£12,129	£10,648	£1,987
Production	9,612	8,417	7,129	12,482
Sales	15,269	18,498	17,619	18,997
Personnel	4,689	(3,429	8,261)	7,269
Financial	8,621	7,498	7,631	8,921
Admin.	4,619	4,218	2,649	5,621

[1] Figures to be ʌ in my office by 12 noon (insert today's date).

Please emphasise the first column, by emboldening or underlining words, and rearrange in alphabetical order.

Change the style and use spaces instead of commas.

ADDRESSING ENVELOPES

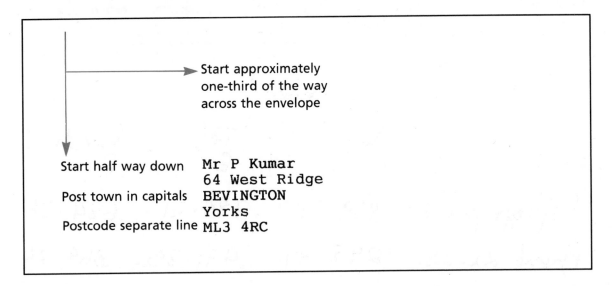

Start approximately one-third of the way across the envelope

Start half way down   Mr P Kumar
                      64 West Ridge
Post town in capitals BEVINGTON
                      Yorks
Postcode separate line ML3 4RC

Address labels

Labels are usually self-adhesive and come on continuous rolls or in sheets for the printer. They are often used because it is quicker and easier than inserting individual envelopes into the typewriter or printer. In addition it is necessary to have labels for large envelopes or parcels.

Labels are typed in exactly the same way as envelopes. However, because they are smaller, it might sometimes be necessary to put longer lines on two lines or abbreviate words, eg 'Road' to 'Rd'.

If you are unsure how to produce labels on your word processor, you will need to refer to the manual or ask your tutor.

Forms of address

Courtesy titles, such as Mr, Ms, Mrs, Miss, should always be used on envelopes and on letters in the address and salutation where a person is called by their surname.

Messrs is sometimes used when addressing a partnership, eg Messrs Barker and Dennison.

Courtesy titles are not used before the name of a limited company or public limited company (PLC), eg Harris Travel Ltd or Littleton Stationers plc.

■ TASK 4

Type or key in the following as envelopes or labels.

1 Sunshine Products Ltd   PO Box 18   24 Union Terrace   ABERDEEN   Grampian   AB1 1NJ

2 Mr Philip Watson   Midland House   64 Bank Avenue   BOURNEMOUTH   Dorset
BH2 5QY

3 Monsieur Maurice Couteau   Director   Credit Agricole   89 rue de la Bain
78119 Dieppe   FRANCE

4 Madame M Lefevre   St Laurent Boulevard   Montmartre   41189 Paris   FRANCE

5 Herr Helmit Russmann   8 Venistrasse   Hamburg   GERMANY

The following figures are needed for a meeting tomorrow on departmental expenditure. Please prepare these using the layout indicated.

Production Department¹

	Jan £	Feb £	March £
Reprographics	469.98	784.21	684.86
Phone Lines	298.41	491.85	369.74
Petty Cash	69.82	84.61	72.91
Hospitality	198.24	176.90	82.45
Travel	1,698.29	1,182.95	1,642.82

¹ This includes all members of staff in the Production Department both in the offices and factory.

Please total the above figures on the table, and embolden the first column if you are using a word processor.

6 Franklin Partnership   18 Rochester Drive   Mayfield Park   Harare   ZIMBABWE

7 The Marketing Manager   FREEPOST   Elgin House   180 St Margaret Street
  CARDIFF   CF1 1ND

8 Rev J Johnson   St Mary's Church   Riley Road   COVENTRY   Midlands   CV1 2RG

9 Ms M Cookson   Bakerstown Health Centre   Donegal Street   BELFAST   BT1 5JP

10 Dr R Smitherson   Institute of Science   57 Farlington Road   LONDON   WC1 4XY

11 Purchasing Manager   Hotel De La Ville   48 Petrovisky Prospekt   Moscow   RUSSIA

12 Mr J Harris   Cramphorne Merchants   Abbey House   169 Notte Street
   PLYMOUTH   Devon   PL1 2ER

Points to remember

- Post Office regulations require that you have the longer side of the envelope at the top.

- The address should start at least half-way down the envelope and one-third across.

- The postal town should be in capitals. This is consistent with the address on the letter.

- The postcode should always be the last line of the address and should have a line to itself. The code should be in block capitals with one character space between the two halves of the code.

- Special marks such as PRIVATE AND CONFIDENTIAL, FOR THE ATTENTION OF, should be 1 clear line space above the address.

- RECORDED DELIVERY, REGISTERED MAIL, AIR MAIL and SPECIAL DELIVERY should be in capitals and placed in the top left corner of the envelope or label.

- FREEPOST is used by organisations wishing to receive a reply or response from an advertisement without the customers having to pay postage. This must be typed in block capitals after the name of the addressee and before the address.

- POSTE RESTANTE is used by people who are travelling and have no fixed mailing address. They can arrange to have their mail sent to a particular post office – for a three-month period only – to await collection by them. POSTE RESTANTE must be typed/keyed in block capitals after the name of the addressee and before the address.

- BY HAND in capital letters should be typed/keyed at the top left corner when the envelope is to be delivered by someone rather than posted.

- Road, Street, Avenue, Square, etc, should be typed/keyed in full. Co, Ltd, St (as in Saint) are retained. Abbreviations for counties, eg Yorks, Middx, Lancs, are acceptable.

■ **TASK 11**

You can now type or key in the following exercise. Centre vertically and horizontally, giving emphasis to the heading. You can do this by either emboldening or underscoring. The total needs to be added.

SALES FOR THE LONDON AREA

	1st Quarter	2nd Quarter	3rd Quarter	4th Quarter
	£	£	£	£
NE	123,789.00	145,798.67	158,007.86	198,135.78
SE	43,898.45	45,678.99	47,789.98	49,889.45
NW	35,765.34	37,543.67	39,478.23	38,678.56
SW	67,995.89	69,458.67	68,674.82	78,489.55
	=========	==========	=========	==========

In the above example commas were used to separate the thousands from the hundreds. Sometimes you might be asked to leave a blank space instead of a comma so that your table would look like this:

SALES FOR THE LONDON AREA

	1st Quarter	2nd Quarter	3rd Quarter	4th Quarter
	£	£	£	£
NE	123 789.00	145 798.67	158 007.86	198 135.78
SE	43 898.45	45 678.99	47 789.98	49 889.45
NW	35 765.34	37 543.67	39 478.23	38 678.56
SW	67 995.89	69 458.67	68 674.82	78 489.55
	=========	==========	=========	==========

This method of leaving a space is used frequently in Europe although there has been a reluctance to use this in the UK, as extra figures can be fraudulently added.

MEMORANDUMS

Memorandums – often referred to as memos – are internal communications within an organisation and are never sent outside the organisation. They are usually in note form and can be informal. They contain no salutation or complimentary close.

The layout can vary considerably. Margins will be governed by the printed forms that are normally used. One example of a printed form is:

```
M E M O R A N D U M

From

To

Date

Ref
```

You will find a blank memo form at the back of this book, which you can copy and use for your work. You may have a skeleton memo set up in the memory file of your electronic typewriter or on your word processing disk.

Leave 2 clear character spaces after `From, To, Ref, Date,` before you type/key in the insertions. If you have a typewriter, use the interliner to ensure that you have lined up the text. If you are using a word processor/computer printer, you will have to adjust the paper in the printer and work out exactly how it should be placed to ensure correct alignment. As in a letter, the date should always be in full.

If there is a subject heading, this will normally go 2 clear line spaces below the printed heading (ie leave 2 line spaces after `Date`). If there is no subject heading, the body of the memo will normally start 2 line spaces after the printed heading. It is usual to type a memo in single line spacing.

You will need to check if an enclosure or enclosures have been mentioned in the memo. If so, type/key in **Enc** or **Encs** at least 1 clear line space below the body of the memo.

Distribution lists

Sometimes a memo has to go to several members of staff. Before you start the memo, you will need to know the names of everyone who is to receive it. Often their initials only will be used. If there is not enough space at the top of the printed form, you can put the circulation list at the end of the memo.

SUMS OF MONEY

When using sums of money you must be consistent within a document. For example:

1 You must be consistent not only with words or figures but also in the way you show the £ sign, ie £5, £20 *or* £5.00, £20.00, £24.90.

2 If you have only pence, leave no space before the pence sign, ie 5p, 10p, 88p.

3 Note that you *never* have both a £ sign and a p sign, ie £0.50 or 50p.

4 The decimal point is used to separate pounds from pence, with no space before or after the point.

Figures in columns

It is better to type units under units, tens under tens, and hundreds under hundreds, as this is easier to read and to add up:

```
  1
 24
307
```

The decimal point will then be at the same position on each line. The unit of currency (eg £) should be at the start of the column and is repeated in the totals column.

■ **COLUMNS – EXAMPLE**

The following is an example of money in columns which you can type or key in. If your word processor or typewriter has a decimal tab facility, you can use this. If not, you will have to tab to the first column and line up the columns by using your space bar. For the last line under the total you can use the equals (=) key.

£	Ff	$
45.95	5000.50	34.00
123.45	400.50	1289.00
65.98	1250.00	1349.99
45.00	10.50	229.99
£280.38	Ff6661.50	$2902.98
======	=======	=======

If columns are not totalled it is acceptable to align either to the right or the left – although aligning to the right is much more popular. Above you aligned to the right. For example:

Aligned to the right	Aligned to the left
£45.99	£45.99
£369.00	£369.00
£789.00	£789.00
£8.99	£8.99

Did you note that there is *no* space after a £ sign?

■ TASK 5

Type or key in the following memo, using the form following page 121.

MEMORANDUM

From Patrick Dubuc

To   Mr N Edwards

Date (Insert today's date)

Ref   PD/(Your initials)/ED345

NEW CUSTOMER

Can you please call on Mrs M J Johnson, Computer Plus PLC, 169 Rock Avenue, Lewisham, London, SE13 4TP, tel no 081-461 1908 on Monday next (please insert next Monday's date) at 2.30 pm to discuss her requirements. A copy of our new catalogue has been sent to her. She has not received details of our price reductions and I am enclosing a copy so that you can take it with you.

I feel we can offer her a 35% discount on all prices in the catalogue for orders up to £10,000. Any orders over that will be subject to a 40% discount. It is important to stress that payment must be made one month from the date of delivery.

■ TASK 6

Type or key in the following memo to All Secretaries with a copy to F Gerard, and L Jones. Use today's date and insert the ref PD/(your initials)/work.

It is important that all work ~~that goes~~ out from this company *going* is error free and it is important that you therefore check your work/before it is put in the signature book. *carefully*

You should pay particular attention to the following: *for signature*

Spelling, punctuation and grammar
Typing/keying errors
Figures correct
Inconsistencies in spelling, punctuation, style. *double line spacing*

emphasize

ALL WORK MUST BE PROOFREAD. DO NOT EXPECT THE ORIGINATOR OF THE DOCUMENT TO HAVE TO ~~SIT~~ THROUGH AND FIND YOUR ERRORS. *READ*

The following is to be added to our catalogue. Use your own judgment on how it should be displayed. Insert today's date at the bottom and the reference SM/(your initials).

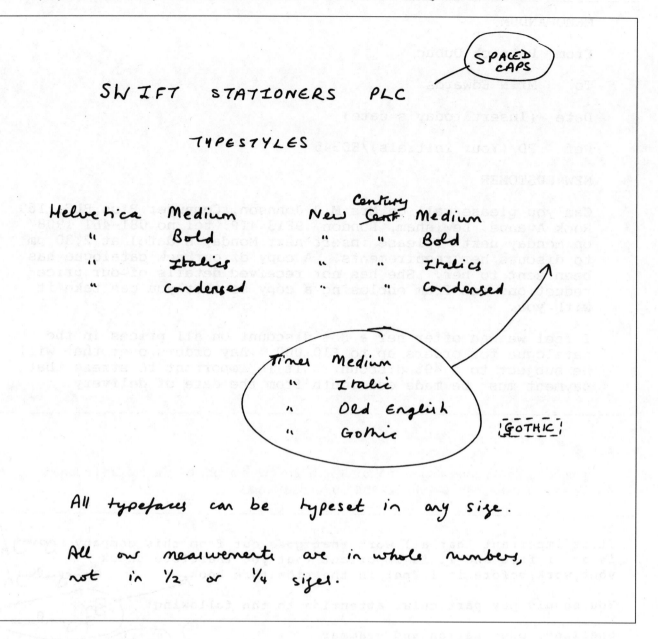

Type or key in a memo to Mr J McDonnell, use ref PD/(your initials)/ED/Paris and today's date. The subject is Paris Exhibition.

Tell him that arrangements have now been made for his trip to Paris from 29 April to 6 May for the Paris Stationers Exhibition. His tickets are in the office ready for his collection. He has been booked into Hotel De Lafayette, Place De La Republique, 76119 Paris Cedex 4, which is a short distance from the exhibition hall. We have not yet received a detailed programme from the French company, Papier Plus, but I am expecting this very shortly. I am arranging for 3000 of our catalogues to be sent to the exhibition hall in advance. As he knows, we are very keen to enter the French market. It would appear that our main rival in Paris is Le Stylo et L'Ordinateur but I feel that our prices are very competitive. If there is anything else he wishes to know, he can always ring me.

Checklist of achievements in Section 2 – Business correspondence

Performance criteria	Date	Signature
Produce letters and memos ready for signature	————	————
Check work against original for errors in spelling, punctuation, grammar, layout and omission	————	————
Correctly indicate enclosures	————	————
Place address on envelope/label accurately	————	————

The following is for staff information. These are the exhibitions I will be attending in Europe together with dates and my contact name. Insert today's date at the bottom and use the reference SM/(your initials). Please centre horizontally and vertically.

EXHIBITIONS IN EUROPE [1]

(circled note: underline headings ←)

Venue	Date	Contact
Paris	22-24 Feb	Monsieur J Valency
Rouen	26-28 Feb	" P Golard
Toulouse	6 - 9 March	" " W Matthieu
Bonn	6 - 11 May	Herr W Fritz
Cologne	7 - 12 June	" M Schult
Madrid	16 -18 June	Signor A Adriáno
Rome	17 - 20 July	" R Lorenzo _(LORENZO)_

[1] These dates are only until the Summer. I have not finalized the other dates.

UNIT 3   DATA PROCESSING

Element 3.1

Produce alpha/numerical information in typewritten form.

Performance criteria

3.1.1   approximately 150 words or numeric equivalents are produced in a 10-minute working period to a tolerance of no more than 2 uncorrected spacing or typographical errors

3.1.2   all corrections are unobtrusive

3.1.3   security and confidentiality of information is always maintained

3.1.4   faults are identified and dealt with in accordance with manufacturer's instructions and/or promptly reported

Competence must be demonstrated on a minimum of 3 separate occasions, within a 10-minute working period.

A different set of materials must be produced on each occasion.

RSA Stage I Typewriting or Word Processing require performance criteria 3.1.1 and 3.1.2 only. For NVQ these may be taken as more than adequate evidence for this Element, provided that 3.1.3 and 3.1.4 are otherwise assessed. This could be in conjunction with other Elements and/or through oral questioning on principles and procedures.

■ TASK 8

Now prepare the following list of new members of staff who will be starting work next month. You will need to keep extra copies of the previous task for them. Centre the heading and underline it. You can use the reference SM/(your initials)/NS/25. Please arrange the names in alphabetical order.

In addition, embolden text where indicated if you have this facility.

<u>NEW MEMBERS OF STAFF</u>[1]

NAME	**DEPARTMENT**	**TELEPHONE EXTENSION**
Peter Jarvis	Forward Planning	2356
Alan Schumakker	Advertising	4578
Michael Davies	Production	6578
Luciana Vedemuttu	Legal	2345
Kamaljit Sindhu	Accounts	2567

[1] As from 1 January (insert current year).

■ TASK 1

Type or key in the following letter on letterheaded paper to Mr Michael Bridge, 10 Park Avenue, MAIDSTONE, Kent, ME9 4PQ. Use the same layout as the specimen letter on page 105. Use the reference number PD/(Your initials)/ED367. Mark the letter URGENT. Produce an envelope.

> Further to your telephone call earlier today I have now looked into the matter and find that the reason for the delay is that there has been a rush of orders for fax paper and we have had to reorder. We expect to receive delivery from the factory tomorrow and your order will be despatched immediately.
>
> We are very sorry for any inconvience caused to you.

■ TASK 2

Type or key in the following memo to Mr D Douglas, use ref PD/(your initials)ED/Com and today's date. The subject is Complaints.

> We have received several complaints that orders in the north of London have been arriving late. As you know it is Company policy that all deliveries will be made one day after rec. of the order. Will you please look into the matter immed. and report back to me.

■ **TASK 6**

Type or key in the following tabulation. Allow 3 spaces between the columns. Embolden the heading if you have this facility.

DAYS OF THE WEEK

ENGLISH	FRENCH	GERMAN
Monday	Lundi	Montag
Tuesday	Mardi	Dienstag
Wednesday	Mercredi	Mittwoch
Thursday	Jeudi	Donnerstag
Friday	Vendredi	Freitag
Saturday	Samedi	Samstag
Sunday	Dimanche	Sonntag

■ **TASK 7**

It has been decided at Swift Stationers that, because we are now going to expand in Europe, all new members of staff should know certain facts about Europe – in particular the capital cities and the currencies of various countries. Prepare the following as a memo for circulation to all members of staff. Date it at the bottom and use the reference SM/(your initials)/EEC/ 190.

EUROPEAN COUNTRIES

COUNTRY	CAPITAL	CURRENCY
Austria	Vienna	Schilling
Belgium	Brussels	Belgium Franc
Denmark	Copenhagen	Kroner
France	Paris	French Franc
Germany	Berlin	Deutsche Mark
Greece	Athens	Drachma
Holland	Amsterdam	Guilder
Ireland	Dublin	Irish Punt
Italy	Rome	Lire
Luxembourg	Luxembourg	Luxembourg Franc*
Portugal	Lisbon	Escudo
Spain	Madrid	Peseta

* The Belgium Franc is also widely used in Luxembourg.

5

National Vocational Qualification
Business Administration
Level 2

Section 3 Business display and tabular work

Section 4 Business forms

Section 5 Business correspondence

When you have completed these sections you should have the underpinning knowledge and skills to take the National Vocational Qualification Business Administration Unit 16 – Text Processing competency:

Element 16.1 Produce a variety of business documents from handwritten/ typewritten drafts.

On a word processor

On each system this will be different so you should check that this will work on your system or consult your tutor or the program manual.

1 Enter into tab mode. Very often you will find this under the formatting commands.

2 You will notice that tab stops are already set, probably every 5 character spaces. Information on the screen usually shows you how to clear these. You will now have to set the tab stops where you want them to be. On the screen you will be given several options:

   L (to justify to the left of the column)

   R (to justify to the right of the column)

   C (to centre the column)

   D (for decimal tabs when you want to keep all the decimal points under each other – particularly if you are keying in sums of money).

   For the purposes of the first exercise we will set to justify to the Left which is usual.

3 Press the space bar for each character in the longest line in column 1. Press the space bar 3 times. Set a tab (your screen usually gives you the commands to do this).

4 Now press the space bar for each character in the longest line in column 2. Press the space bar 3 times. Set a second tab.

5 Continue in this manner until you have set a tab stop for each column.

6 If you want to centre across a page you can use the method given below for calculating tab stops on a typewriter.

Alternative method

There is an alternative method for calculating where to set your tab stops on either a typewriter or word processor. You can try out both and see which you prefer.

1 Calculate the longest line in each column. Allow 3 (or 5) spaces between each column. Add these figures together, including the spaces between the columns.

2 Subtract the total from 82 (pica)/100 (elite) (the number of character spaces across the A4 page) and divide the figure by 2. This will give you the point at which to start your left margin.

3 From the left margin, tap the space bar for each character in the longest line in the first column, plus 3 or 5 spaces between the columns and set a tab stop for column 2. Continue until you have set all your tab stops.

4 Return to the left margin. You can now type or key in the first column. Then press the TAB key. This will take you to the start of the second column. Continue until you have completed the first line. Return to the left margin and continue as for the first line.

Section 3 Business display and tabular work

NVQ Level 2

Refer to Section 1, page 85, if you need to recap on tabulation and indenting.

For this section you are working for Stephen McKenzie, Production Director (refer to the organisation chart on page 80).

DISPLAY WORK

Sometimes work you are given will need to be displayed so that the information stands out, or looks more attractive. This will be necessary for notices, advertisements, announcements, invitations, menus, and so on. If you have the facilities on your typewriter or word processor, you can use these to centre horizontally and/or vertically. If not, you will have to do the calculations yourself, using the instructions given below. In any case, it would be useful for you to do at least one task manually.

HORIZONTAL CENTRING – MANUALLY

To centre a piece of work across the page (ie horizontally), find the centre of the page – usually 50 (elite), 41 (pica), or the central point between the margins. With this as your typing point, identify the *longest* line in the display and backspace once for each pair of characters, for every character and space, ie:

BARGAINS IN THE NEW YEAR

Backspace once for   every 2 characters, including spaces.

When you have done this, set your left margin at this point and use it for each line in the display. (It is not necessary to set a right margin.) You can use the same method to centre each line in the display. In this case it is not necessary to set the margin, simply backspace and type.

TABULATION (COLUMN WORK)

You may be asked to arrange work in columns. This makes it easier for information to be read and understood.

You will have already found out the position of the tabulator (Tab) key or bar and its function. As explained on page 85, if you are using a typewriter, the TAB- (TAB CLEAR) key clears existing tabs, the TAB+ (TAB SET) key sets new tabs, and the TAB ⇆ key is pressed when you wish to move from column to column. If you are using a word processor, you will have to find the menu to clear all the existing tab stops – usually set every 5 character spaces – and then set new ones.

To calculate where to set the tab stops:

On a typewriter

1 Clear margins and all existing tab stops (on most manual and electric typewriters you will have to tab to each tab stop and press the TAB- key).

2 Move the typing point to the centre of the page. This is usually at point 50 on the scale of a typewriter.

3 Identify the longest line in each column. From the centre point on the page backspace once for every 2 characters or spaces in these longest lines. Allow for 3 (or 5) spaces between columns. (In the tasks which follow, 3 or 5 spaces have been allowed between columns.) Set a left margin. This will be the starting point of your first column.

4 Now press the space bar for each character in the longest line in the first column, plus 3 (or 5) for the column space, and set the first tab. Repeat for the remaining longest lines in each column.

5 When you have set the tab for the last column, press the space bar for the number of characters in the longest line in this column. You are now at the right margin. Check that this is the same as the left margin. For example, if the left margin is 20 spaces, the right margin should also be 20 spaces. It is not necessary to set a right margin.

6 Return to the left margin. You can now begin to type. Type the first line of the first column and then press the TAB key. This will take you to the start of the second column. Type this and TAB for the third column. Continue until you have typed the first line of each column. Then return to the left margin to follow the same procedure for the second line.

■ TASK 1

This company likes everything blocked, so type the following list using this style. Use the method given for horizontal centring to find out where to set your margins. If you have the facility, embolden the main heading. Leave 1 clear line space between each line, ie turn up 2 line spaces.

Turn up 7 single line spaces

BARGAINS IN THE NEW YEAR

line space

Office Desks

line space

Office Chairs

line space

Printer Stands

line space

Filing Cabinets

line space

Photocopy Paper

■ TASK 2

Now display the following notices, using emboldening, if you have this facility, and underscore for effective display.

Turn up 15 single line spaces

S W I F T   S T A T I O N E R S   P L C

You are invited to the Grand Opening

of the new Showroom

on

Friday   (use next Friday's date)

at

<u>7.30 pm</u>

FOOTNOTES

Footnotes can be used to expand on a point mentioned in the text above, or be listed at the end of a chapter in a book. The following task gives you further information.

In the main text footnotes are shown as symbols or as superscript numbers. Superscript characters are those typed half a line space above the typing line; subscript characters are those typed half a line space below the typing line. Word processor programs have a menu or codes to give these characters.

■ TASK 5

Type/key in the following document and keep it for reference.

FOOTNOTES

Footnotes[1] are indicated by several different methods.

1   In the text a number or symbol such as an asterisk (`·`), single dagger † (‡) or double dagger (type I, turn down half a line space, backspace and type I again to make ‡) is typed/keyed in WITHOUT A SPACE between it and the previous character. Most systems, however, now use numbers. On a word processor the superscript facility is used.

      In addition, if your typewriter or word processor has a footnote facility, you can use this and it will automatically number all your footnotes for you and raise the number in the text half a space above the word to which it refers.

      If your machine does not have this facility then you will have to key in the number half a space above the word. An asterisk will automatically be in the correct position as it is a raised character.

2   At the bottom of the page the number or symbol is typed/keyed in again, but need not be as a superscript character, and a space is left AFTER it and before the information. This footnote is always in single line spacing, even though the document may be in double line spacing.

      The footnote is separated from the text with a horizontal line from margin to margin. There is usually one single line space above and below this line, ie one clear line space between the text and this line, and one clear line space between this line and the footnote.

---

[1] Footnotes can be used for a further explanation, to identify a person or point made in a document, or to give the source of a quotation that has been used.

■ TASK 3

Turn up 15 single line spaces

```
            P  R  E  S  S      R  E  L  E  A  S  E

                    SWIFT STATIONERS PLC


                  are pleased to announce
                   the arrival of their
                      new range of


                    Office Furniture

          For more details phone 0689 543545
          or fax us through your requirements for
             a FREE quotation on 0689 657890
```

VERTICAL CENTRING ON THE PAGE

If you have no facility on your typewriter or word processor to centre vertically, you will have to calculate on which line to start the document. To do this you will have to know how many lines there are down the page. There are:

70 lines using A4 paper – portrait (shorter edge at the top)
50 lines using A4 paper – landscape (longer edge at the top)

Method

1 Begin by counting the total number of typed and blank lines in the document (eg 52).

2 Take this total away from the number of lines on the page (eg using A4 portrait, 70 − 52 = 18). This is the number of line spaces remaining.

3 Divide this remaining number by 2 (eg 18 ÷ 2 = 9). This will give you equal space at the top and bottom of the document.

4 If you are using a word processor, reach the starting line by pressing the Return (Enter) key until the status line shows the correct line number. If you are using a typewriter, turn up the correct number of lines from the top edge of the page.

In this example there will be 9 spaces at the top, so you will begin typing on the 10th line, ie turn up 10. If you have an odd number, leave an extra space at the bottom.

Look at the following menu. If you count the lines and spaces, you will see that there are 35. Take this away from 70 which leaves 35. Divide this by 2 which gives a top margin of 17 and a bottom margin of 18. Start typing on the 18th line.

■ **TASK 4**

Display the following notice in blocked style.

Type the pattern at the top and bottom of the notice. If you have a copy facility (word processors/computers), use this to repeat the pattern at the bottom of the notice.

Underscore where shown, and embolden if you have this facility on your machine (electronic typewriters, word processors and computers).

XXXXXXXXXXXXXXXXXXXXXXXXXXXXXXXXXXXXXXXXXXXXXXXXXXXXXXXXXX
* *

LANGUAGE COURSES FOR STAFF

on site

CLASSES AVAILABLE

in

FRENCH
GERMAN
SPANISH
ITALIAN
RUSSIAN

Courses Commence

January and September

For more information contact:

Patrick Dubuc   Sales Manager   European Division

XXXXXXXXXXXXXXXXXXXXXXXXXXXXXXXXXXXXXXXXXXXXXXXXXXXXXXXXX
* *

■ **TASK 3**

Display the following effectively, centring horizontally and vertically using the blocked style.
Do not type the numbers – they are for guidance only.

```
1    M E N U
2
3    Staff Christmas Lunch
4
5    18 December
6
7    Soup of the Day
8    Prawn Cocktail
9    Melon Cocktail
10   Fruit Juice
11
12   *****
13
14   Roast Turkey
15   Roast Beef
16   Roast Lamb
17   Jacket Potatoes
18   French Fries
19   Brussels Sprouts
20   Green Beans
21   Peas
22
23   *****
24
25   Christmas Pudding
26   Chocolate Cake
27   Raspberry Pavlova
28   Blackcurrant Cheesecake
29   Fresh Fruit Salad
30
31   *****
32
33   Cheese and Biscuits
34
35   Coffee and Mints
```

■ **TASK 3 – final version**

This is how the menu would look if you had centred each line. Do that now, centring both
vertically and horizontally.

```
                    M E N U

              Staff Christmas Lunch

                  18 December

                Soup of the Day
                Prawn Cocktail
                Melon Cocktail
                  Fruit Juice

                     *****

                 Roast Turkey
                  Roast Beef
                  Roast Lamb
                Jacket Potatoes
                 French Fries
               Brussels Sprouts
                 Green Beans
                     Peas

                     *****

              Christmas Pudding
               Chocolate Cake
               Raspberry Pavlova
             Blackcurrant Cheesecake
               Fresh Fruit Salad

                     *****

              Cheese and Biscuits

               Coffee and Mints
```

MEMORANDUM

From

To

Date

Ref

CREDIT NOTE NO:

SWIFT STATIONERS PLC
DRURY HOUSE
10 KNIGHTS PLACE
OXFORD
OX1 4MC

Telephone: 0689 543545
Fax: 0689 657890
Telex: 789678278

To:

VAT Registered No: 47985678

Date:

Invoice No:

Reason for Credit	Quantity and Description	Total Credit £
E & OE	TOTAL	

SWIFT STATIONERS PLC

DRURY HOUSE
10 KNIGHTS PLACE
OXFORD
OX1 4MC

Telephone: 0689 543545
Fax: 0689 657890
Telex: 789678278

Your Ref:

Our Ref:

Registered No: 4798 England

INVOICE NO:

SWIFT STATIONERS PLC
DRURY HOUSE
10 KNIGHTS PLACE
OXFORD
OX1 4MC

Telephone: 0689 543545
Fax: 0689 657890
Telex: 789678278

VAT Registered No: 47985678

To:

Date:

Your Order No:

Terms: Nett 30 days

Cat No	Quantity and Description	Price £	Total £
	Sub Total		
	VAT Total at 17.5%		
E & OE	TOTAL		